The Widening Circle of Us

The Widening Circle of Us

A Theological Memoir

Peter Francis

University of Chester Press

First published 2021
by University of Chester Press
University of Chester
Parkgate Road
Chester CH1 4BJ

Printed and bound in the UK by the
LIS Print Unit
University of Chester
Cover designed by the
LIS Graphics Team
University of Chester

A catalogue record for this book is available
from the British Library

ISBN 978-1-910481-08-0

To Helen

in admiration of your passion for equality, your intelligence,
and the unearned love that lights up my life. I hope this
book will help to explain my own preoccupations and
why I spend time, thought and energy on something
as incomprehensible, in your eyes, as rethinking faith.
It matters to me but not nearly as much as you do.
Valentine's Day, 14 February 2021

There is no longer Jew or Greek, there is no longer
slave or free, there is no longer male and female;
for all of you are one in Christ Jesus.
Galatians 3:28

He drew a circle that shut me out –
Heretic, rebel, a thing to flout.
But Love and I had the wit to win:
We drew a circle that took him in!
Edwin Markham – 'Outwitted' – 1852

CONTENTS

LIST OF ILLUSTRATIONS

INTRODUCTION

This book is a theological memoir. What on earth does that mean? On one level it is quite clear – it charts my life and theological views over 40-plus years of ministry in the Anglican church.

The period of my life, in British terms, is the second Elizabethan age, which has seen a widening of the circle of us – of those no longer excluded. A sadness in this progress has been the slowness of the mainstream churches to respond to this growth of tolerance and acceptance and in the process, they have made themselves seem extremely foolish and out of touch. The churches have lagged behind the liberal spirit of the age and have often been a brake on the forward momentum of society. Strange to think that they claim to worship a truly human being, Jesus, who broke the religious conventions of his society and whose spirit and truth is claimed to set us free. It set me free to be myself rather than following an expected path mapped out for me.

I am thankful that the outriders of my tradition have kept the freeing, widening truth of Jesus alive. There are many who prefer the old certainties of a previous age. They ignore the realisation that the great gift of Christianity to the world was the gift of liberation which underpins all religious and secular movements of liberation. Paul in his letter to the Galatians, probably reciting a well-known song or creed of the early church, states that in the early Christian community 'there is no longer Jew or Greek, there is no longer slave or free, there is no longer male and female; for we are all one'. Or, in contemporary parlance, they were in effect saying 'no race, class or gender discrimination within our community'. It is sad that so often the churches, including my own Anglican tradition, have seen themselves as preserving the status quo and have been slow to recognise those struggling for the fullness of life that Jesus promised.

Why write this book now? I suppose, on a practical level, I have to thank the pandemic which allowed me the time and space to shape and conclude this manuscript which I had been working on for some time. However, there is another rather more essential reason for writing at this time: for the first time in my lifetime the widening of the circle is under threat and hard-won freedoms are threatened by populist movements and populist leaders.

In Hungary (2021), Viktor Orbán limits press freedom, is careless over democratic rights, remains aggressively socially conservative as well as being accused of anti-Semitism and exhibiting Islamophobia. Yet, he proudly considers his government to be Christian. In Poland, the right-wing populist government led by Andrzej Duda attacks LGBTQ and women's rights with connivance on the part of many within the Catholic church in Poland. In the USA, four years of a Trump administration has seen his attempts to roll back on women's and LGBTQ rights and to have a hard line on immigration to make America great again. Trump is lauded and was elected with the help of the Christian right. In the UK, the Brexit vote was secured with fears of immigration and by harking back to the days of Empire – make Britain Great again.[1] For me, the harsh reality is that plenty of those who follow populist leaders propounding views that call for a simpler, whiter, straighter, masculine world can be found in the churches of the West. If not necessarily amongst many of the Anglican clergy – only 6% of whom voted Conservative at the last general election compared to 43.6% of the population[2] – certainly amongst the Anglican laity as 66% voted in favour of Brexit.[3]

What can be done? How can Christianity become a force for justice amidst this right-wing surge of traditionalism and insularity? A focus on the teaching of the historical Jesus and the early church's radical inclusion would be as good a place to start as any.

The current populism is counter to the movements that dominate this book and my own awakening. I want to tell my story in order to defend the widening of the circle of us. My life is set in an age of struggles for justice and fairness – an era of inclusion rather than exclusion. It is about my developing liberal view of faith and exclusions that I had grown up blissfully unaware of. I have come from a conservative home and schooling both lower case and upper case 'C' and shed those often ingrained and insular attitudes in the light of my experience and life choices. It is about my 'widening' as well as that of British society.

To begin at my beginning ...

PART I

BECOMING

CHAPTER 1
SCHOOLED
(1953–1971)

We look at the world once, in childhood.
The rest is memory.
Louise Glück – 'Nostos' – 1996

I was born during the tea interval of the Lord's test match in June 1953 to the soothing and quintessentially British soundtrack of the BBC's ball-by-ball cricket commentary. Well, that's the myth anyway. We lived in Tutshill, a small village on the English–Welsh border a mile from the Welsh town of Chepstow but just on the English side, which was deemed important by my parents, although the postal address indicated Wales. I was the third child of the family but the first boy. The coronation of Queen Elizabeth had just taken place and my parents had bought a television to watch the ceremony. Meat rationing was still in force after the Second World War but there was a feeling that Britain was experiencing a new dawn – a new Elizabethan era – Edmund Hillary and Tenzing Norgay had just conquered Everest and planted the Union Jack on the top of the highest point of the world. Soon Harold Macmillan would be announcing that we had 'never had it so good'. This was the world I was born into. I was destined to become a lawyer like my father, uncle, grandfather and, indeed, great-grandfather. I bucked the trend and became a priest instead.

I have a vivid memory of my parents, Pauline and Richard, kneeling either side of their double bed silently praying. I know, because my mother told me, that the prayers that they both said each night were just a grown-up version of how they taught my sisters and I to pray – God bless Mummy, God bless Daddy, etc. Praying, as Mum taught us, was a recital of the names of those closest to us who we entrusted to God's loving care. It included listing special worries about people we knew who were ill or unhappy. It was comforting to do and created a cosy feeling that we were wrapped in a cocoon

3

of protection and love. I don't think any of us expected God to do anything about our list of requests which included, in my case, a list of childish requests for Christmas presents, harm to those who were beastly to me at school and so on. It was an articulation of hopes and fears. Praying in a sense was 'good manners' like remembering to say 'thank you' and 'please'. So far, so very Christopher Robin. It was a tableau straight out of A. A. Milne's poem 'Vespers': 'Hush! Hush! Whisper who dares! Christopher Robin is saying his prayers.'[4]

I never believed in this method of prayer and instead when left to my own devices as a child I prayed not the conventional 'God bless x, y and z' but rather that God would kill my parents and my sisters, Diana and Clare, that we would be burgled and that the house would burn down – for I believed that God did the exact opposite of what was asked for. I would then sleep soundly totally content that all would be well. Where did that come from? Strange boy! Even stranger that with such a contrary beginning I should become an Anglican priest.

The genteel, almost 'Ladybird book', upper-middle-class world of comfort and entitlement that my parental home exuded gave out strange and contradictory messages about Christianity and its practice. Yes, it was good (required) to say prayers every night and good (required) to go to church. However, church-going was recognised as something boring and a duty that had to be endured – a sort of medicine you took to ensure something – God's protection? A moral compass? Or was it just something expected of us? Something we should be seen to be doing? Values that our attendance showed we subscribed to – I am not quite sure.

In my early years, my mother found an excuse for cutting short our church-going. She used to take me to the main morning service at 11am. It was the service of Matins from the *Book of Common Prayer* with hymns and sermon added. We would always walk out before the sermon thus cutting the tedious hour to just 30 minutes, long enough to hear my Dad read the two lessons. Our exit was always during the hymn before the sermon, during the first verse if it was a hymn we didn't know or during the last verse if it was one of Mum's favourites.

Schooled (1953–1971)

It was not a question of sneaking out surreptitiously but straight down the central aisle from the very front of the church to the door at the back. Nobody else did this.

There was never any thought of sending me to Sunday school, although I asked to go, which would have meant mixing with children of a different social standing. Eventually, the family abandoned Matins altogether and went instead to the early morning communion service at which there was no sermon and the whole thing was over in about 40 minutes. This variation to our routine was because we always had visitors who came to Sunday lunch and we needed to be at home to cook and get ready during the time when the main service was droning on. There was no question about where priorities should lie. Christianity was important – up to a point.

My parents were key figures in the parish – my father was churchwarden and my mother was Enrolling Member (head) of the parish branch of the Mothers' Union, but both these positions had more to do with social status than with devotion. The church fête was held either in my grandfather's garden, a sports field that we owned or, very occasionally, in our own garden.

I don't want to slur my parents' Christianity. It showed itself in their commitment to each other and to a sense of duty and beneficence in the local community. I don't think my father thought about his faith very much. I think for him it was a 'duty'. My mother, on the other hand, had a more enquiring mind. In the 1960s, she read John Robinson's *Honest to God* and the various traditional responses to his book.[5] The book caused a national, even international, stir as Robinson was a Church of England bishop and questioned the whole concept of a God up there; he spoke of God as the ground of our being or, simply, as love. Ethics, for Robinson, was a case of doing the most loving thing rather than obeying prescribed commandments from on high. It is hard to imagine now, but the book was a bestseller and has apparently sold more copies than any other theological book apart from John Bunyan's *Pilgrim's Progress*. It raised questions and doubts that ordinary people had and was part of the questioning spirit of the

1960s. Robinson himself had been part of that spirit of cultural and moral change when he had given evidence in support of lifting the ban on D H Lawrence's *Lady Chatterley's Lover*. Robinson's book, *Honest to God*, was written quickly when he was laid up with a bad back and was trying to explain to his wife, Ruth, in what he believed and why. It was her sceptical questioning that inveigled the 'honest' response. In reflecting on the people who have influenced my thoughts on religion from my mother onwards, *Honest to God* plays a significant part in their lives, it is a common denominator. Not that the book was saying anything new or unthought but a person in authority, a bishop no less, was publicly pronouncing these views and this enabled other public responses that altered the theological conversation. It became a 'marker' for liberal theological thought, it was something you were 'for' or 'against', theologically liberal or conservative.

Years later, when I was going through my training as a priest, Mum professed an interest in progressive Christian theology. Neither parent was a biblical literalist in any sense. I never, for instance, thought that creation stories, the great hero stories of the Hebrew Bible or the virgin birth and miracles of the New Testament were anything other than myths and fables. The resurrection seemed to be an exception and was believed or at least outwardly believed. I noted, even when I was quite young, that it was not included in the list of Christian fairy tales.

Not always totally at ease with all progressive Christian thought and especially anything that was to do with life after death, Mum worried about the souls of my sister Clare's two daughters, Penelope and Deborah, as their father, Jeremy, was a Buddhist and Mum feared his spiritual influence over them. She, in the old-fashioned phrase, feared for their mortal souls. I wonder what nonsense she had been taught by clergy and schoolteachers that made her think that Buddhists would be excluded from heaven? She wrote to John Hick, a world-renowned theologian with a pluralistic approach to world faiths, to express her worries. He wrote back a very sweet letter about the benefits of the Buddhist way and a confidence that there was only one God but many paths. The letter pleased her and, I think, removed some anxiety for her.

The upper-middle-class faith that I was brought up with was strong on morality and family values. I was cocooned, secure and protected from anything subversive or threatening. It was a loving and caring home, and provided all three of us children with a supportive and happy background. It had its boundaries, it governed who we could and should play with and taught a strongly ingrained politeness of manner. Class and our God-given position in society were clearly defined. It taught a sense of entitlement and expectation of a certain position in society just as England (and I use the word deliberately rather than saying Britain or the UK) was entitled to a prominent place in the world. Those were the days when school rooms proudly displayed a map of the world with the countries of the British Empire marked red on the map and Britain presented as the very centre of the world. The church, especially the established Church of England, was one of the stakeholders in protecting that entitlement. All of this I subconsciously imbibed at a very young age.

Life experience determines our understanding of faith, consciously or unconsciously. So why was it, many years later, if I was dreaming of home, did I nearly always had the same image of a large room full of sunlight with large French windows but where the carpet should be there was beautiful tranquil, blue sunlit water? I always told my therapist that I thought it represented a happy, loving and secure home. Diana, Clare and I would and could proffer witness to that, we had a loving mother and a supportive father. Throughout my childhood years, home represented happiness, warmth, log fires, nursery puddings and playing Racing Demon in front of the fire with Mum and my sisters. There was no violence, no money problems, it was all very secure and privileged. Why then did that same recurring dream always have me in the corner of the room hunched up, naked and cowering in fear with my hands shielding my head from some unseen but anticipated blow? What is it about? Freedom and happiness balanced against fear, constraint and, perhaps cowardice?

I remember vividly when as a young child I was ill I always asked Mum to read *Peter Pan* to me. I presume it was a children's version, but the end of the book had a disconcerting phrase about the corner of Mrs Darling's mouth that never smiled. Mum always made a point of explaining this disconcerting image to me as a 'worry'. It was a symbol of worry and as she explained this, she said that we all have worries which stay with us. I loved that book but the bit I was most intrigued by was the corner of Mrs Darling's mouth. It was obviously important to Mum as well, as we always dwelt on the phrase. Strangely, I have looked this up in several versions of the story and in the original J M Barrie text it uses a different yet more understandable image of Mrs Darling (and it was at the very beginning of the book not the end). My childhood was a happy, cossetted world but there was perhaps a corner that was a 'worry'. Re-reading *Peter Pan* now I see it is all rather more complex.

> She was a lovely lady, with a romantic mind and such a sweet mocking mouth. Her romantic mind was like the tiny boxes, one within the other, that come from the puzzling East, however many you discover there is always one more; and her sweet mocking mouth ... which had one kiss on it that Wendy could never get, though there it was, perfectly conspicuous in the right-hand corner.[6]

My mother, avoiding the subject of the one kiss that Wendy could never get, gave me the worry of that conspicuous worry! Is it a parallel image to me cowering in the corner of a sunlit room? Nevertheless, despite the cowering worry, or perhaps the kiss that eluded me, home was basically secure and happy; it was school that was the antithesis.

When I was seven years old, I was sent away to a 'prep' school that was 240 miles from home. It was a bewildering experience. At Charing Cross Station in London, I was handed over to a master from the school and we boarded the school train with about 30 other boys. I remember that I was the only 'new boy' on the train.

I sometimes wonder, almost certainly wrongly, whether the experience of a bespectacled boy with a scar above his eye, which

Schooled (1953–1971)

I received from climbing on railings at Tintern Abbey and being pierced by a spike when I slipped and almost impaled my head when I was about three, ever impinged on the consciousness of our village neighbour at home, J K Rowling. Our two mothers knew each other well, my mother often visiting Anne Rowling when she was ill. Anne used to work for my mother for a while. What gives me pause for thought is that I used to play in a den under the stairs at my parents' home. If at the end of the Harry Potter saga Harry had become an Anglican priest I might have had a case for a tiny percentage. I have written to J K Rowling once or twice, not to make any preposterous claim, but to tell her something that my mother said often in her later years about how happy Anne would have been at Joanne's success. Alas, my missives have not got beyond her gatekeepers.

The school I went to was not Harry Potter's Hogwarts but Tormore in Deal on the Kent coast (1960–1966). The school was chosen because my uncle, a man I had never met before, was headmaster. He told me some years later that he was very careful not to show me any favouritism and perhaps had been rather hard on me. During the first months, new boys felt especially vulnerable with no parental visits or phone calls allowed. Even sending letters home was controlled with the weekly Sunday letter written on the blackboard for us to copy. Other letters could be sent but they had to be left open in the school post box – some, I guess, just disappeared. It was like living in a police state.

The dormitory of new boys was a sad place with all of us crying ourselves to sleep during those first weeks. We were told repeatedly that things would get better and that it was character building and would make us strong leaders. There were frequent short early morning runs before breakfast and then a dunk in fairly cold water in a bath with Matron presiding and holding a sponge with which she washed what she termed as our undercarriage.

I remember being told during a period of unhappiness that if there was another world war, and if I was captured and imprisoned, then I would easily survive as concentration camps would not be as bad as school. Come the war, I would be able to be a leader supporting those less fortunate than myself. It still gets me angry when I think about it. It was quite clear that we were expected to hold significant positions in society, positions with power and influence. This entitlement would be the reward for this hard schooling – you have to be cruel to be kind.

Daily prayers, consisting of a couple of hymns and a reading from Scripture, were held for the whole school seven days a week, usually with my uncle presiding. We all had to pack a Bible and a combined prayer and hymn book to bring with us to school. My great-aunt Phyllis had given me a honey-coloured hymn book that became my comfort blanket. It had a plastic faux-leather cover, and, in my anxiety, I nibbled away at it until the cover looked chewed and had a significant area missing from each corner. Of course, my nervous nibbling had been observed and one day the book was taken off me by my uncle at the end of morning prayers as he processed out with other staff. Embarrassment enough, but it didn't begin to prepare me for the next day when it was publicly returned to me at the start of prayers by him with a short speech about defacing holy objects and my wickedness in so doing. Of course, duly humiliated, I became the laughing stock of the whole school. I had a further mild scolding when I went home for the holidays and we had to set out to buy a less enticingly chewable replacement.

At Tormore, I learned huge gobbets from the Bible in the 4th Form under the tutelage of Myles Raven, a fearsomely large presence to us 10-year-old boys. He, all six-foot-three and 24-stone of him, took us through selected highlights of the whole Bible in one year. What he did was simply tell the stories with some strange embellishments of his own and get us to copy down famous verses. There was no distinction between history and myth – but at least, I suppose, we learnt the stories. He was a good storyteller like his brother the novelist Simon Raven. We were not allowed to copy down his embellishments – for instance, 'The Lord said unto Moses all Jews shall have long noses, except for Aaron and he'll have a square one.' In fact, despite his storytelling gift, Myles Raven peddled insulting Empire views and jokes on religion and race to children who knew no better. To our shame we laughed and giggled and probably repeated them – certainly they have stuck in my memory. Misogynistic too; for him the story of Adam and Eve was a divine warning that you couldn't and shouldn't trust women – women led you astray. When I was a little older and one of his favoured cricket players, he used to refer to women in crude and derogatory terms. These are not the ideal values that you should want children to imbibe.

The school inculcated not only a strong sense of personal entitlement but also a sense of national entitlement and in some strange way it was all tied up with the brand of Anglicanism to which we were subjected. The attitudes promulgated provided the seedbed for the awful views that have risen to the surface in the UK's 2016 Brexit referendum.

We were taken once a term to the local church for Sung Communion. None of us boys were confirmed and, therefore, we were not allowed to receive the sacrament, but it was a hated Sunday for us all. It lasted about an hour and a half and seemed interminable. To help us follow and understand the service we were given a small pamphlet, *Our Bounden Duty*.[7] Aged eight or nine we had no idea what 'bounden duty' meant but knew that for sure it was boring and long. It strikes me now as a perfect way of describing this upper-middle-class understanding of Christianity.

Tormore no longer exists. It has disappeared as part, I hope, of a vanishing age. The industrialist and former Chairman of ICI, John Harvey-Jones, even filmed a sequence of Tormore being demolished in his popular *Troubleshooter* (BBC) series about industry in the 1990s. In *The Independent* newspaper (9 December 1993)[8] he gleefully reported that demolishing the place was 'something I always wanted to do when I was there, and now I'm going to take a jack-hammer to it. I hated the place.' In his autobiography, he confessed to the misery that he felt at Tormore: 'for many years I could not even bear to think back to it, as I was aware that I could bring no balance or fairness, or generosity of spirit to my view of the place'.[9]

11

Like, I suppose many similar institutions, there was a culture of cruelty that was inflicted but tolerated in the name of character building. But who would ever want characters to be moulded like this? Aged nine or ten, I was taught Latin by, let's call him, Mr Smithers. One day he found an ingenious way of punishing us for getting things wrong. He took a broken wooden coat-hanger with a tack sticking out of the wood and if we got something wrong he would tap us on the hand with the exposed tack. Imagine my surprise when many years later I arrived in Glasgow as Provost (Dean) of the cathedral to find he was a member of the congregation.

The wise way to survive this trainee concentration camp was to make enough friends to feel secure and protected. Those who were loners were picked off by the groups, teased and their lives made hell. The other way of ensuring security was to be good at sports. Excel at sports and you became a school hero, untouchable by the bullies. On the other hand, being in the school team didn't necessarily make you immune from the casual cruelty of the school. For instance, a myth abounded that a year or two earlier after playing a neighbouring school at rugby and winning on a bitingly cold and frosty day, with the frosted ground almost like concrete, the team were deemed not to have tried hard enough and the whole team were caned by the headmaster. This story was told often by staff and pupils and was a myth which ensured that come rain, snow, frost or thunderstorm we would always give 100% or risk punishment.

Such tales are common to those of us 'privileged' to have had this sort of education in the 1950s and 1960s. Apart from the sense of entitlement, perhaps the most harmful thing of all was that we had been schooled in a culture of cruelty and bullying that can persist from generation to generation and somehow religion was seamlessly enmeshed into this culture. I often wonder why my father, who clearly knew what boarding schools were like, inflicted it on us. Perhaps he thought they were character building.

Character building, maybe, but I remember running away from the school to my grandmother's house where my mother and sister,

Schooled (1953-1971)

Diana, were staying. I was being bullied at the time and longed to get away. The cause of the bullying was a second-hand towelling dressing gown that was multi-coloured and had belonged to Diana before it was passed on to me. The dressing gown still had Diana's name tag in – so for several weeks whenever I walked into a room or tried to sit next to someone, they called me 'Diana' and mocked and shunned me. It had become unbearable and I was extremely unhappy. My mother's visit to see my grandmother in Deal offered a chance of escape and I took it. The house was about a mile away, if that, but it seemed to me a great escape. On the way to the house, I was shouted at and punched in the stomach and generally shoved around by a group of local boys from whom I tried to flee but they pushed me to the ground and kicked me. It wasn't very serious, it hurt and caused me to cry, mainly out of loss of dignity, but it remains the abiding memory of my futile escape attempt. I can understand that when this small teenage gang, dressed casually and laughing, found a young boy in school uniform, with short trousers, a neat tie and a silly cap on his head, it was an irresistible target. They were venting their scorn at class privilege and the yawning gap between the haves and the have nots. Little did they know that I wished so much to be in their shoes and clothes rather than my polished Clarks lace-up black shoes and a uniform purchased from Swan and Edgar of Piccadilly.

When I rang the doorbell of my grandmother's house, I tearfully blurted out my unhappiness with school but said nothing about the boys; it was too humiliating. I was soon bundled back to school, but the lasting impression was of that hostility by the boys, all a bit older than me, that made me think perhaps for the first time that there were two nations and I was very firmly, despite my unhappiness, in the privileged nation and there was a sense of conflict seething under the surface.

Theology is not something you consciously think about much before the teenage years. My concept of God was based on the sleeve of the record album of *My Fair Lady*, the soundtrack from the musical play based on Shaw's *Pygmalion*. The picture shows George Bernard

13

Shaw as an old man with a beard, sitting on a cloud and controlling the puppet strings of Henry Higgins below him who, in turn, controlled Eliza Doolittle on strings beneath him. With no understanding of who George Bernard Shaw was, I assumed that the figure on the cloud was God.

To my young mind God was called 'Father' and the attributes associated with this father figure were remoteness (never seen or heard), control (seeing every move and knowing every thought), awe, and obedience with a threat of possible punishment – even eternal punishment. Nowadays, I hope, the attributes of God would more likely be seen as love, justice and forgiveness but then, and within the regimented life of a boy's prep school and a polite upper-middle-class home, the wrathful God-King was more prevalent, and we were to be obedient subjects.

This (mis)understanding of God was in some way mirrored by my father and my grandfather. My father never visited Tormore during my six years there and came only at the end of the final term to transport me and my stuff home. Like so many of us from my generation with professional fathers he was largely absent. When I see the loving relationship that friends and especially my daughter and her friends have with their fathers, I would have to say there was something lacking – I was rarely, if ever, kissed or hugged by my father. On formal moments like going to Tormore or other key events it was a shake of the hand, a warm shake of the hand but nevertheless just a shake of the hand. It was respect and an awareness of a behind the scenes sort of love. It was there but you didn't see it or necessarily feel it. At school, a letter from my father usually meant I had done something wrong as he was also the parent to administer punishment. Reflecting now, I just think that was the way he had been brought up.

My grandfather had those same remote God-like qualities. I remember he gave me half a crown and a bar of Cadbury's Dairy Milk chocolate for what must have been my eighth or ninth birthday. I was at Tormore and I never had a birthday at my parent's home from seven years of age onwards. I can't remember having any other birthday present from my grandfather and this special occasion was because he came to stay nearby at the White Cliffs Hotel in Dover on his way to the continent. A taxi was sent to take me to him for Sunday lunch. We had Dover Sole on the bone, something that as a 10-year-old I didn't know how to deal with – what 10-year-old would? I picked at it and was constantly spitting out bones. I was told off, as much as was seemly, in public. There were at least chips in which to take some sort of comfort. As I didn't finish my fish I wasn't allowed a pudding. I remember he ate apple pie and ice cream. Relief came at last when a taxi arrived to take me back to Tormore, and I could stop silently watching him have coffee in the lounge. Rather unfairly, I thought, the bar of chocolate was confiscated when I got back to school. Three weeks later, I received my first ever letter from my father. It contained a sharp rebuke for not writing a thank-you letter to my grandfather for my birthday present and giving me lunch. I remember wishing that my grandfather would die – and within a year he did. I was convinced I had killed him by willpower. Willpower was my current enthusiasm because we had just been told the story and watched the film of *Reach for the Sky*[10] about Douglas Bader, the Second World War flying ace who lost both his legs in an accident, and the sheer willpower that got him flying again, and we were led to believe that with willpower almost anything was possible. I soon forgot my wilful attempt to 'murder'.

In the midst of my Tormore years, I experienced a strange 'spiritual' moment. Of course, I didn't recognise it as such at the time, but the scene has from time to time come back to me in thoughts and dreams so that it continues to haunt me – not in a frightening way – but because both then and now I don't quite understand it, although I recognise it as somehow important. I can almost date it – somewhere between 22 October and 28 October 1962 or, in other words, between Kennedy's television announcement about the Cuban Missile crisis and its resolution. I was just nine, the initial unhappiness of being at the school had faded, I knew its routines and how to survive the harsh regime. I was standing in the forecourt of the school in the early evening, it was drizzling and foggy, but I remember it as being very still and eerily silent. Word had leaked out to us that the world could be facing nuclear war. It was actually difficult to get news; we saw no newspapers, we weren't allowed to watch television or have our own radios, but somehow Kennedy's alarming message had reached us through, I guess, a series of Chinese whispers that no doubt distorted and increased the sense of alarm and impending doom. I was standing there alone, I don't think there was anybody around me, and I was overtaken by a sense of calm and what I can only describe as reassurance and certainty that all was well whatever the outcome of this news. Time seemed frozen as though I was standing there for a long time, but in fact it can only have been a minute or two at most. Some veil had been lifted, some insight felt but what I am at a loss to say. I think every now and then of that inconsequential moment as though it had great significance. When I think of it now the overwhelming feeling was of being alone and yet not alone – invisibly supported. I can't quite rid myself of the feeling that it was important, but I have no idea what the importance was. An isolated moment or two – it passed, life went on, the world was saved but the moment haunts me. Ineffable. Was it God? I certainly find it difficult to write it off as childish anxiety.

That 'spiritual' experience remains as vivid as anything else in my Tormore experience. I recognise that it wasn't my parents who 'f**ked me up', as Larkin would have us believe, but it was the ridiculous schooling they subjected me to. It shaped me in ways I regret but at least I will survive better than some others in a concentration camp! It also probably laid a groundwork of belief and anti-belief that became my career choice. A final meeting with my uncle in his study to shake my hand and wish me well and to recite the final verse of Kipling's *If*. It is a poem I have found it difficult to listen to from that day forward.

> If you can talk with crowds and keep your virtue,
>   Or walk with Kings – nor lose the common touch,
> If neither foes nor loving friends can hurt you,
>   If all men count with you, but none too much;
> If you can fill the unforgiving minute
>   With sixty seconds' worth of distance run,

Schooled (1953–1971)

Yours is the Earth and everything that's in it,
And – which is more – you'll be a Man, my son![11]

My uncle gave me a copy of the Bible, the King James version, and on the flyleaf he had written the school's mottoes – interestingly, I think he got the Latin slightly wrong: Stimulos adde (spur on) and possum quia posse videtur (I can because I think I can). Has there ever been a more succinct rallying call to entitlement?

I left Tormore for the comparative freedom of my public school, Malvern College. I was aged 13. That was the same age as C S Lewis was when he moved from his prep school to Malvern College in 1913. He found the fagging and bullying hard to bear and wrote to his father begging to be taken out of the College.[12] One of his biographers, Colin Duriez, sums up the function of public schools in 1913 which was 'to produce a standardised article … they were factories turning out the spare parts and replacements needed to keep the imperial and commercial machinery functioning efficiently …'.[13]

Lewis's experience was still recognisable but the second half of the 1960s began to see a change, a growing truculence in the ranks of staff and students balancing the old Empire values. There was a palpable feeling that change was coming even if I never witnessed it.

Fagging and bullying was still rife; fags were junior boys who when a house prefect yelled 'fag' had to run and the last one there would be made to do some task or errand for the prefect like taking a message to another boarding house, for instance. There were also personal fags who were 'the servant' of a College prefect of which there were usually two or three per house. The personal fags were basically the 'slaves' of their masters. They cleaned shoes, made beds, went into the town to do some shopping, even warm lavatory seats in the cold outside toilet block. At the end of the term they would get a tip for the service rendered. The perk was that personal fags were exempt from running every time the 'fag' call rang through the corridors. When I was head boy and under the auspices of a new headmaster, Martin Rogers, the role of personal fags was abolished.

The Widening Circle of Us

At Malvern, Christianity still played a part in daily life. Each morning all 600 of us would go to chapel where we would sing hymns and listen to readings from Scripture and say prayers. In the evenings, there would be house prayers, presided over by the housemaster and prefects of each boarding house. It provided a sort of scaffolding to daily life. On Sunday, it was a longer service in chapel which included a sermon by the chaplain or a visiting preacher. Sundays were also treated as a day when we could read, do academic work or go for a walk, but virtually nothing else. We were not allowed to play any sport or indoor games or do anything frivolous, like play records, listen to the radio or watch TV as we were supposedly keeping the Sabbath day holy. I see now that it was designed primarily to be a day of rest for the teaching staff rather than an opportunity to reflect on the things of God. They were probably relieved that we went up into the Malvern Hills, not for fresh air and the contemplation of God's natural grandeur, but to smoke and nearly talk to the girls from other local boarding schools – at least we were being no trouble to the College staff.

In the daily services that we attended, form was more important than content and duty more than spirituality. Nevertheless, somehow the wonderful resonance of Coverdale's translation of the Psalms, Cranmer's Prayer Book, verses of *Hymns Ancient and Modern* and snatches of biblical quotations in the Authorised Version still lurk in my memory nestled side by side with chunks of Shakespeare, Chaucer and other snatches of poetry dutifully learnt by heart for English lessons and exams. All of this was more to do with Englishness than the things of God. Remembering it now, I have a sense of order and discipline, processing in and out of chapel while giving due deference to school prefects and staff. It was very controlled and emotionless. It was duty and it was boring. It sucked out any sense of spirituality or interest in anything except the music. The message about Christianity – duty not joy – was much the same as I had received from my parents which was not surprising as they had been moulded by the same educational process. Church attendance was certainly a duty and not a joy.

Schooled (1953–1971)

More than one visiting preacher at chapel on a Sunday quoted Sir Henry Newbolt's poem 'Vitai Lampada' (1892) exhorting us 'to play up and play the game' as though life and especially war should be played in the same spirit as a game of cricket. The camaraderie, concentration and will to win not for one's own glory but for the sake of the whole cricket team was a metaphor for past wars and wars yet to come. The thought of the possibility of war obviously haunted our teachers, many of whom had served in the Second World War. It did not haunt my generation who had grown up in peace and if we feared anything at all it was nuclear war which would have been played to different rules and ignored entirely the class hierarchy of the army and society. Peter Watkins's still chilling pseudo-documentary *The War Game* (1966)[14] had alerted us to the real perils of nuclear war. We were caught between these two worldviews – our teachers adhering to one, but their pupils living in another.

Just occasionally, a preacher would come to chapel on a Sunday, grab our attention and talk about our world. Anthony Bird, a medical doctor and a priest, came and delivered a sermon about masturbation. His message was clear: masturbation was good, healthy and to be expected, even encouraged, in teenage boys and we shouldn't feel guilty. I came across Anthony later in life when he was my Principal at Queen's Theological College in Birmingham. He remembered the sermon. He chose to talk about masturbation because he knew it was something that we were more than likely being told was sinful and he wanted to add a scientific and medical corrective. He told me that he was roundly told off by the headmaster who wrote not only to him but to the church authorities. We laughed at the memory and I was also able to tell him that later that day we were gathered in our houses and told by our housemaster that the preacher was in error and that there were grave psychological consequences for those who masturbate. We would, he said, be less likely to find a wife and the practice would make us lethargic and less likely to be able to study to the best of our ability. Masturbation was firmly reinstated as a sin. No surprise to know that ever since I went away to school aged seven, I had been warned to keep my hands above the bedclothes. Of course, this injunction did nothing to curb our masturbation although it probably reinstated our guilt and feelings of sexual inadequacy. Isn't it just typical of the church and Establishment to correct the 'person' who was telling the scientific truth and being pastorally astute?

If you lock up hundreds of pubescent boys without any female company, there is going to be a good deal of sexual experimentation. Most, of course, was the stuff of jokes, crushes on pretty boys and teasing but all a consequence of our age, our developing sexuality and the lack of girls. It did, I think, give many of us an understanding that sexuality was more fluid than we realised and that most of us are not exclusively homosexual or heterosexual. That awareness, honestly faced, can create more empathy and understanding towards people with different sexualities. That might be a rare healthy by-product of the unhealthy sexual environment of the British public school in the 1960s. It also made us terrible at speaking and relating to girls – so desperate were we at trying to prove our heterosexual masculinity. This was the era of sexual freedom, but we seemed to still be in chains. Grabbing what education we could from illicit copies of *Men Only* embarrassingly bought from corner shops – and, of course, that was no education at all but a dehumanising and desensitising experience. Everywhere, in film, and even on the records we played, like the soundtrack of the musical *Hair*, a freer sexual, spiritual and political world was proclaimed. We sang along to the soundtrack of *Hair* with adolescent glee at the 'dirty' words – some of which, I suspect, we didn't quite know the meaning.[15]

Boarding school taught those of us unfortunate enough to be sent away to school from an early age that sex was somehow dirty, furtive and illicit. We were often being told not to play with ourselves or each other. This together with a strong parental steer (and from those *in loco parentis*) that you shouldn't show affection in public screwed up many people who went through the same system and it has been a slow relearning process. Reflecting, I am rather proud that an Anglican priest taught us in the school chapel the only wisdom I can remember hearing on sex throughout my privileged education.

If the world was experiencing freedom – and our minds were aching for this new world – we were trapped in compulsory chapel, the combined cadet force and serious games four times a week all within an entirely male environment. The combined cadet force was compulsory for us to join. Once a week on a Wednesday afternoon we would play soldiers – learn to fire guns (the targets were life-size models of German soldiers with a target painted on them), take exams and we were told that if there was another war that we would be conscripted as officers because of passing these exams. The conflict that we were preparing for might be against the communist world or it might be against undesirable factions in our country. I remember vividly being told this by a visiting soldier who came to train us one Wednesday. Most of us thought this was silly but some talked earnestly to the visiting officers and signed up instead of, or sometimes as well as, going to university.

It is easy to write something that is a diatribe against my schooling, my early experiences of Christianity and church-going but I want to try to be positive. For there was a moment when for me faith moved from being a duty to being a way of life. I was still at Malvern and it was the autumn of 1970. I must have been 17 and in my last few terms when I and another boy were sent to Birmingham to stay with a Christian couple, Guy and Helen Horden, for a weekend. They were heavily engaged in Christian social work. It had a profound effect on me and transformed my understanding of Christianity.

Late on Friday night we were nervously helping on a soup run at a deserted Midland Red Bus Station in Birmingham. Arriving in a Land Rover with urns of hot soup and sandwiches, we began to set up our stall when gradually there appeared out of the shadows about 40 people. All were sleeping rough in the city. After a while, with the soup finished, the conversations over, we packed up the Land Rover, and the homeless vanished again into the shadows and we went off to a warm house and comfortable bed. An image of that scene stays

21

with me vividly – men and women appearing out of the shadows of a misty, drizzly night and 40 minutes or so later disappearing back into the anonymous shadows.

The conversations during that time in Birmingham were eye-opening to me. Many of the stories started with normal almost humdrum lives but job loss, broken marriage, financial chaos, addiction, mental illness or violence suddenly ripped these men and women out of normality and comparative safety into this shadowy world that was barely living. I realised, probably for the first time, how fragile life could be and how thin was the veneer of respectability.

The next day over breakfast we talked about the problem of homelessness in Birmingham, but by mid-morning we were visiting a house for prostitutes and drug addicts in Balsall Heath and listening to their stories and struggles. It was fascinating and eye-opening, and, God knows, I had never consciously met a prostitute or a heroin addict in my life before. On to another coffee room for the homeless and there I remember speaking to a homeless man sitting in the corner of the room who quickly and calmly finished *The Times* crossword. He did it at the same time as we were speaking to him, it took just 20 minutes. His story was less about addiction and more about just giving up. He had walked away from a prestigious job, marriage and home. He had just disappeared.

In the evening we met, 'Steve', a former drug addict who had become a Christian and now set about trying to 'save' other drug addicts and homeless people. It was striking testimony and this and the other people he had helped, many of whom were there, gave me my real glimpse of an active and committed faith. Soon, however, we were being prayed over and the prayers urged us to give our lives to the Lord. I don't remember that having any effect on me at all but I do remember that these people who outwardly seemed to spend all their time and money sacrificially helping other people were the happiest people I had ever met. It all seemed a long way from 'our bounden duty'.

Schooled (1953–1971)

That first weekend, a subsequent weekend a few months later and a visit I arranged for Guy, Helen and Steve to make to the school were, for me, life changing. It was a glimpse of a Christianity that was fully engaged with the real world. It was rather shamefully, I thought, my first real experience and understanding of those who are left behind in society. It was a conversion to socialism (and if not socialism per se then certainly to social justice) as much as to Christianity. For me, forever, there has to be a link between Christianity and the least, the last and the lost in the world. Any other understanding of faith just will not do.

My understanding of faith had shifted from a sense of bounden duty that was deathly dull to something that offered a different focus on life. It was not about entitlement and 'spurring on' or arrogantly thinking 'I can because I think I can' – it was about noticing that not everybody had the same range of opportunities and possibilities that I had. It began to dawn on me that a real Christian faith was about the poor, the hungry and those who society had either ignored or failed. It was nothing to do with upholding the status quo and a 'nice' (but nevertheless often hypocritical) middle-class morality. I could no longer be indifferent to the plight of the excluded and victims of society. I have the Birmingham experience to thank for that.

It was at that time that I stumbled upon the writing of G A Studdert Kennedy, the famous First World War chaplain who was nicknamed Woodbine Willie, so called because, unlike many chaplains, he actually shared the experience of the trenches, talked to the men and gave out Woodbine cigarettes. He was awarded the Military Cross 'for conspicuous gallantry and devotion to duty. He showed the greatest courage and disregard for his own safety in attending to the wounded under heavy fire ...' He was so much more than just a heroic war chaplain. He was galvanised by what he saw in the First World War, the horror and squalor but also the elitism and class system. After the war he took his campaign of empathy into the factories and slums of the UK. For relaxation and to help get his message across he wrote accessible but powerful poetry:

23

When Jesus came to Golgotha they hanged Him on a tree,
They drave great nails through hands and feet, and made a Calvary; ...

When Jesus came to Birmingham they simply passed Him by,
They never hurt a hair of Him, they only let Him die:
For men had grown more tender, and they would not give Him pain,
They only just passed down the street, and left Him in the rain.[16]

The compulsive thing about Studdert Kennedy was that he played against type and class expectations both during and after the war and that intrigued me. He had crossed a boundary of privilege and class.

Little did I know that I still needed to learn that I shouldn't be in a position of power dispensing soup. I had probably a rather romantic view of helping the poor and helpless. I needed to be battered around a bit and humbled. Without a kind of levelling there could be no real empathy, no real compassion. There is a poem by Monica Furlong that expresses that thought very accurately.

A slum is where somebody else lives,
Help is what others need.
We all want to be the priest, social worker, nurse,
The nun in white habit giving out the soup –
To work from a position of power,
The power being
That we are not the shuffler in the queue
Holding out a bowl ...

Hide me from those who want to help
And still have strength to do so.
Only those who get on with their lives
And think they have nothing to give
Are any use to me.
Let your bankrupts feed me.[17]

My whole schooling was designed to ensure that I was officer class and that I was in a position of power dispensing the soup rather than an awkward shuffler in the queue. I think that the 'Birmingham experience' taught me to be angry. Angry at inequality, angry at the often casual indifference of my class to the least, last and lost of society. Angry with myself for … I'm not sure what – perhaps for being born into the wrong side of those societal equations, to the privileges I enjoyed and would continue to enjoy.

On reflection, the 'Birmingham experience' was perhaps the most important 'life' lesson that my public schooling taught me. Despite that priceless experience, there were times from the age of seven onwards throughout my schooling that I was bitterly unhappy, so I vowed never to inflict boarding school on any children I might have.

Shamefully, I confess that despite my antipathy to the experience I had quite a successful school career: I received some recognition in all three sports, cricket (perhaps deservedly), rugby (not really) and soccer (no idea why). I became head boy, or senior chapel prefect as it was termed, and isn't that an interesting conflation of secular 'power, position' and established religion! There is a telling scene in Lindsay Anderson's powerful 1968 film *If….* (with its longer ellipsis flouting the conventional rules of grammar).[18] The film is set in a public school as a microcosm of the Establishment, when the headmaster opens a drawer in his study and the chaplain pops out, shakes hands with boys who had played an unpleasant trick on him and then lies down, and the drawer is shut again by the headmaster. That's it! The church as a useful appendage to the powers that be. Stored away and pulled out when needed.

The Birmingham visits opened my eyes and woke me up to social realities beyond my privileged schooling. During the last terms we were given some wonderful extracurricular lectures on philosophy by our history teacher, Ralph Blumenau, that were as important as anything from the curriculum that I learnt in my school career.[19] He had been a Jewish refugee in the 1930s. Shamefully for my generation our reflections on the war were full of war comics and trashy films about the heroic British and Americans. Ralph Blumenau in these post A level sessions seemed to be intent, compelled even, to feed his pupils with these essential tools for life. You felt that this was his personal curriculum that he felt was the most important he could impart to us.

It was here that I first read or thought about Aristotle, Plato, Voltaire, Rousseau, Mill. It was as powerful, inspiring, gripping and useful to life as anything I had ever been taught – the thoughts that emerged, the intellectual excitement that these thinkers triggered were enlivening and exciting. Perhaps out of admiration for Ralph Blumenau, I started to read works of holocaust survivors like the psychiatrist Viktor Frankl, whose book *Man's Search for Meaning* is based on his experience under the Nazis in Auschwitz.[20] It was Frankl's assertion born out of his experience in Auschwitz that we need a 'why', a belief or philosophy, to help us survive.

Alongside Birmingham and Ralph Blumenau's guide to philosophy and living, I studied off my own bat John Hemming's book *The Conquest of the Incas*.[21] Choosing this massive book had been prompted by reading and re-reading Peter Shaffer's wonderful play *The Royal Hunt of the Sun* about the conquest of Peru which he frames as a battle between the civilising barbarity of European Christianity, led by the atheist Pizarro, and the God-like ruler of Peru, Atahualpa. I had seen the play at the Bristol Old Vic in 1969 which had piqued my interest in the subject. Its themes haunted my teenage mind. Shaffer writes about the 'God of Europe with all its death and blooding' contrasted with Atahualpa of Peru whose 'spirit keeps an empire sweet as the corn in the field'. As the narrator expresses at the end of the play: 'So fell Peru … we gave her greed, hunger, and the cross: three gifts of the civilized life. The family groups that sang on the terraces are gone. In their place slaves shuffle underground and they don't sing there …'[22]

Pizarro's atheism and anger at the church's mission in which he is complicit in enacting is contrasted with the primitive religion which he was busy annihilating. This contrast initiated a dialogue in my mind about faith, doubt, social justice and human rights. I can remember coming to the same conclusion as Shaffer does in the play that human beings need religion, or if not religion, a strong belief in some creed or standpoint to help us give our lives meaning and direction. Without that we lack vitality, hope, and life seems meaningless. We need a 'why' to help us live effectively. Shaffer, Frankl and Blumenau had a significant and lasting effect on me and perhaps in their different ways the same answer – the need for a philosophy or religion to believe in.

I was told, by Donald Lindsay, the headmaster, when he asked me to be head boy at Malvern, that I was destined to be not only a leader in the hierarchical world of a public school but in my career and in the nation. It sounded as silly and pompous then as it does to write it now. It no doubt boosted my sense of self-importance, my arrogance and sense of entitlement but on some level that was what my parents' investment in a private education was buying.

Please don't think that I went through most of this first period of life with any sense of awareness of my privilege, it was something that dawned very slowly. For the most part I accepted these years as normal. This is not a question of a poor little rich boy, I lapped up the privileges without much thought; I assumed there would always be enough money, food and freedom to do and be what I wanted to do and be. It was a cosseted life and the hardships, while often silly, could be easily borne by me. Nevertheless, there remained a hint of something 'other'.

CHAPTER 2
CALLED
(1972–1980)

… a long conversation in my heart. Who
knows what will finally happen or
where I will be sent …
Mary Oliver – 'Thirst' – 2006

The Birmingham episode gave me a glimpse of 'real Christianity' but
it still wasn't real to me; it could be picked up and put down easily
enough. I still found church-going a duty and a chore and as soon
as I left school it became one I happily avoided. Then out of the blue
something happened.

I had always lazily taken it for granted that I would become a
solicitor. My father, uncle, grandfather, great-grandfather and even
my great-great-grandfather had all been solicitors. It was expected
that I too should take my place in the family firm. I wanted to get
qualified quickly, so I chose to go to College of Law, Guildford as I
wanted the quick route to qualification rather than the longer route
through university and then law school.

On my last weekend at home before leaving for Guildford in
September 1972 I was helping my parents pack as they were setting
off on a holiday. They wished me good luck as I finished packing their
car, we said goodbye and I waved them off and they drove down the
driveway. I remember spontaneously shouting at the disappearing car
'I don't want to be a lawyer, I am going into the church.' Of course,
they couldn't hear me but it was a turning point and the first time I
had ever articulated that thought or, frankly, ever had that thought. It
came out of the blue. Perhaps even from God? Surely not.

For many years I would tell this story as though I had been chosen,
seeing it as my personal version of the burning bush story. But re-read
that story of Moses listening to the voice of God from the midst of the
burning bush, or watch it in Cecil B DeMille's grossly over-blown film

Called (1972–1980)

The Ten Commandments[23] and you will notice in the film that the voice of God and the voice of Moses are the same – both played by Charlton Heston and displaying unexpected subtlety by DeMille. We might feel these events are from outside, but they are really only a dawning of what the self wants.

For me that moment seemed divinely inspired. However, I put the thought behind me and the following day I went to Guildford to start my legal studies. Frankly, it was painstakingly boring, with lectures from nine to five but not in any sense did the lectures engage the mind. We simply had to take notes during the day and look up cases at night – it was, more or less, education by dictation. I plodded through this for several weeks but the feeling that I wanted to go 'into the church' became stronger and stronger. What was strange was that I felt no desire or compulsion to start going to church. I think if our law lecturers had given us reasons 'why', a sense of the philosophical need and purpose of law, then I might have been more engaged.

I tried to push the religious 'calling' aside, thinking it was just a stupid fantasy, it began to make me physically ill with headaches, restlessness and vomiting. Long conversations with one's heart tend to have a physical manifestation. Eventually I resolved to go and talk to someone about it. I chose my old headmaster, Donald Lindsay from Malvern, who was now retired and living on the South Coast and thus within quite easy reach. He had always seemed supportive of me. He couldn't have been more helpful, listening to my story, such as it was, and then arranging for me (and this is typical of a well-connected public school headmaster) to go and talk to his friend Launcelot Fleming, Dean of Windsor. So, in November 1972, about six weeks into my legal training I found myself sitting in the Dean of Windsor's study in Windsor Castle. This was a more probing interview than Donald's and included a good deal of questioning about my church-going. It seemed to me that he was relieved that I wasn't someone who had always wanted to be a priest and had done all the churchy things like serving at the altar, helping at Sunday school and so on. My vocation, and he seemed to think I had one and that it was genuine, had come unexpectedly, uncalled for and from God. But was it God?

I think now if I was confronted by my young self, I would have recommended a psychiatrist or certainly some form of counselling. Donald and Launcelot did, I believe, want it to be a genuine vocation. I wasn't a born-again enthusiast or a high church altar boy; I was someone, as Donald expressed it, who was not 'chasing a vocation but someone being chased by God'. I had been a head boy of a public school and a cricket and rugby player, so as Donald claimed, I was 'just the sort of young man who the church could do with'. This was very flattering and I was, of course, taken in but it was wishful thinking by them and, I suppose, by me.

After visiting Donald Lindsay, but just before the visit to Windsor, I went to see my parents. If all the signs so far had been encouraging, this certainly was not. I understand my father's disappointment, as I was breaking a line of succession in a family legal practice stretching back to the mid-nineteenth century. For them, it came out of the blue as well. They were, however, impressed by the invitation to Windsor Castle!

I tried to explain that I had a 'vocation' and that I wanted to start training to be an Anglican priest. I also came up against my parents', especially my father's, 'up to a point' view of Christianity. He argued that Christianity was all very well and, yes, important, but it shouldn't get out of hand, it should remain a hobby and something one supported – not something to throw away your life and social standing by following. I remember him saying that I wouldn't be able to live the sort of life that I had been brought up to live and more devastatingly he stated, 'After all, I haven't noticed you going to church very often.' My mother was more understanding and just about kept the peace between us – after all I wasn't trying to do something that was totally disreputable.

An agreement was reached. I could do this but I had to go to university first to read theology before taking any decisive steps. I agreed and found a place at the University of St Andrews for the

Called (1972–1980)

following academic year and put the law behind me after a term and a half at Guildford.

There remained flaws in my new chosen direction. I still hardly ever went to church and when I did, I found it unengaging and a rather soulless going through the motions but for what? Probably to try and prove to whoever was noticing that I had a vocation. I hardly ever consciously or formally prayed although I recognise that I was having just such 'a long conversation in my heart', a phrase the North American poet Mary Oliver uses, and maybe that inner conversation is what prayer truly is.

Did I have a vocation and, if I did, where on earth did it come from? Well, everything I have learnt since has made me quite convinced that I was not singled out by God to do a particular job of work. I think the answer lies far more in the indelible example of Christian social work in Birmingham.

The desire to be ordained and the steps I took towards that goal suddenly translated me into a worldview that thought in terms of 'vocation'. For me, it was something I wanted to do and to be – I hadn't ever thought that this had come directly from God, but those from whom I sought advice spoke in terms of vocation from God, so suddenly I was being 'interpreted' by a new vocabulary which I had to learn. Certainly, Donald Lindsay and Launcelot Fleming used that kind of vocabulary. I began to translate my antipathy to the legal profession and my wish to be a clergyperson into rather grander theological concepts.

I think I was caught up in religious language and the baggage that goes along with ordination as my vocation was tested by the church. I was horrified to read, in a book to encourage vocations, a phrase proclaiming that a 'priest is a walking sacrament of God'. I now know that it was a slight (and sleight) misquote from the theologian Austin Farrer who wrote that a priest is a walking sacrament of the grace of God – which is better – but still implies that God chooses some pet lambs for his religious work. Such language is unhelpful. Why can't we just admit that it is a job we want to do? That doesn't take away

31

from the role of the church to test each candidate's suitability – but we should try to prevent the voice of God from entering the picture. I know that my 'out of the blue' vocation was tried, tested and accepted by the church as a call from God and at the time that is how I too would have described it. With hindsight and worldlier wisdom, I don't think it was anything of the kind. It was, I believe, the first bud of a seed that had been planted in Birmingham a few years earlier.

Oh, the naïveté of my first attempt at being a serious card-carrying Christian! I arrived at St Andrews in the autumn of 1973 to read theology, or divinity, as it was called north of the Scottish border. The first disappointment was realising that divines didn't wear the red gowns that had adorned the university's prospectus. We divines wore a rather drab black one with a St Andrew's Cross stitched on the front. But my naïveté was most apparent when I fell amongst the Christians. Somehow, I had escaped ever hearing about the Christian Union at school and it was far beyond my parents' experience of faith. The day after my arrival in St Andrews, a very pleasant public school-educated student knocked on my bedroom door and invited me to tea at his flat the next day. I will call him Paul, not his real name as he has become a leading figure in the British evangelical world. Paul was also a 'divine' and a Church of England candidate for ordination. He assured me that at tea I would meet some like-minded Christians.

Tea, the next afternoon, was surprising. It was held in a damp basement flat in a terrace of solid and worthy Scottish houses on Hope Street and it seemed to be packed with first-year students and a few older students. A short introduction by Paul began, 'We like to contact Christians as soon as they arrive. We need to support each other in prayer and fellowship. There is a full range of activities throughout the week,' he explained, 'Bible study, prayer groups, and a large meeting on a Friday night. On Sundays, you might like to go to the university chapel or if you want something more Christian then there is a Baptist chapel on South Street. Or you could go to both, as the Baptist chapel has an evening service with strong biblical preaching.' To my mind, it seemed strange to say that the chapel was not sufficiently 'Christian'.

Called (1972–1980)

Paul went on, 'The first weeks of university are full of temptations – drink and sex – be on your guard because the Devil likes to lure you away from the straight and narrow.' He then read a sermon, I can't remember the name of the author, but it was, I think, called *Keeping the Rules*. It was about a train driver who had ignored safety procedures and exceeded speed limits so he could arrive early for some nefarious liaison he had planned. It ended in disaster, the train wrecked, many passengers killed and the driver muttering on his deathbed, 'If only I had kept to the rules.' Our host then gave a short homily on keeping God's commandments and living exemplary lives as a witness to our faith.

The meeting finished with prayer. 'We just want to thank you Lord for gathering us here today, for the fellowship we enjoy. We pray, Lord, for those who face temptations. Make them strong, Lord. And we pray for our meeting on Friday night that each of us might bring a friend so that they too might know you Lord.' And we joined in saying 'Yes, Lord.'

I began to realise that I was going to have to be more serious about religion and church-going than I had been before. But this was different, a more earnest and committed faith than I had known before. The battle with the Devil was a new concept to me. I had never envisaged the Devil as a real entity trying to catch me out. Drink and sex was another matter, I probably drank too much and had, in my few days at the university, frequently gone to the pub or student bars with more secular friends. In fact, I had wanted to be a student and do studently things. I saw now that I must take my 'vocation' seriously and 'fight valiantly against sin, the world and the Devil' and put away any such impure thoughts or the need to quench my thirst at the Cross Keys on Market Street.

What followed was a strange tug of war for my soul. On the one hand, I was a perfectly normal busy student – playing cricket, acting a bit, doing some voluntary service work with old people in St Andrews, going to the cinema, drinking in the pub as well as a little bit of student politics. On the other, a Bible study group on one evening, a prayer group on another and the big Friday Christian Union meeting. I got sucked into this Christian ghetto and this began to take over my life while other activities became more and more sporadic.

And then there was the theology degree. The lectures seemed at odds with what I was being taught by the Christian Union. The first year I did badly, largely I think, because when I asked my Christian friends about what I had been learning, I was told that too was 'a devilish trick to undermine my faith. Did I not know,' they said, 'that most of the teachers in the theology faculty were not Christians.' That perplexed me because they were nearly all ordained. The Christian Union believed in the absolute authority of the Scriptures. To even deny the creation stories of Genesis was thought to be the start of a slippery slope to unbelief.

I was looking through some of my old books and I found one from that stage of my life, *My God is Real* by David Watson, a clergyman and perhaps the most influential evangelical in the Church of England at that time. I quickly re-read it and was amazed at the emphasis on sin, on hell and judgement. All served up with biblical quotations that were treated as though they were the very word of God. There was no room for questioning a text. The choice of texts was highly selective and always taken out of context. The texts largely focused on damnation and the atoning death of Christ. Good works or other faiths would not get you to heaven which, of course, was seen as a real place. Hell was seen as the place of godlessness whereas heaven was for God's chosen – the sinners who have repented. Watson writes: 'Of course, if this doctrine of hell is not true, then heaven itself is meaningless. How could heaven be heaven if it were full of people who had no time for God?'[24] This was the book that we were encouraged to give to those who we were trying to convert. It was suggested that I give it to my parents for Christmas as they clearly weren't Christians. To my shame I did.

To excite us 'real' Christians there was to be a mission in which it was our duty to lead our friends to Jesus. I remember a Sunday afternoon meeting in the basement flat when a few of us were being taught how to convert people. A sort of technique tutorial. We were to get to know the person as a friend. When the time was right we were to talk about sin, especially sexual thoughts and the desire to use another student to gratify those feelings, and to make the friend feel guilty. Then to tell him the scriptural texts that spelt it out so clearly: 'All we like sheep have gone astray.' We are all guilty and deserve punishment for 'the wages of sin is death'. And that would be eternal death, hell in other words. The poor friend would now be full of guilt and along comes the get-out clause, 'The Lord had laid on him the iniquity of us all.' The atoning death of Christ was explained and another fish was safely landed in the Christian net. Of course, it wasn't quite as crude as that and could take a long time to take the friend through the process. In fact, the more you got to know 'the man' the easier it was to play on his guilt.

This is not a sudden burst of non-inclusive language on my part but because it was deemed inappropriate to try to win the soul of someone of the opposite sex. I had already been stopped from that a week or two earlier. I had been attracted to a medical student, Judy, who was part of the Christian group and we clearly liked each other. So, unsubtle though it was, I invited her to my room to come and read the Bible together – it was the prophet *Amos*, one of the few books of the Bible I knew enough about and could show off a little. She had agreed but it clearly must have troubled her as when she knocked on the door she was accompanied by Paul. We prayed together briefly and then she went home and he then gave me a short lecture on the inappropriateness of discussing and sharing such emotionally deep things with someone of the opposite sex especially if the two were attracted to each other. The Devil would use it to undermine our Christian morals. Damn.

In fact, it wasn't just my hormones planning a cosy night in, I wanted to talk to someone about *Amos* seriously and Judy seemed more open to what I needed to think through than Paul. Amos was a dynamic prophet who challenged the status quo and was clearly on the side of the poor and oppressed. He was especially hard on religious people who did not champion the cause of the poor. I wanted confirmation that this was the core concern of true Christianity. But Judy disappeared and Paul and I were left alone and studied Paul's *Letter to the Romans* and the great justification by faith not works debate instead. Remembering the incident now, it shows that even in thrall to Paul and his friends I was beginning to have doubts and wanting a more socially responsible (and even slightly irresponsible) faith and life.

I was soon being groomed to be one of the committee members and leaders of the Christian Union. Paul said to me that we, with our privileged background and position, were required to take the lead as God expected much from us and we shouldn't hide our talents under a bushel, although what he really meant was that we shouldn't hide our privilege and entitlement. A very typical officer-class attitude which I suspect is how Paul saw us, part of an army being marshalled for God – who is on the Lord's side?

Returning home for the Easter holidays, I had been prayed with and for so that I would find the strength to 'convert' my parents. It shows how insidious this form of religion is. My parents lived good and, I would say, Christian lives. They were practising Christians and in many ways pillars of the church community. Why, therefore for God's sake, bother with converting them? But duly armed with key texts and a range of questions, I hesitatingly started to question their faith. Thankfully, it fell on deaf ears. As I reflect on it now, I cringe with embarrassment at my presumption of the superiority of my faith over theirs. I think that the absurdity of this failed attempt did mark the start of my disillusion with this brand of distorted faith.

The break with this type of religion came in four ways. The first was the attempted 'conversion' of a friend. He was a great guy, intelligent and a good citizen spending his free time doing student voluntary service. He had a busy life full of activities and was politically engaged. As I tried, badly probably, to take him through the stages of the conversion process, I could see that it was going to work. The manipulation of this process suddenly made me stop. Did I really want this nice guy to stop his good works and all his fun activities and enter the same Christian ghetto that I was in? Surely, God didn't want that either. I cooled my involvement and found excuses for not attending the Friday meetings and other groups. I remembered that it was 'doing good' and the social commitment of some Christians that was responsible for the path I was now on. I drifted away, although much prayer was employed to try and get me out of the Devil's hands and back into the fold of the godly.

The second loosening of the chains of quasi-fundamentalism slipped away when I started going out with Denise, who was not in this holy clique but who was a Christian, in that she was a church attender and always had been. She was thoughtful about her faith and enjoyed church music and the aesthetic of Christian worship. Her parents were also solid church-going liberal Presbyterians. They had warned her before going to university not, whatever she did, to get involved with the Christian Union. Her father, a distinguished university professor, dismissed their narrowness as a lack of culture.

My choice of girlfriend did not go down well with the Christian Union. Biblical texts were quoted at me: 'Do not be bound together with unbelievers; for what partnership have righteousness and lawlessness, or what fellowship has light with darkness? (2 Corinthians 6:14.)' It seemed absurd that this good person who called herself a Christian should be regarded as some sort of agent of the Devil trying to lure a child of light away from truth.

I was moving away from a narrow understanding of faith that was supernatural, sin laden and which prevented me from being me. The Christian Union quasi-fundamentalism was at worst manipulative but at best it did at least teach me a working knowledge of the Bible. It was also hypocritical and unrealistic about the real needs and thoughts of young people. I remember talking to several Christian Union couples who were having sex and who simply said they had asked the Lord and the Lord replied that in his eyes they were married already. Having left the fold, I remember with glee going to deliver a political election notice to the bedroom of one of the office holders of the Christian Union. I knocked on the door and thinking I heard him say, 'come in',

I entered and found him frolicking on the bed with two girls. I wonder if the Lord had told him that this was OK. At least you might have thought that the Lord would have told him to lock the door.

The split from this narrow 'sect' was made more painful because towards the end of my first year I had planned to move in to a flat with Paul and other members of the Christian Union the following academic year. As the next year began and my complete split from the CU became more complete, things in the flat became tense and frankly annoying, probably for them as well as for me.

Our flat was frequently the place where speakers for the Christian Union meetings came to stay. I found myself having breakfast one day with an evangelical charismatic Canadian, as I hurried about getting him something to eat he asked me whether I had ever spoken in tongues. When I said that I hadn't, he asked me whether I would like to here and now. He obviously hadn't been told by my flat-mates that I had gone over to the dark side. So, amidst a bowl of Frosties and the toast and marmalade, we prayed and began to speak in the strange gibberish of 'tongues'. Initially that was a puzzle to me, but I began to interpret it as complete nonsense that proves absolutely nothing. Even then I knew that it wasn't confined to born-again Christians and that even some communist cells had been known to speak in 'tongues'. Nevertheless, that scene lingers in my mind no matter how rationally I might have tried to dismiss it at the time as nonsense. I found it an unexplained comfort – a confirmation that I was not deserting God.

The third agent of salvation for me was a theological awakening that was transformative to how I thought of the world and the role of Christianity within it. This was due in no small part to endless conversations over coffee with a fellow theology student, Gordon. He was ex-Salvation Army. His family were very involved in the Army but he, because of his gay partner, had chosen to leave the fold. As we discussed the theology of the great German Second World War martyr Dietrich Bonhoeffer over coffee in our favourite café, Peppita's, I think that we both began to forge our own honest theologies and to find an excuse to eat their wonderful gooey chocolate cake. For me, theology was more and more about social justice which is how I understood the central Christian phrase 'the Kingdom of God' – a proper understanding of which meant making the world a better place. It was these discussions that convinced me of the centrality of the kingdom as a hope for this world. Later, a friend and mentor explained that he thought the meaning of this phrase 'Kingdom of God' was rather like the socialist longing for a Jerusalem. It is a secular hope, the age-old dream of a good society here on earth.[25]

The icon of this theological awakening was for me Bonhoeffer, the German pastor and disciple of Gandhi's teachings on non-violence. A devout and serious man, a teacher from a well-connected upper-middle-class background. To cut an inspiring story short, Bonhoeffer was part of the conspiracy to assassinate Hitler; he was arrested on 5 April 1943 and executed two years later on 9 April 1945 by the Nazi authorities. In those two years in prison, he reflected on his theological position. His transformation is chronicled in his book, *Letters and Papers from Prison*, a seminal work of modern theology.

In his early years as a student and as a theologian Bonhoeffer had been a traditional believer and his focus was very much on the 'ultimate questions of life' – death of Christ, the atonement, judgement, heaven and hell – the transcendent and the other worldly. As the world goes bad around him he begins to give all his attention to the penultimate – to the questions of living and acting responsibly in the world. In John's gospel the text 'for God so loved the world' does not demand that people of faith concentrate on promises of eternity, but that they love the world as God does even to the point of suffering and loss. In a meditation on Psalm 119:19 he indicates the shift from ultimate questions to penultimate questions, from the next world to this world. 'There is a very godless homesickness for the other world, and it will certainly not produce any homecoming ... I am not to close my heart indifferently to the earth's problems, sorrows and joys.'[26]

Talking to a fellow prisoner in the Tegel prison yard, Bonhoeffer explains his decision as an ordained pastor to participate in a plot to assassinate Hitler by simply saying that if you see a madman driving down the street mowing down pedestrians, the point is not to pray for the victims and console the bereaved but to wrench the wheel from the madman. Bonhoeffer's insistence of the call of Christians to act responsibly in the world for this and future generations also raised ethical and moral questions. Was it ethical for a Christian to try to assassinate Hitler? Didn't that violate God's law? Bonhoeffer's response was not to take texts from the Bible and try to apply them uncritically and out of context but to look at the underlying moral precepts of Christianity and decide, as mature people come of age, what is the right thing to do in the circumstance. He moved from a list of 'thou shalts' and 'thou shalt nots' to focus on the underlying question of what sort of society are we leaving future generations? How do you act responsibly in the world? These were the key questions for Bonhoeffer and lay behind his prison thoughts on 'religionless Christianity' in which he believed that human beings had to act responsibly and maturely on society's behalf. We have come of age and we are responsible for both the mess of the world and clearing it up. For Bonhoeffer context defines what is right and what is wrong and what God requires of us. We might, of course, get it wrong but deciding and acting on that decision is what a Christian come of age must do. We might have been taught that taking a life is a sin, but sometimes for the greater good we need to take that sin upon ourselves. That is not to deny that it is a sin, but one we have to do for the sake of others. A mature decision.

Bonhoeffer's shift in theological emphasis is key in understanding the shift to contextual and liberation theologies in the late twentieth and twenty-first centuries. Reflecting on this shift, he writes in an essay hidden in his parents' attic just before his arrest: 'We have for once learnt to see the great events of world history from below ... from the perspective of those who suffer.'[27] A shift from the static old certainties and truth to those that take their context with absolute seriousness and shape their theologies within that context. In other words the view not of Pharaohs, but of slaves.

To me, Bonhoeffer's writings articulated in a stark way my own dilemmas (although my shift was far from being life-threatening) and my move from an understanding of Christianity that focused on the ultimate and the transcendent, to one that was fully engaged in the world and questioning the sort of society in which we live and that we are creating. This might be termed a theology of liberation, but for me it was also the liberation of theology itself.

This understanding was undoubtedly 'thickened' and developed by listening to a lecture by the Brazilian educator and Christian socialist Paulo Freire, who was on a visit to Scotland. Through him I began to understand the difficulty in moving from the primacy of theory to that of practice and from talk to action. Silent protest can so easily become collusion with the status quo; change has to come from the oppressed themselves not people talking and making decisions on their behalf from afar.

The importance of context seemed to me the most important theological concept that I learnt, and this tied in completely with my understanding of the Kingdom of God as making the world a better place. Not just a nebulous wish and hope for a better world but something that is worked out practically in your local context. The 'local' was part of a popular mantra at the time – Think Global, Act Local – emerging from reflection on the work of E F Schumacher whose book *Small is Beautiful: A Study of Economics As If People Mattered*,[28] was then much discussed and lauded.

A fourth and parallel agent of salvation for me was 'the arts'. I had a strange encounter with the radical artist Joseph Beuys in the Demarco Gallery at the Edinburgh Festival (I think in 1975) that shook me up. This extraordinary man, wearing a wide-brimmed hat, stood in the middle of the gallery floor and was talking to a group of students who were making notes coolly and casually but somehow fervently. I felt out of place and slunk about in the furthest corner of the room, looking at the exhibits, suddenly he turned around and shouted at me (or so it seemed) in his strange accent 'Who are you? Why are you here? Have you anything to contribute?' I quietly spluttered something in return and he turned back to his students and said, 'What did I tell you? They come but they have nothing of value to give.' Duly chastised I sloped out, followed by laughter at my expense. But the questions continued to pursue me. Did I have anything of value to give?

This chance encounter tied into my understanding of the role of theology. As did my choice of dissertation for my Master of Theology degree. I chose to write on 'Prophetic Theatre – A Christian Approach to Contemporary British Drama'. I focused on three contemporary British dramatists: Peter Shaffer, Edward Bond and David Storey. I took as my starting point two sentences from an essay by the American theologian Harvey Cox on the prophetic purpose of theology: 'The task of prophecy is to illuminate contemporary history, to clarify the crucial options and to summon humanity to a responsible stewardship of the world. The task of theology is to guide, criticize and deepen prophecy.'[29]

I liked the quotation for two reasons: firstly, it resonated with how I now understood theology and secondly, it removed the popular interpretation of prophecy as some sort of quasi-soothsaying role. It was about looking realistically at the world and the direction it was heading. These playwrights personified this same clarity of vision and seemed to summon us to responsible stewardship.

I have already written about the importance of Peter Shaffer's play *The Royal Hunt of the Sun* to me and the same themes of innate spirituality and talents versus reason and craft dominate his other great plays – *Amadeus* (the tension between the virtuoso brilliance of Mozart and the competence of Salieri), *Equus* (rationalism of a psychiatrist against the out of control ecstasy and spirituality of a teenager) and, less successfully, in *The Battle of Shrivings* (a philosopher pitted against a poet).[30]

I chose David Storey because of his extraordinary ability to capture the essence of a community through a central event, frequently an event that happens off stage or between Acts. Often his plays take naturalism of dialogue to the point where the text on the page can sound like a sequence of banalities. The rhythms and surface banalities reveal the depths and tragedies of life.

Called (1972–1980)

With Storey, it is often the spaces around the words that one listens to most intently. I can remember being enchanted by listening to these spaces – the silences that said so much. Storey articulates and pinpoints the tensions in working-class life. His plays are naturalistic, in *The Contractor* a marquee is raised on stage as we listen to the work force, *The Changing Room* focuses on a rugby league changing room and *Life Class* listens to the would-be artists. Many of his other plays, *In Celebration* and *The Restoration of Arnold Middleton* and *Mother's Day* explore the tension between middle-class and working-class values and outlooks through family members who have transitioned from one to another.[31] For me, Storey's plays represented the start of a love of poetry, of the magic of words although I accept that it is ironic that Storey's lack of words should introduce me to the marvel of beautifully crafted words. To listen to the exchanges in his play about a retirement home, aptly called *Home,* is to listen to wonderful poetry with the words and spaces between the words carrying a wealth of meaning.

Edward Bond, the other playwright that I chose to study was bold, visceral and revolutionary. His creed was one of what he calls 'optimistic pessimism'. His firm belief that people are not born violent by nature, there is no original sin.

> The natural condition in which people are born is love, the aptitude for loving and being loved … Children are made competitive, aggressive – society does not control the beast in men, it makes men animals to control them.[32]

This sense of optimistic pessimism is strongly present in his early plays, *Saved* and *The Pope's Wedding.*[33]

In Bond's play *Saved* there are two haunting scenes. One is pessimistic, and the other is optimistic. The pessimistic scene is the stoning of an unwanted baby, and the smothering of it in excrement. This is horrifying and startling and caused the play to be banned in 1965 when it was first produced at the Royal Court Theatre. It was only in 1968 that it was seen by the public after the abolition of the Lord Chamberlain's role in licensing plays in the Theatres Act of 1968.

Indeed, the case of *Saved* and the outcry by writers, actors, directors and critics helped to end the Lord Chamberlain's role as the censor of the theatre.

This pessimistic scene of the stoning is shown by Bond to be the consequence of social deprivation and of the bored lovelessness of the character's lives in deprived areas of South London. Bond believes and dramatises the consequences of the situations in which people live in such areas of deprivation. Bond calls the play almost 'irresponsibly optimistic'. The central character, Len, remains good in spite of his upbringing, environment and the pressure of society revealed in the play. In the almost entirely silent last scene, Len doggedly mends a chair that has been broken in a fight in the previous scene. Len repairs as Harry, the man who has broken the chair fighting Len, does his football pools. Many critics saw it as a high point of modern drama, others as the low point of drama in an increasingly permissive age. It is certainly an arresting image which eloquently encapsulates Bond's optimistic pessimism. It is a life changing image for me.

I remember being asked in a tutorial on our dissertations at St Andrews if I could think of a scene in a play that clearly articulated an aspect of Christian theology. I was castigated when I relayed this 'optimistic' scene. 'But he wasn't a Christian,' they all said. They wanted to talk about concepts of redemption and salvation. It was my first strong inkling of a great chasm between two theological stances, one that was earth bound and practical and the other that still talked in terms of theological concepts. In short from below or from above? I was firmly pitching my tent on the ground.

Bond's 'optimistic pessimism' that pervades this and many of his plays has been something that I have taken as part of my credo although I reverse the two words and speak instead of pessimistic optimism. Bond is 'adapting' an idea from Gramsci – the pessimism of the intellect and creative optimism of the will. The novelist and activist Elif Shafak expresses well what I want to affirm:

> A dose of pessimism is actually not necessarily a bad thing in itself. It makes the mind more alert, more cognisant of what is happening here,

there and everywhere. But too much pessimism weighs the heart down, drains us of energy and motivation. It is emotionally and physically debilitating. Perhaps in an era when everything is in constant flux, in order to be saner, we need a blend of conscious optimism and creative pessimism.[34]

I believe essentially in the goodness of human beings and in their ability to advance humanitarianism. I believe in the goal of a Kingdom of God as a sort of Utopia so that if we call ourselves followers of Christ, then we have to try and contribute to making the world a better place, always starting with the local context. Good can triumph little by little, despite appearances of seemingly opposite evidence. Optimism doesn't mean that we all have to do huge significant projects that are going to alter human history, but it does mean we do little things of which Len's mending of the chair in the midst of a violent situation is just one example.

The act of prayer is also an act of pessimistic optimism. I found these words that I wrote about a collection of prayers that I compiled for a university Christian event:

Some find these prayers too pessimistic, too gloom laden and overwhelming. But the world and its oppressions are overwhelming and frightful and prayer should not be an escape but should 'bite and sting us and rouse us with a blow to the head'. Our intercessions are tears shared with God at the thwarting of God's purpose for the world. To borrow a phrase from Franz Kafka, I want to say that prayer must be 'an axe for the frozen sea within us'.[35] Some will find these prayers too optimistic and naïve in their Christian hope. Yes, in everyday life 'if' is a fiction, in prayer 'if' is an experiment. In everyday life 'if' is an evasion, in prayer 'if' is the truth. Prayer is always the place of dreams and vision, of longing, of glimpses of how things might be. In our imaginations and our dreams, we realize the Kingdom of God. Prayer is above all a place to flex our imaginations … Too pessimistic – too optimistic, perhaps pessimistic optimism is the only stance for a Christian who faces up to how things really are but has a clear vision of how things will be in God's kingdom.'[36]

The plays of Storey, Shaffer and Bond, the brief encounter with Joseph Beuys, the discussions with Gordon in Peppita's, and the inspiring stance both theologically and politically of Dietrich Bonhoeffer all helped me to grow up in my faith and to understand my priorities.

I was beginning to find my theological voice, enjoy my studies and play an active part in university life. I was now branded a 'liberal' Christian, meaning that I didn't believe in the infallibility of the Bible and didn't accept it as my guide and authority in all matters. I became enthused by Liberation Theology. I became charity convener for the theology faculty and attended political meetings at the Students' Union. I played cricket, even making the university's six-a-side team for a Scottish competition which we managed to win – the prize was 144 Black Shadow condoms by Durex who had sponsored the competition. Assuming I was a God-fearing future vicar the captain did not give me my share.

Thank God, I was saved. Well – to a point.

From St Andrew's University, Denise and I, now married, came south to Birmingham for me to train as an Anglican priest and for her to attend the University of Birmingham. During my four years at St Andrews I had gone through the selection board of the Church of England successfully. Thank goodness I had shed my naïve Christian Union views before I attended the interviews. In September 1977 I started at The Queen's College in Birmingham (1977–1978), or more properly known as the Queen's Foundation for Ecumenical Theological Education. We settled into our married quarters and experienced the strange life of a theological college with its somewhat enforced sense of community.

If St Andrews had managed to allow me to start to find my own theological voice, then Queen's Birmingham was there to teach me how to be an Anglican priest – learning the nuts and bolts of the job. The four terms I spent there were stimulating for me, a time to process what I had begun to learn at St Andrews. I had very little academic work to do, my four-year Master of Theology degree at St Andrews exempted me from most of the exams that the other trainees were taking, and I focused instead on learning about pastoral care and attending lectures at the university. It was a time of very good deep conversations as all of us argued and worked out our theologies.

One harrowing day I was sent to meet an undertaker and to observe his work. At his office and the adjacent chapel of rest he flung open the fridge door and I was confronted by 23 dead bodies all in open coffins. The first time I had ever seen a dead body. At least the next time, if I was asked by a parishioner I could honestly say that I had seen lots of dead bodies. In the afternoon, I and the local curate who escorted me on this visit and to whose church, St Mary's, Moseley, I was seconded on a placement as part of my training, visited the local crematorium. It was interesting to see how it worked but I wasn't expecting to be taken on a tour of the ovens. We even had the viewing window of each oven opened for us. There were two bodies burning and one other oven being cleaned. 'You see in this one, the flames are just beginning to cave in the chest,' the attendant cheerfully told us. 'Now this one is nearly finished, look you can just see, it's mainly the bones that are left. That's what we grind up for ashes.' The oven being cleaned, he told us, was in readiness for a child's funeral that was taking place later that afternoon. 'We always give it a thorough scrub before a child's funeral.' I then went upstairs from the ovens to the chapel and listened to a minister take the child's funeral. Harrowing, but I couldn't help thinking that this child and his parents deserved better than being told that the child was 'so special that God wanted him in heaven now'. He then went on to say that this football-loving child would be playing football with other boys in heaven. I found his words of comfort the most gruesome and the least professionally competent part of this day of death.

I had chosen Queen's deliberately because it was ecumenical. I did not want to go to one of the Oxford or Cambridge theological colleges as I thought that would be the more comfortable and expected route for a public school ordinand. It would not have widened my social, political or religious experience. I was still painfully aware of the entitlement and expectation that Paul had talked about at St Andrew's

University. The ecumenical side of Queen's was good - we trained alongside Methodists, United Reformed ordination candidates and even shared a term with a Roman Catholic Seminary. Friends were made less on the basis of which denomination, but more on political and theological positions. It has meant that I now take ecumenism for granted - the variations in how we worship, what happens to the bread and wine, what form of church government our denominations favoured or what we wore when leading worship all seemed like human creations and of very little importance. To uphold one way as the true way would seem to be ridiculously arrogant and wrong.

It was the time (1977) of the publication of a theology book that caused a scandal, *The Myth of God Incarnate*.[37] As the title implies, most of the authors saw Jesus solely as a human being. It was edited by John Hick, a professor at Birmingham and many of the contributors also came from Birmingham. By chance I seemed to be in the right theological place at the right time. Hick was one of our lecturers and quite frankly one of the best I have ever experienced. He could make Kant sound as easy as A–B–C. He was also a very committed Christian social activist and he was particularly active in bringing together different faith traditions and races in Birmingham. *The Myth of God Incarnate* caused heated discussion in the College. Large and crowded public debates were held in and around Birmingham with Hick speaking. I remember attending one with over a thousand interested people; the majority of the public always seemed to be on the side of Hick, that is on the side of the liberal against traditionalist and orthodox views, and it was always an ordained clergyman who seemed to argue against Hick.

What a boost this gave to those of us on the liberal side, who like Hick and his co-contributors, did not think of Jesus as God but preferred to think of him as 'the centre of Christianity' or a 'window into God'. We were convinced that the virgin birth was a myth and many of us were more than hesitant about the literal bodily resurrection of Jesus. Geoffrey Wainwright, one of my tutors and like me a fanatical cricket enthusiast, told me something which I have always found to be true, that if you work out your Christology (your understanding of the nature and role of Jesus) then everything else falls into place. So, if Jesus is just a human being then a virgin birth, resurrection and an atoning death for our sins all become fanciful nonsense.

What is striking is that it was a substantial percentage of those training for the Anglican, Methodist or United Reformed ministry, who believed like Hick and his co-authors, that Jesus was a truly human being. What would our future congregations make of this? Sadly, many of us succumbed to an incomprehensible fudging of this central Christian doctrine and preferred a bland orthodoxy to a theology that people could actually believe in. It seemed as though the church was publicly holding out against the insights of theological scholarship that had frankly demolished much of the biblical story of Jesus.

Those of us on Hick's side, who would regard themselves as theologically liberal, shared an enthusiasm for the ministry of Jesus and his central message of the Kingdom of God with almost all the supernatural elements taken away. The excitement was that this led not to a safe religious ghetto but action to try to make the world a better place, for that is how we understood Jesus' central message of the Kingdom of God. The Hick enthusiasts amongst us had bookmarks made which stated in large gold letters, 'THE HICK IS COOL'.

It was this period and especially the Hick controversy that confirmed my now unshakeable view that Jesus was wholly a human being. In those days, I used to carefully frame my understanding of Jesus by saying in following this human being you find that you are following God (what I meant by 'God' would take several more years for me to work out). The Hick controversy confirmed for me that it is Jesus' message of the Kingdom of God that had to be central. Put simply, Christianity was concerned with this world not the next world and Christians were called to make the world a better place.

Reflecting on my training, I relished conversations with fellow ordinands as well as the time to stop and think whether this was something I really wanted to do. I believed it was but I had already abandoned any sense that I was called by God – picked out to be special. It was just the job I most wanted to do. Indeed, I think that the language of vocation can be dangerous nonsense and lead to unhelpful models of ministry that encourage the priest to think literally that he or she is God's gift to the church. Training requires practical pastoral and teaching skills and the ability to understand the social, cultural and political context of any parish or chaplaincy that you serve. It also requires leadership skills, especially the skills of working as a team. My training taught me some of these but most had to be learnt on the job. I confess that I still felt something of a fake, a sham priest. I still found church-going profoundly boring, I hardly ever prayed in any recognisably formal way. I just hoped I would fall into the habit of prayer and that church services would become more enjoyable rather than something of a chore.

I left Queen's after just over a year to be ordained. Before I left, Anthony Bird, the Principal of the College, to whom I had confessed my misgivings about prayer and church-going, told me not to worry and kindly said, 'you are just rather more honest than many who come to see me'. After he had blessed me and wished me well he gave me (for the second time) some very sound advice. As I was reaching for the door handle of his study he simply said, 'Peter, make mistakes.' That was my commission.

I have always thought that Jesus' great parable of the loving father, the younger adventurous son and the resentful risk-averse stay-at-home elder son was meant as a challenge to those of us who by inclination are 'stay at homes' (Luke 15:11–32). To call it the parable of the prodigal son is to immediately side with the elder stay-at-home son's reading of the story. Aren't we often resentful but secretly jealous of those who take risks? I have always read the parable with a feeling that the teller, possibly Jesus, was urging us to go out, leave safety and take risks and to learn who we really are and where our future lies. Certainly, the sympathies of the gospel writer, Luke, seems to be with the prodigal.

Called (1972–1980)

Thus, I took Anthony's instruction to 'make mistakes' as a challenge to my timidity and my tendency to seek the safe and comfortable road. Maybe, life is a battle between those two selves: the stay at home and the risk taker.

My 'job' as a real ordained clergyperson began in Hagley in the West Midlands (1978–1980). A dormitory village for Birmingham on the edge of the Black Country with a population of about 10,000. I was ordained deacon by the Bishop of Dudley, Tony Dumper, in Hagley parish church[38] and became the curate to the parish.

Becoming a priest in the Anglican church was a two-stage process. Usually about a year was spent as a deacon. This in a sense is a period of probation in which what a deacon can do is slightly limited. They can take funerals, baptisms, but not preside at a Communion service or take a wedding. If all is well there is a further ordination when the deacon is ordained a priest.

Some nine months after being made a deacon, I went to Worcester Cathedral to be ordained a priest. Worcester Cathedral overlooked the County Cricket Ground, where I had once hit the South African-born star of the English cricket team, Basil D'Oliveira, for six. The cathedral was packed with friends, supporters and parishioners of those who were about to be ordained priest. The Bishop of Worcester, Robin Woods, asked all the candidates to make these declarations:

> Do you believe, so far as you know your own heart, that God has called you to the office and work of a priest in his church?
> I believe that God has called me.
>
> Do you accept the holy Scriptures as revealing all things necessary for eternal salvation through faith in Jesus Christ?
> I do so accept them.
>
> Do you believe the doctrine of the Christian faith as the Church of England has received it, and in your ministry will you expound and teach it?
> I believe it, and will so do.

51

Will you accept the discipline of this church, and give due respect to those in authority?
By the help of God, I will.

Will you be diligent in prayer, in reading holy Scripture, and in all studies that will deepen your faith and fit you to uphold the truth of the Gospel against error?
By the help of God, I will.

Will you strive to fashion your own life and that of your household according to the way of Christ?
By the help of God, I will.

Will you promote unity, peace, and love among all Christian people, and especially among those whom you serve?
By the help of God, I will.

Will you then, in the strength of the Holy Spirit, continually stir up the gift of God that is in you, to make Christ known to all men?
By the help of God, I will.

The Bishop prayed for the Holy Spirit to come upon us and then we knelt one by one and the Bishop with about 40 priests from the diocese placed their hands on my head and I swear I felt something transcendent, numinous even, at the centre of that intense ecclesiastical ruck. Was it God? Nerves of the moment? The impressive pomp of the moment? A sudden realisation of what this strange archaic tradition linking back to the earliest days of Christianity would mean for my life? Did God's spirit really descend on me? Was there indeed such a thing as God's spirit?

Was it God? I remember being sceptical about all the declarations before the service and indeed was assured by Robin Woods, that I would grow into understanding as I lived the life. 'I, indeed all of us, think you are called to be a priest. Think of this ordination as a launching of a ship. Peter, you have a vocation.' Now, I think it is dangerous nonsense to think that individual people are called out to be God's agents in this world, as that encourages the ultimate sense of entitlement and power (unearned privileges that have often been and still are abused). This ambivalence about vocation left me on the border between faith and doubt, between being comfortable and competent as a priest and wondering what on earth I was doing here with my shaky faith. In some ways border living is a good thing, it demanded asking myself constantly where I belong and questioning what I am doing and being wary of what I sign up for. It makes contact with others not inside the holy flock perhaps easier to navigate.

Throughout the first three years of ministry, as part of our continued in-service training, the curates of the diocese would meet about once a month and listen to a speaker and share our experiences and difficulties. At one of the first of these, we were told by a retired bishop (Oliver Tomkins, a former Bishop of Bristol) that we should have two theologies – one for the study, in which we could explore doubts and modern interpretations (indeed we were positively encouraged to read contemporary theology and wrestle with the big theological questions with intellectual rigour), and the other for the pulpit and parish where we had to teach an orthodox Christianity. 'The Shepherd must lead the sheep,' declared Bishop Tomkins. I argued, and still do, that this is fundamentally dishonest and the lack of sincerity wins no one to Christianity. In some ways the Tomkins solution was tempting, if dishonest. I would rather try to straddle the middle ground (the muddle ground) between doubt and faith. I wanted to be honest about what I believed and what I didn't believe. I didn't want to be like the Emperor in Hans Christian Andersen's story and think I was wearing the most beautiful clothes. I wanted to wave the flag for honest doubt. I remember listening to the late Gerald Priestland talk (he was the BBC religious affairs correspondent) about the number of 'disgruntled of Tunbridge Wells' letters he received telling him that he was a wicked man destroying people's simple faith. But he had never received a letter saying you are a wicked man you have destroyed my faith. I think we fear needlessly. Clergy should not pretend to believe 'firmly and truly' as many of us are hovering on the border between faith and doubt just like the people in our congregations and those on the edges of those congregations.

Remembering my College Principal's parting words to 'make mistakes' which I interpreted to mean to be bold and to be prepared to take risks. I took him at his word. The first sermon I preached as a deacon was just before Christmas and the reading was about the Annunciation to Mary. Wisely or foolishly, I spoke about the virgin birth stories and explained that they were myths or poetic stories that weren't meant to be taken literally. That was the cause of my first mild telling off by my boss, the rector of the parish. He had received complaints and it wasn't, he warned, my 'right' to challenge people's simple faith from the pulpit. However, I was pleased to see that the next time I preached on the Sunday after Christmas (usually a Sunday of low attendances) there were over twice as many people in church.

As a curate, my life was largely taken up with funerals. In my first year, I took 56 funerals. The first funeral I ever attended, apart from that strange day of death when I was training, was at one that I ministered. Funeral visits took up most of my time and it was rewarding experience, if stretching pastorally. I was not a believer in the literal bodily resurrection of Jesus or of our own bodily resurrection. I was aware that this was not the right time pastorally to throw that sort of theological bombshell into the midst of a grieving family so like so many others I fudged it. Of course, people should be encouraged to think about the mystery of death in the normal teaching role of the church's life but not, I think, in the midst of a pastoral funeral visit. However, many people did raise questions about what happens after death when confronted by the death of someone close and I replied as honestly as I could. I relied a great deal on Paul's description of the resurrection in 1 Corinthians 15:44, which also hedges its bets but draws a parallel between a human body and a kernel of wheat: 'it is sown a physical body, it is raised a spiritual body'. Earlier in the same passage he refers to his meeting with the risen Christ as a dream, a vision which I think is the proper interpretation of the so-called resurrection appearances. I just about maintained my theological integrity without alarming the church-goers.

Called (1972–1980)

I began to wonder if being a priest required any other skill apart from the ability to support people through death and funerals. Most of the funerals I took were for people I didn't know, and most were not church-goers. Funerals became less a religious observance and more a memorial and celebration of the deceased person's life. It was as though nobody (clergy, family or congregation) quite believed that there was an afterlife.

Occasionally, of course, funerals were for people I knew who were key members of the church community. I remember sitting with one old lady, a widow, who had been ill for a long time. She was extremely frail but had a strong faith and an absolute certainty that she was going to be with God in heaven. I guess I had been sent to be with her by the rector to experience her faith and acceptance in the face of death. As it became clear that she would not last much longer. I sat by her bed and read some psalms, said a few prayers and waited with her. I think I was much more anxious than she was; I had never been with someone in the last hours of their life. She quietly, said to me, 'Don't worry, vicar. I have read the gospels and I have seen *Ben-Hur*.' She died a few hours later and those were, I suspect, her final coherent words.

It is a great privilege to be alongside people at these key moments of life, birth, death, marriage. In funerals, I always feel more valuable than in other pastoral services – it is good to have someone who takes away the worry of the service and knows the practical mechanics of what is going to happen and why. It helps to have someone alongside the bereaved as they go through the stages of grief. I enjoyed trying to gather the stories and memories of the deceased and get a real sense of the person. In fact, turning the funeral away from being a gateway to another world to being a memorial and celebration of the deceased's life.

Young curates are usually given schools and youth clubs to look after – it is typically something that the training clergyperson is eager to avoid. I took assemblies, in junior, middle and high schools and was met with blank indifference until I took the funeral of a 16-year-old boy who died on his motorbike. They saw the need for a clergyperson then and continued to speak to me about their concerns and worries.

I also ran a youth club. It was successful with about 40 members. It was meant to be a place of Christian instruction leading up to confirmation as well as a place to have fun. I also wrote and put on a couple of plays/liturgical events with the group. One of the bits of drama was a re-working of the parable of the prodigal son. We changed it to a prodigal daughter who ran away from home (using the Lennon/McCartney song *She's Leaving Home*). The rest of the story follows the parable closely, but instead of a cloak to wear at the party, she is given a multi-coloured woolly jumper as she is welcomed back home by her mother and a party is held to celebrate. What I remember most is two mothers who came to see me the following day and complained that the girl wasn't punished by her mother. They thought my teaching was not Christian and endangering morals. This baffled me as it seems to be the whole point of the story about the unearned and undeserved welcoming love of God. A complaint was sent to my boss.

Not unrelated to the re-working of the parable, I also remember a young girl of just 16 who became pregnant. Her boyfriend was the same age. They came to see me having just told their angry but, in the end, supportive parents. We spoke and I assured them of the church's support, and they said they were grateful and that they would come to church the following Sunday. They did and thankfully seemed to be accepted by the church community. On the following Monday, my boss told me that that they were not to come back to church until they were properly repentant and that in future, I should refuse them communion. 'They need to be made aware of their sin,' he argued, 'we cannot be seen to tolerate immorality'. It was a moment of strong disagreement between us as I felt that it said a great deal for the church community that they felt comfortable attending and that they felt acceptance in spite of what had happened to them. My boss went and visited the parents of both and told them that it was not appropriate for them to come to church. I was furious, but my bluster was trumped by his seniority and there was nothing I could do other than visit and offer support in that way. The incident upset me – it seemed counter to everything I understood about Christianity.

I left the parish shortly after the incident with the young couple. I had wanted to see whether liberal theology in a place like Hagley would be accepted. The answer was both 'yes' and 'no'. 'Yes', in that I found young people, once I made the breakthrough and earned their trust, were quite receptive. I found, too, that talking to the bereaved was a time when they and you could be honest and struggle together to understand the meaning of life and death. 'No', in that the church authorities (national, diocesan and local) were unwilling to take risks or be very honest about faith and the result was often a boring blandness. The Archbishop of Canterbury of the time, Robert Runcie, had spoken of 'the bland leading the bland' and that seemed an accurate description of much of normal church life.

The two worries that I had before I was ordained about lack of prayer and not enjoying services in church had partly been answered. I confess, and this is not very honourable, to only finding services that I was taking or participating in quite enjoyable. I enjoyed the performance aspect which is hardly a spiritual plus. As far as prayer is concerned, I still struggled. The clergy team and a few laity said morning and evening prayer in church each day. As a way of bringing pastoral concern to the fore and talking about them afterwards I found this helpful, as a way of meeting and reflecting together as a team it was also helpful. As a form of spiritual discipline, I found it wanting. The recital of the same few canticles day in and day out, the reading aloud of huge chunks of Scripture from the Hebrew Bible and the New Testament was not very enlightening as the pieces lacked any pastoral context. There were moments when I just sat quietly in the church and waited for my colleagues, or times when they were away and it was just me on my own in a large church, it was then I began to feel something, some connection, some deep thoughts – not so much a presence but (and this is not quite the right word but the closest I can get) a direction. Frankly, I liked sitting still and reflecting. To move through the noisy clatter of thoughts to a kind of peace in which my other self can be found and a direction gradually suggests a way.

The Widening Circle of Us

While at Hagley, I read Don Cupitt's 1980 book *Taking Leave of God*, which was causing a stir as it implied that this ordained Anglican theologian was an atheist. I liked the book and was especially struck with his idea of Christian Buddhism. He lists a number of religious practices and values that should remain and be the solid core of faith. They are:

> It is good that one should appraise oneself and one's life with an unconditional religious seriousness that tolerates no concealment or self-deception.

> It is good that one should cultivate meditation and contemplative prayer, and especially the inner fortitude and resilience needed to combat evils of all kinds.

> It is good that one should come to transcend the mean defensive ego and learn absolute disinterestedness and purity of heart.

> It is good that one should commit oneself to existence in religious hope and receptivity to grace.

> In spite of all the ugliness and cruelty in the world, it is good that one should at least sometimes experience and express cosmic awe, thanksgiving and love.

> It is good that such values as these should not only be cultivated in and for oneself, but that they should shape our attitudes towards other people and be expressed in our social life.[39]

These simple 'goods' felt right, a raft of sense in the midst of so much that had been written about all the ideas, disciplines, creeds and spiritual exercises that I am sure are useful to many people searching for a spirituality but not for me. I think we all need to find our own path, our own way of pondering, praying, focusing on what matters about the world, about self, about those we care about, the confusions of daily living. Cupitt's list of 'goods' provided a basis of what works for me. It articulated and summarised what I believed, and they have remained my touchstone of what faith should and could be. It was time to move on.

CHAPTER 3
LONDON E1
(1980–1987)

But learn to learn and try to learn for what.
Bertolt Brecht – So you could Sit here ...

We moved to London in August 1980. I was to be chaplain of Queen Mary College, part of the University of London. In London, we lived in Sidney Square, an area full of East End history. It was just behind the London Hospital and south of Whitechapel's Blind Beggar pub where Ronnie Kray murdered George Cornell in 1966, and in front of that same pub was where William Booth preached his first sermon in 1865 which led to the foundation of the Salvation Army. If you cross the road from the pub you enter Sidney Street where in January 1911 the Police and Army united to lay siege to Jewish Latvian refugees, who later proved to be innocent. It was an over-zealous blunder that led to loss of life by the then Home Secretary, Winston Churchill. Just a few streets away, there was Cable Street, the scene of the battle in 1936 between Mosley's black-shirted fascists defended by the Metropolitan police on the one side and the Jews, Irish, socialists and communists on the other. But it was always Christian Street, London E1, that fascinated me most for there was a mosque in a building that had been a Jewish synagogue but which started life as a Welsh Baptist chapel. There was a Bangladeshi grocer in the street but above the door I could still make out the previous name of the shop – 'Cohen'. The street's name was itself, I was told, a hangover from an earlier wave of immigration, that of the French Huguenots in the sixteenth and seventeenth centuries. The street charted the waves of immigration that swept through the East End of London.

Walk a mile further on and there was evidence of another wave of immigration with Limehouse's Chinatown that in those days had very good Chinese restaurants and, still then in existence, a Chinese laundry. As the waves of immigrants became more settled and prosperous so they moved further East or North. We lived in the East End at the end of the Jewish era still with a few Jewish bakeries hanging on – Bloom's restaurant in Whitechapel, the most famous kosher restaurant in Great Britain, closed down while we were there.

The East End was a very cosmopolitan community. Each tide of immigrants or refugees left some of its community in the East End and traces of their culture. Of course, the East End was still in the 1980s a slightly rough place to live, with a lurking air of criminality still detectable. The gentrification had hardly started to happen. There were also obvious racial tensions that meant at night you needed to be cautious.

Walking along the Commercial Road in London's East End in the early evening I became involved in an incident that is open to two widely different interpretations. It was just before seven in the evening and I was returning a video to the video shop (remember them?) when I literally bumped into three black guys coming out of a pub, or rather they bumped into me. I mumbled 'sorry' in a typically awkward British way although to be honest it hadn't been my fault at all. I carried on walking and out of the corner of my eye I was aware of them pointing at me and talking amongst themselves and then they started to run towards me. Thinking that I was about to be mugged. I quickly turned around and faced the attackers and said, surprisingly calmly and with my hands far apart and wide open, 'Please don't hit me. I'm a priest. I will only have to turn the other cheek and it will be frightfully painful for me.' They stopped in their tracks and from an aggressive stance, with fists ready to strike, they suddenly begged for forgiveness and mumbled their embarrassed apologies. We started to talk, and I listened to their brief explanation. A friend of theirs had been beaten up by white skinheads and they had gone to the pub to drown their sorrows and plan revenge. Their plan was to attack the first white guy they saw who gave them any bother. Clearly I was the 'bother' that gave them the excuse. They asked for my forgiveness on the pavement of the busy Commercial Road. I obliged and assured them of my prayers and of my sympathy, we shook hands and I went on my way to return the video to the store.

A lucky escape? Yes, but was it divine intervention? No, it was just quick thinking or maybe reflex cowardice. It was lucky and very surprising that they believed me as I wasn't wearing a dog collar or anything to imply that I was actually a real priest – indeed, the only thing I was carrying was an 18-rated Ken Russell video. I put it down to luck and perhaps an awareness that violence met with more violence only begets yet more violence – God knows I had platitudinously preached it often enough.

The experience of living in the East End was a formative experience for the students and staff of Queen Mary. Often from safe middle-class backgrounds, the ever-present poverty and racial tension of the areas surrounding the College opened many eyes to the reality of life for the left behind and the immigrant. After the leafy middle-class world of Hagley, it was quite a contrast for me as well.

Having struggled with the fundamentalist evangelicalism of the Christian Union at St Andrews and, having become more liberal, I very much wanted to act as a bridge between these two Christian communities on campus. It was a good intention but doomed to failure. I, and by association students and staff who frequented the chaplaincy, were branded as non-believers by the Christian Union who clearly wanted nothing to do with me and the chaplaincy crowd. And the students who hung around the chaplaincy certainly didn't want to be associated with the Christian Union. I realised that many people join the Christian Union but many also leave and have an experience not unlike my path away from it at St Andrews. They needed somewhere that was obviously different to turn to. To offer something that was markedly different in tone was a help for those wanting something other than the certainties of the Christian Union. Something that wasn't opting out of student life but fully engaged. For instance, we held short services in the College building during sit-ins.

We, the Roman Catholic chaplain, the Methodist chaplain and I made the chaplaincy almost aggressively ecumenical. Each Tuesday evening, we would hold a Eucharist and the three chaplains took it in turns to preside with one of the other chaplains preaching. There was no question of excluding other denominations from full participation, although the church authorities, especially the Roman Catholic, looked on askance. But it worked, and I like to think that all those students who attended will never be satisfied with anything that segregates Christian denominations. Strangely, the only time it didn't work was in the week of prayer for Christian Unity, an official UK-wide ecumenical event, for then we examined our differences. But by working on projects together and naturally enjoying the diversity of worship styles together week by week it was a good experience. I suppose, we lived and believed in John Wesley's dictum that Stuart Jordan, the Methodist chaplain, quoted to me:

> If it be, give me thy hand. I do not mean 'Be of my opinion'. You need not: I do not expect or desire it. Neither do I mean 'I will be of your opinion'. Keep your opinion; I mine; and that as steadily as ever ... Let all opinions alone – on one side and the other: only 'give me thine hand'.

In Hagley, I had been aware how excluding church could be for young people, even to the point of actively pushing them out. I was determined that a university chaplaincy would be welcoming, inclusive and open regardless of age, gender, class, religious denomination or sexual orientation. Nowadays, that seems almost trite and just sheer common sense but that doesn't take account of the dos and don'ts of church authorities who tried to curb our practice of intercommunion between denominations, our insistence that everyone was welcome to receive the sacrament regardless of whether they were baptised or indeed belonged to a different faith.

My main support in chaplaincy work was not primarily my fellow chaplains who were only part time at Queen Mary but a mature student Nerissa Jones. She helped to shape the chaplaincy into something that was active politically and strongly ecumenical. She and her husband, David, had spent time in Ghana and had been transformed

London E1 (1980–1987)

by the experience. David had been a soldier seconded to support and advise the new Ghanaian democracy. The experience of that posting led him to apply and become deputy director of Oxfam. Nerissa was studying German and spoke to me of her sense of vocation. She was invaluable support in chaplaincy matters and a remarkable socially and politically committed Christian. When she left the university with a first in German, she trained for the ministry and was appointed as curate to St Botolph's in Aldgate, a church with a strong and valuable ministry to the homeless. From there she went to Coventry to one of the most deprived areas of the city, Wood End, where through hard work and constant political agitation she achieved much. These were perfect postings for her because she had a clear-sighted understanding of the gospel as having a bias to the poor and marginalised.

The activism of the chaplaincy also suited Nerissa and indeed was partly shaped by her commitment and social conscience. The chaplaincy was run on the basis of generous hospitality to the students, an atmosphere that was open and friendly and had a strong commitment to the social gospel. All of these characteristics Nerissa embodied and she and David were happy to invite groups of us down to their cottage in Dorset for weekends of discussion and relaxation. She provided invaluable support and friendship to students and staff.

I valued her friendship and companionship in the chaplaincy and beyond. Discussions with Nerissa helped me shape a more robust political theology and, of course, articulated very vividly the discrimination against women in the Anglican church. On a personal level, she often supported me in my own life and was always someone who would listen and offer shrewd but practical and realistic advice. Her career, and the support of David, took her to selfless hard inner-city jobs before moving to Dorset for a more peaceful life. I admired the political cut and thrust of her ministry and the feeling, especially in the deprived area of Wood End, that she was making a difference even if it was at some personal cost.

I still quite often ask myself 'what would Nerissa say or do' when I have preached something controversial or have made a choice that determines where or how I should minister. I often feel that I have ducked out of hard ministry committed to the poor. I sense her disapproval which is an absurd thing to say as you could not meet anyone kinder or more tolerant and forgiving. And yet, I think, it was partly the chaplaincy experience that helped to shape her future ministry and life.

The activity of the chaplaincy was often political: raising funds for a black South African student to study at Queen Mary College's law faculty; running our own weekend soup kitchen – the chaplaincy building was on the Mile End Road and the number of homeless that passed the door was very large; and there was always some demonstration or another to march on each weekend – anti-apartheid, CND, against the Falklands War, in support of the miners, save the GLC – there were no end of causes in Thatcher's Britain.

The advantage of being in London was that we could invite well-known speakers to chaplaincy meetings, speakers that would attract more than just the usual Christian crowd. Amongst whom we invited Bruce Kent, the Catholic priest who headed CND; the Roman Catholic Archbishop of Westminster, Cardinal Hume; Richard Kirker of the Gay Christian Movement; the veteran anti-apartheid campaigners and Bishops Trevor Huddleston and Colin Winter of Namibia; David Jenkins, the notorious Bishop of Durham and Lionel Blue, the wonderful witty gay Jewish rabbi, who I remember telling me of his horror at reading the minute books of a church that was beside the tracks leading into Auschwitz. As the terrible human cargo rattled by Lionel told us that the minute book revealed their concerns and priorities: a church social raising funds for a new roof.

One of the most compelling and memorable speakers was Sister Irene Brennan, a Roman Catholic nun, who was also general secretary of the British Communist party. A group of traditional Roman Catholic students from all over London flooded our meeting with hostile intent. In the questions at the end of her talk, the leader of their group asked very bluntly how she could justify her communist activities with being a Christian nun. 'Oh,' she replied, 'It is quite simple, every day at twelve I go into church and pray for the party!'

The work at the university was engrossing and stimulating. Part of the time I was counsellor, sometimes a chef cooking supper for large groups of hungry students in the chaplaincy and part of the time an activist priest. In the university holidays, I helped at local churches; they were often very small struggling East End congregations of elderly people.

Chaplaincy life was not immune to the political life of the wider Church of England. *Faith in the City,* a report published in 1985, was the fruit of work done by Archbishop Robert Runcie's Commission on Urban Priority Areas.[40] The report suggested that much of the blame for the spiritual and economic malaise in the inner cities was due to Thatcherite policies. The commission had toured the country and worked with inner-city groups and clergy to compile their findings which were based on the testimony of those they met. I was included in some of the East End clergy group discussions and we had Canon Eric James, who was perhaps the prime mover behind the report, to speak at the chaplaincy. He became a friend who kept on popping up throughout my life – always witty, always radical. Thankfully, his archive has now come to Gladstone's Library.

I came across a piece of paper that was part of the submission of the East End clergy group to the report. It was short and pithy and, of course, uncomfortably accurate:

> God is with us in our brokenness and powerlessness.
> Yet the church aligns itself with the established and the powerful.

> God values everyone.
> Yet the church picks its leaders by worldly standards.

> God is good news for the poor.
> Yet the church isn't.

> God is present in a mixed community.
> Yet the church presents God as an educated Englishman.

God calls people together to send them out.
Yet the church acts like a social club for private members.

God sets us free from all that enslaves us.
Yet the church shackles us with convention.

God, how dare we call ourselves your people?

Faith in The City was far reaching for the Church of England and helped to launch a sea change that valued inner-city ministry and saw that its mission was properly financed and supported. It was predictably rubbished by the Thatcher government and frequently labelled 'Marxist'. In reality, it was reality.

A key movement which came to define my time at Queen Mary College was involvement in the struggle of women to be ordained into the Anglican church. A number of students from Queen Mary, including women, wanted to 'go into the church' and during my six years there I can think of seven people who have been ordained from that small student community. At Queen's I had trained alongside very able women who were at that time barred from fulfilling their vocation to be a priest because of the bigotry of many members of the Synod of the Church of England, who prevented the legislation from being passed by a sufficient majority. I felt too, the pain of women students who felt they wanted to be priests but the required two-thirds majority of those voting in the house of laity, house of bishops and the house of clergy could not be achieved.

In 1975, the Synod of the Church of England had voted that there was no fundamental objection to the ordination of women to the priesthood. In USA, Canada and New Zealand women were being ordained into the Anglican priesthood. It is a lamentable chapter in the Church of England's history. At a debate in 1987 – 12 years after agreeing that there was no fundamental theological objection to women's ordination, – Synod speakers claimed that women were 'dismembering', 'disembowelling' and 'destroying' the church. In that same debate, Graham Leonard, the Bishop of London, referred to those women as an 'an ineradicable virus in the blood stream of the church'.

London E1 (1980–1987)

A vote in Synod in July 1986 perniciously prevented women lawfully ordained abroad from celebrating the Eucharist or any other priestly activity in England. For some that was the final straw and they demanded action. It seemed mean-minded and another piece of blatant discrimination and institutionalised misogyny. The hurt to women who felt 'called' to the priesthood was palpable. The group, headed by the author and broadcaster, Monica Furlong, could wait no longer and wanted to take some positive action. Monica, it should be noted, was not doing this on her own behalf but on behalf of those who felt called.

I was on holiday in Portugal in mid-December 1986 searching for a bit of late sun and a modicum of warmth. In those days, long before newspapers could be read on tablets or mobile phones and before the advent of 24-hour rolling news channels, those of us who were obsessed with knowing the latest news when we were out of the country used to search for newsagents that had a copy of an English newspaper. It was usually a couple of days old but a precious, and often rather expensive, fix for us news obsessives.

I eventually found a two-day-old copy of *The Independent* in a small newsagent in Albufeira. As I got my news fix, I read an article by Monica Furlong about the ordination of women in England. In the article, Monica complained about liberals in the Church of England who were quick to voice their support, but when some action was required were not to be found. She singled out liberal bishops, but it applied to most liberal clergy. The ordination of women did not, she felt, seem to be a justice issue to them but rather a women's problem with which they sympathised but, perhaps, only to a point (and that point was usually their career and reputation). The strange thing is that I have searched and searched through digital archives for Monica's article in *The Independent* but to no avail. I have tried other papers thinking I might have misremembered – I have searched all the broadsheets and nothing has come up. Did I dream it? Was it some strange premonition that I had as I wandered beside the sea in the Algarve? Another one of my moments? God knows! I can remember thinking I had to do something and a feeling that faith required greater commitment than I was giving.

Back in England, I was surprised when less than a week after reading this article I got a phone call from Monica Furlong asking to see me. We met a few days later in my office in St Benet's Chaplaincy at Queen Mary College. Monica came straight to the point. Would I allow the chapel to be used by a small community of women and men who would invite women ordained overseas to come and celebrate Holy Communion? Monica and the rest of this small group were fed up and wanted to do something that would bring a bit of hope and above all support for women who felt called to the priesthood. I must realise, she reminded me, that what she was asking was illegal within the Church of England and might lead to some trouble. The community would start quietly and build itself up so that it wasn't just formed to do a delinquent thing. Remembering the article that I had read just a week before, I felt my 'liberal' credentials were at stake and I agreed and indeed became part of the community from its first meeting on Sunday 1 February 1987.

I knew that my bluff had been called. If I wanted to call myself 'liberal' and if I wanted to face those women I trained with and the students who felt called to ministry with a clear conscience I had to do this whatever the consequence for my career.

The decision was not hard to make, not to make it would have been going against not only the women I trained and worked with but the whole thrust of the secular feminist movement.

In those first weeks of the community in the early months of 1987 we gathered and gradually worked out a way of worshipping that suited us. It was a given that the language was non-sexist as we called it. The community began with a few students from the chaplaincy and some from Ripon College, Cuddesdon, two of whom, Nerissa Jones and Sally Theakston, had been key figures in the chaplaincy congregation and were now training for ministry at Cuddesdon. Among the other attendees were members of the *Movement for the Ordination of Women* and from the small group *Women in Theology*. Other people began to hear about it and our inclusive community attracted many who felt attracted by the ethos – a number of gay men and women and others who felt marginalised by their local churches. Within a few weeks, we had selected a name for the community, St Hilda. We wanted a woman saint who had been a strong leader, not just another virgin who starved herself to death, as Monica insisted. We chose Hilda who had founded a community at Whitby and had been a leading figure at the Synod of Whitby (CE 664). She was intelligent and brave. The choice predictably caused howls of protest not least from the Prioress of the Order of the Holy Paraclete at Whitby who objected to the use of the name of Hilda.

We advertised the St Hilda gatherings at the chaplaincy in the *Church Times* and numbers began to grow. It transpired that there were a lot of people who felt alienated by the sexism of the church and its lack of inclusion. In those first weeks the community settled down to regular ways of celebrating. Sermons were replaced by group reflection. Absolution was given not by the priest but by making the sign of the cross on our neighbour's forehead while announcing their sins were forgiven – which was extremely powerful. Intercession was quiet and meditative – simply coming forward and placing a lighted candle in a tray of sand and either saying 'I light this candle for …' or, lighting it in silence. A period of silence would then follow as the candles burned and the thoughts, hopes, pain – articulated or unarticulated – hung in the air. The simplicity of the community's liturgy is something I have been trying to recreate ever since. These simple symbolic gestures were for me transformative of my understanding of what worship could and should be.

The celebrant was always a woman. A variety of women priests from USA and New Zealand visited and became guest celebrants. Suzanne Fageol from the USA who was living in London became our regular priest. It was a very creative community. A fresh liturgy was produced each week and we were blessed in having the support of skilful writers like the liturgist Janet Morley and Monica Furlong. Sometimes students from the chaplaincy and I would create the liturgy.

The Widening Circle of Us

By Easter Sunday on 19 April 1987 the community had grown to about 100 people. We advertised the Easter service in the *Church Times*. It was to be a Eucharist celebrated by Suzanne Fageol. Janet Morley had written the liturgy. The advertisement was like a red rag to a bull and the Bishop of London, Graham Leonard, tried to prevent the service from taking place. He let it be known that I would lose my licence if it went ahead. My response was that the chapel was university property and the chaplaincy was ecumenical, therefore he had no jurisdiction over the place. The Bishop of London and the Bishop of Fulham, Brian Masters, who looked after university chaplaincies in London, were not impressed by the arguments. My licence and career were saved by the kind support of Jim Thompson, Bishop of Stepney and Alan Webster, Dean of St Paul's, whose wife Margaret was a core member of the St Hilda Community. Behind closed doors a deal was struck that this Easter Eucharist would not be in the chapel but in the adjoining common room and my licence and job were safe for the time being. It was made clear to me that I wouldn't get another job in the Diocese of London. A fellow clergyman reported to me that Bishop Leonard had said to him that I would be leaving soon, which was news to me.

With a great deal of press attention, the Easter Eucharist went ahead in the common room of the chaplaincy filmed as part of a documentary by the BBC. A light burned in the adjoining chapel just beyond the room's makeshift altar. It was in itself a symbolic metaphor of inclusion and exclusion. Monica Furlong remembers that some, 'who wrote afterwards felt they had a unique Christian experience, found themselves in an "upper room" where truths that had been theoretical had become a matter of experience'.[41]

The aftermath of the Eucharist led to a number of interesting responses. A group of women who wanted to be ordained wrote a letter to me complaining that we had put the cause of women's ordination back several years. The point, they argued, was to work responsibly and well in parishes and let the pastoral work speak for itself and then the case would be overwhelming. Women needed patience, they argued. Many women seemed to want to rely on careful diplomacy and to make haste slowly. It was about building up confidence in women's ministry and winning the argument that way. I disagree. I think delinquent acts like this help to push causes forward providing a bit of practical eschatology (the study of last things) – a taste of 'the already' in the 'not yet'. It is worth remembering that the first Anglican women priests in USA were ordained irregularly, but it hurried the process along and wouldn't have happened for years without the 'irregular' ordinations of the Philadelphia Eleven and the Washington Four. I knew also because of letters I received from people who came and participated each Sunday evening that it brought hope to many and made the possibility of women priests seem real and, in the end, unstoppable.

Stranger, and in a way laughable, was a death threat. I thought it was unpleasant and pathetic, almost comical but indicative of the strength of feeling. It was a venomous letter which concluded by saying, 'I hope you die and go to hell.' It was on a printed letterhead from an address in Tufton Street just beside the Church of England offices and Westminster Abbey. It was signed 'Yours in Christ' and followed by an illegible scrawl of a signature.

The St Hilda Community provided a wonderful creative experience. A glimpse of an inclusive community where we would all take roles with no hierarchical structure imposing who does what – baking bread, bringing wine, writing liturgy, sharing simple meals at Indian restaurants in the East End. It complemented the life of the chaplaincy which was also strongly inclusive.

When I was asked (or challenged) by Monica Furlong to help create the community, I didn't think for a moment that I was doing anything wrong or unchristian. I thought it was profoundly true to the synoptic gospels (Matthew, Mark and Luke) for they showed Jesus' community was inclusive of women. Speaking, more recently, to the novelist Naomi Alderman, whose extensive research for her novel about Jesus, *The Liars' Gospel*, as well as writing from the perspective of a Jewish feminist, believes that, although the uniqueness of Jesus' message is often overplayed by Christians, Jesus' inclusiveness to women, is unique and startling for first-century Roman-occupied Palestine.[42]

Jesus' community of followers counters the negative status of women in first-century Palestine. He rejects the blood taboo which barred menstruating women from any cultic action;[43] rejecting the treatment of women as sex objects;[44] similarly, in a world where divorce was easy and could only be initiated by men, forbidding divorce to protect women and insisting that women and men were to have the same rights and responsibilities in their relationships.[45] Consider the gospel evidence to demonstrate the key role of women played amongst the first followers of Jesus: Mary Magdala is chosen as the first apostle of the resurrection;[46] amongst the closest listed followers of Jesus were Mary of Bethany who became a disciple sitting at Jesus' feet and was commended by him (or the gospel writer) for choosing 'the better part' rather than accepting a woman's traditional role.[47] Amongst the closest listed followers of Jesus were women who financially supported the mission of Jesus: 'Joanna, the wife of Herod's steward Chuza, and Susanna, and many others, who provided for them out of their resources.'[48] The prominence of women and the support of wealthy women continued after the death of Jesus in the early church. *The Gospel of Mary Magdala*, which some authorities see as containing very early accounts shows the pre-eminence of Mary Magdala amongst the post-crucifixion disciples.[49]

It is possible to find evidence of Jesus' community as preaching and practising an equality between the sexes although those stories are often sadly missing from many of the lectionaries used by the major denominations. For instance, in a parable (Luke 15:8–10), Jesus speaks of God as a woman searching for coins. We are quick to grasp hold of other parable images of God – the loving father is often used but the searching woman looking for the lost coins is seldom, if ever, used in the authorised lectionaries, but is equally likely to have been part of Jesus' teaching.

The Essenes, the Pharisees and the Sadducees – the three significant Jewish religious groups at the time of Jesus – all had laws, rules and customs that discriminated against women. Jesus flouted these laws and displayed an attitude to women that was revolutionary for his day. It is reported that he associated with, talked and argued faith with foreign women, adulterers and prostitutes; he told stories and parables that upheld women as examples of faith. My reading of the biblical evidence alone would have compelled me to get off the fence and accept Monica's challenge.

The early advertisements in the *Church Times* advertising the St Hilda Community stressed the use of inclusive language. The use of inclusive language and especially the rewriting of the Lord's Prayer to begin, 'Beloved, our Father and Mother, in whom is heaven' caused a ridiculous amount of press coverage when the community's *Women Included* was published in 1991. The Church of England had been overly cautious about inclusive language.

For those of us in the community, it was so refreshing to hear liturgy that was completely inclusive and used a plethora of images to talk about God and faith. It presented such a contrast to the Church of England's Alternative Service Book, the new prayer book produced in 1980 to be used alongside the *Book of Common Prayer*, which had deliberately failed to address the issue of inclusive language. The preface to the book states that 'Christians are formed by the way they pray, and the way that they pray expresses what they are.' The words of the new prayer book did not speak to the many women who felt alienated by the Church of England's language in prayer and worship. The worship of the St Hilda Community, with its non-sexist language and inclusive liturgical practice, was by contrast affirming and spoke to many women's spiritual needs.

I began to be almost fanatical about correcting the overwhelming imbalance of male and power images in traditional worship. I really do believe that the language we use for God in liturgy does damage our understanding of faith and warps our image of the Christian faith. Father – Almighty – King – Shepherd – Lord are the almost exclusive range of titles for God that dominate worship and praise. Brian Wren in his book *What Language Shall I Borrow?* proves this point.[50] He takes the *Hymns and Psalms: A Methodist and Ecumenical Hymn Book* and analyses the first 328 hymns. There are 290 different names for God: male authority titles dominate (73%); clear male reference (76.6%); clear female reference (0%); names associated with power as rule (81%). It is an important book and well argued. Perhaps it needed to be written by a man respected as a theologian and hymn writer for it to make a significant difference but I remember clearly that many women liturgists and theologians found it rather tiresome that it was not until the publication of a book by a man that the subject of inclusive language was taken seriously by the churches. Before then it was considered by most church authorities that it was a trivial complaint by extremist women.

The acceptance of feminism in the academic mainstream, coupled with the painfully slow move towards the ordination of women as priests in British Anglican churches and the widespread acceptance of gender equality in society (e.g. in employment law – although the church was exempt) meant that the demand for inclusive language became increasingly insistent. The debate about inclusive language had become inseparably bound up with issues about leadership and ordination. The St Hilda Community played a small but significant role in raising awareness of the need for change.

The St Hilda Community was an agitator aiming to encourage the Church of England's development of a spirituality and a new language for prayer and worship based on the insights of feminist theology – a language that empowered women to articulate their spiritual journey. Many women found, like the liturgist Janet Morley, that 'access to God through woman centred language is the beginning of a costly and intimate struggle of a journey' that would not have been possible with the old male-centred language.[51] Different biblical images for God began to be used: 'images of friendship, giving birth, motherhood, nurturing which produced a very different feel from the images of God as rich aristocrat, judge or king in the panoply of power'.[52]

If the St Hilda Community was ground-breaking in its challenge to the Church of England, it was in fact building on work of earlier

74

pioneers. It had been Mary Daly's books *The Church and the Second Sex* and *Beyond God the Father* that determined the agenda for a generation of feminist theologians with their critical analysis of women's experience.[53] The search was for new terminology, and a thorough critique of patriarchal ideology and the gendering of God as male – 'if God is male, the male is God' as Daly so succinctly sums up.[54] It was important to recover the often-overlooked women's story in Christian history.

Rosemary Radford Ruether's 1985 book *Women–Church* was influential to many of us involved in the community. Her book lays the ecclesiological foundation for a feminist church, offering guidelines for developing communities of worship and mutual support. However, it was difficult to see how many or indeed any of these resources could easily be used in mainstream churches. Indeed, Ruether's powerful 'Exorcism of Patriarchal Texts' from *Women–Church* was one of the few unsuccessful liturgical events at the St Hilda Community.[55] I found Ruether's liturgy liberating. As 'patriarchal' was read we all shouted, 'Out, demons, Out.' And at the conclusion of the exorcism, this passage was read aloud:

> These texts and all oppressive texts have lost their power over our lives. We no longer need to apologise for them or try to interpret them as words of truth, but we cast out their oppressive message as expressions of evil and justifications of evil.[56]

The passage was liberating to those of us who wanted to find a communal way of dismissing literalism or holding the Bible up as God's infallible word, to others it represented an uneasy step that they were not yet prepared to make.

When the St Hilda Community's book *Women Included* was published it was in many ways far less radical than Ruether's book but what it managed to do, which Ruether's book did not, was to provide resources for worshipping and celebrating the Eucharist that were practical and possible even within comparatively conventional church communities.

The issue of inclusive language was eventually addressed in the Church of England's 1988 report *Making Women Visible*, partly as a result of consciousness raising by the St Hilda Community and other groups.[57] The report provided a range of suggested replacement words and prayers of a more inclusive nature. The report was carefully even-handed, but at least began to address the issue. The main essay in the report relies heavily on the work of Deborah Cameron. She argues that languages are not used in a social and political vacuum:

> the important difference between those who consider language symptomatic and those who consider it casual. Is a sexist remark simply the outward manifestation of an unacceptable misogyny or is it also, as many feminists believe the very mechanism by which misogyny is constructed and transmitted ...? If we look closely at the regulatory mechanisms which grow up around languages, it is clear that they are rather closely connected with the power structures of their society.[58]

Language, of course, is not really the core issue but it is representative of a mindset. The name we use for God determines who and what we are and our position in the divine plan is reinforced by clericalism where the basic relationship of a clergy to a layperson is that of husband to dependent wife, shepherd to sheep, father to child (although how that squares with Jesus' injunction in Matthew's gospel – call no man father except your father in heaven – always baffles me).[59] The St Hilda Community was not about language but about the justice issue of not permitting women to be ordained. It was part of the feminist movement's demand for equal rights (and rites).

What Will Happen to God? was a book by William Oddie who was an Anglican priest but converted to Roman Catholicism over, amongst other things, the issue of women's ordination.[60] He understood the true significance of inclusive language. His book expressed a horrified belief that inclusive language was the start of the slippery slope that would dismantle traditional Christianity. I would have to admit that he was right, feminism has irrevocably changed (although I would say corrected) Christianity. William Oddie might bemoan it but plenty of people uttered a joyous 'Hallelujah'. My experience with the St Hilda Community meant that I was quite often asked to speak about either the experience of the community or more generally on women and their role in the church. I had to deepen my thought from an instinctive feeling that this was right towards a coherent analysis of the inclusion of women and the effect on the church. In reality, as I attended groups and conferences, I was being educated and I received far more wisdom than I ever gave. I had thought that it was a basic question of justice that women should be equal in the church. I learnt it was more profound and deep rooted than that.

It is men who have been in control and who have shaped the tradition, the doctrine, determined the canon of Scripture, and held power in almost all churches. It is men who have predominantly led worship, heard confessions and thereby controlled behaviour. Men have had all the power. Feminism is liberating the church from that patriarchal control.

Since the 1960s, social institutions had been increasingly criticised for their patriarchy and sexism. The theologian, Catherine Lacunga, describes feminist consciousness as 'a blinding flash of light: it blinds in that it disorients and disturbs the viewers; it is light in the way that it vividly illumines the whole landscape'.[61] The American Unitarian theologian, Gaye Ortiz, explains how this blinding light touched her and her sisters throughout the 1960s and 1970s:

> The realisation is that men have formulated beliefs, written and transmitted sacred writings, and have been sole interpreters, have created and controlled institutions, worship and rituals. This insight is followed rapidly by another, which is simply the principle of contemporary hermeneutics; that all interpretation is conditioned by the presumptions and prejudgements of the interpreter, the revelation for budding feminist thinkers is, 'It's not all carved in stone after all! They (the male dominated powers that be) only say that it is![62]

There are three stages in the feminist critique of religion. The first offers a feminist critique of the Christian tradition, a long history of subjugation, an absence of women's voices and an awareness that in the Bible there are many texts that treat women as property, tools, objects or stereotypes. The second stage is the recovery of women's story in Christian history. A careful uncovering of the legacy of women in the Christian story. Sometimes reinterpreting, re-visioning and uncovering stories to provide new insights of women in the Bible and Christian history. The third stage is the work of theological reconstruction: the reframing of Christian doctrine, readings of the Bible from a feminist perspective, new interpretations of Christian ethics and the offering of models for Women–Church.

Daly and others were right to consider central Christian theological ideas like kenosis, the self-emptying of God, which demonstrate the harm Christian doctrine has sometimes done to Christian women. Kenosis, for instance, has contributed to the powerlessness of women. How often congregations are exhorted from the pulpit to leave self behind and take up your cross. This is considered Christian and loving – emulating Jesus' self-sacrifice; love, we are told, doesn't count the cost, is self-sacrificial and self-giving in order to nurture others. But and it is a very significant 'but', losing your life to save it has enslaved and abused countless numbers of women (and even some men). Women are prized for their virtue of self-giving, wives for sticking with abusive or painful marriages. Mothers are hailed for living for their husband and children; the Virgin Mary is worshipped as the ideal woman. The feminist theologian, Daphne Hampson rightly points out that 'the gospel of powerlessness has been appropriated by those to whom it should never have been directed. Resistance to injustice then comes to look unChristlike.'[63]

It is easy to see why many feminists have given up on the tradition as being irredeemably patriarchal and flawed. There remains a major divide within feminist theology. There are those who are reformist and revisionist wanting to work within the tradition to make it truly inclusive of all humanity. On the other hand, there are those who believe that Christianity is irredeemably sexist. For these feminists the only solution is to abandon the tradition altogether. That divide was apparent within the St Hilda Community. Nevertheless, it managed to offer a model of Women–Church that was new and refreshing. It offered not only new liturgy but new ways of making decisions and reflecting on Scripture that were not hierarchical. It certainly changed my understanding of institutional Christianity.

It is not that Christianity's problem with women and power is unique to the religious sphere. Mary Beard referencing ancient history and contemporary politics is equally insistent that 'you can't easily fit women in to a structure that is already coded as male; you have to change the structure'.[64] What theology and Christianity (and indeed all religions) suffer from is the idea that this inequality is somehow the will of God in creation and approval for the power imbalance is part of God's revealed truth.

The great step forward that was feminism's gift to the whole of Christianity was that it emphasised that there is no single orthodoxy. It all depends on context. The patriarchal mindset took a range of male metaphors for God like Father, Judge, King, and instead of treating them as metaphors enshrined them as Christian truth and actual descriptions of God. No metaphor is an exact description – the city isn't actually a jungle, all the world isn't literally a stage, you ain't truthfully nothing but a hound-dog! Look with different eyes and from different contexts and you will find a mass of feminine metaphors that can equally well describe aspects of God. For God is no more a father than a mother. God is no more a being than simply being itself. God is no more a warrior – the God of Hosts – than a peacemaker or indeed peace itself. God is no more the lawmaker than simply 'wisdom'. God is not so much the Almighty, King of Creation than the Word. These metaphors are all attempts to 'eff' the ineffable. God is no more a noun than a verb. All metaphors for God will be partial and inadequate.

I find it difficult to be civil to clergy who still, all these years later, hold out against the ordination of women and keep on using non-inclusive language. I think they are siding with forces of injustice and prejudice and being anti-Christian in a very literal sense for they are not replicating the powerful support that Jesus gave to women as disciples and the way he included them as members of his inner circle of supporters.

I decided to leave the chaplaincy because after a while university chaplaincy has a sameness that repeats itself in a cycle year after year. I had learnt a lot and been educated by the context of the East End and perhaps above all by the women of the St Hilda Community. Proudly, I remain the only male priest who has presided at a Eucharist for the St Hilda Community. I was the celebrant on my final Sunday before I left for my new job in Scotland. A few women members of the community stayed away because a man was celebrant, that hurt me but was only a tiny glimpse of the week in week out treatment many women felt in their churches. I thought then and still do, that the hurts that a patriarchal church has inflicted on women will take a very long time to heal, even after all the obstacles allowing women priests, bishops and all those man-made hurdles have been successfully negotiated. Feminism has altered Christianity for good and 'the' good.

I had, I suppose, come off the fence in a number of issues and no longer tried to hold the middle ground, or to shelve difficult problems muttering 'let's make haste slowly on this one' but rather to speak the truth as I saw it. Something else was happening, I had engaged with the foundation texts of faith and they had for me come alive as the issue of the role of women was explored. They became not just holy words enshrined by years of tradition but words that shaped the present. It is ironic that when I was being most faithful to Jesus, I was closer than ever before to being thrown out of the church. I suppose there was a parochial inkling of this in Hagley over the acceptance of the pregnant teenager. That too was a time when adherence to the reported behaviour of Jesus got me into trouble with my superiors. I think I was realising that I was 'for' the radical message of Jesus and possibly 'against' many of the traditions and the stultifying caution of the church.

I had often been told to 'make haste slowly'. It was a phrase that was used by Bishop Jim Thompson to me about the St Hilda Community and the need, as he expressed it, for time and caution rather than upsetting the status quo. Off to Scotland I went, where the man who some years later became my Bishop (John Taylor, Bishop of Glasgow) proudly quoted a former Scottish prelate who said that the role of bishop was to be 'a brake on the forward momentum of the church' which was the exact opposite of what I wanted to hear. His and Jim Thompson's caution seemed the very opposite to the idea of my commission to 'make mistakes' or of the cutting edge of what Jesus said and did.

As I set off for a new pastoral ministry, I was eager to see whether the inclusive nature and new ways of being church would have any resonance in an ordinary church community, for I realised that both the chaplaincy and the St Hilda Community were very much the exception. I had learnt in London that Jesus' gospel was one of radical inclusion. It was about creating and living the future now. Would that kind of model work in a normal pastoral setting?

CHAPTER 4
SCOTLAND
(1987–1996)

Scotland small? Our multiform, our infinite Scotland *small*?
Only as a patch of hillside may be a cliché corner
To a fool who cries 'Nothing but heather!'
… –How marvellously descriptive! And incomplete!
Hugh MacDiarmid – 'Scotland Small'?

London was exciting and energising and I left somewhat reluctantly. I had been at the chaplaincy for just over six years and it was probably time to move on. I toyed with two possibilities. I could have gone to Taiwan to teach Liberation Theology but in the end, I chose to go to Ayr in Scotland as a rector in the Scottish Episcopal Church, which is the Scottish province of the Anglican Communion. Following the St Hilda experience, it had been made very clear to me that I should not expect to have another job in London. I spoke to Jim Thompson, the Bishop of Stepney, about this and he suggested that Bishop Richard Holloway in Scotland would, he thought, be very keen to have me and so I found myself heading north.

I now knew that it was possible to create a 'liberal' and 'inclusive' church in a university context. That was hardly surprising. I wanted to see if it was possible in conventional pastoral situations such as Holy Trinity, Ayr. I had an inkling, based on the experience of Hagley, that it might not be possible. I chose Scotland not only because of Jim Thompson's suggestion but also because I had enjoyed the University of St Andrews just 10 years before and Denise, my wife, was Scottish. I suppose, I was going back to border living; back from the exceptional, a university chapel, to a conventional parish.

What a cultural shock. After the East End of London, Ayr seemed uniformly white. The west coast of southern Scotland seemed very different to the Scotland I had experienced before at St Andrews and in Edinburgh, where my in-laws lived and we frequently stayed. In

London's East End I was used to graffiti, even racist graffiti, but I was surprised in this white community to find racist graffiti and it was all Catholic versus Protestant and vice versa. I was startled how much affinity there was with Northern Ireland and how fierce the sectarian divide was in the West of Scotland, defining where you lived, where you went to school and who you could work for. Orange marches and corresponding violence were a regular problem. I remember visiting a parishioner in a Glasgow hospital and having to drive my car through the crowds spilling out of Ibrox stadium after a Rangers–Celtic match. Rangers are traditionally Protestant and Celtic are their Roman Catholic arch-rivals. In my car amidst the thronging Protestant crowd I was dressed in suit, black shirt and clerical collar and looked very much like a Catholic priest. The car was thumped, rocked and jeered at until a policeman on foot and another on a horse cleared the way for my car to break free. God, how I hate the tribalism of religion. This was a small example but across the water in Northern Ireland people were still being killed for belonging to the wrong religious tribe and today Middle East divisions are as much about Sunni–Shia antipathy as anything else.

A significant early problem for me was the problem of language. I am not thinking of the rarely spoken Scottish Gaelic but the ordinary Ayrshire accent. On my first day of work I visited a council house in the north of the town. A young girl of 16 had died after a joy-riding incident. I went to arrange the funeral; it was a difficult pastoral situation, but it was certainly one of my very worst pastoral failures. I literally couldn't understand a word they were saying and even more surprising to me was that they didn't seem to understand a word I was saying. Muddling through doesn't begin to define the visit and the subsequent funeral.

As the weeks and months went on, I became attuned to the Ayrshire cadences and the strange little linguistic touches – for instance, a personal statement frequently finished with the phrase 'I am, amn't I?' Glaswegian was a doddle after broad Ayrshire!

What I hadn't expected was that large numbers of working Scots in Ayr proudly belonged to what they called 'the English church'. In Scotland, because of the sectarian divide it was important to belong to a church although you didn't necessarily feel any obligation to attend. You just knew whose side you were on. This meant a large number of funerals, baptisms and weddings for non-attending, yet fiercely loyal, members of the English church.

A little bit of research showed there were two main reasons for this. Firstly, a lot of coal-miners had come to Ayrshire from the pits of South Wales and England who were traditionally Anglican, and secondly at a time in the early twentieth century when Catholic membership was strong but clearly defined and membership of the Presbyterian Church of Scotland was hedged around with duty, respectability and expectation of attendance, it was the Anglicans who went into the poorer areas and were happy to baptise, marry and bury anyone from either side of the religious divide. The Anglicans expressed an unconditional acceptance of people at a time when other churches had very clear conditions. This, especially in Ayr, seemed to have built up a proud loyalty for their church.

Although outwardly a prosperous seaside town, sectarianism was very evident in Ayr in the 1980s and early 1990s. Religious allegiance, Catholic or Protestant, was important and was immediately defined by your name, by the school you attended, the job you were likely to get, the area you lived in.

In the midst of the sectarian divide, the Episcopalian (Anglican) tradition was an exception. I liked the openness which was a distinct part of the Scottish Episcopalian tradition. I suppose the attraction of 'Piskies', as we were known, was that we were not one of the dominant Scottish religious tribes. It is not dissimilar to Glasgow football clubs – those who don't like the Protestant Rangers or the Catholic Celtic often proudly associate with Partick Thistle. That historical reason that differentiated the denominations remained in force in the 1990s. Scottish Presbyterianism was somewhat colourless and very dominated by a rather old-fashioned (and lengthy) form of preaching;

Catholicism, especially in the West of Scotland, was equally old-fashioned which was good news for the Piskies which seemed a more liberal alternative and also bridged the sectarian divide.

I have always advocated an open approach to baptisms, funerals and weddings. If the church is unable to say 'yes' to people, then people are unlikely to say 'yes' to the church. My wholehearted 'yes' to anyone who came asking for baptism, wedding or funeral led to complaints of poaching parishioners from my Church of Scotland Presbyterian colleagues. I wasn't consciously poaching, just offering an alternative view of the role of the church, to which some people responded. This included a willingness to baptise, marry and bury anyone who asked without hedging it around with conditions, just as I always accept that anyone can receive communion and that there are no barriers to full participation.

I relished the pastoral round of life in Ayr in a way that was very different to the pastoral needs of students. I found that the younger members of the parish had felt unsupported by my predecessor. He was old and not very well and rather out of touch with the warp and weft of contemporary life. In fact, he died while I was in Ayr and I ministered to him and his family through that process. What I found was that many people were willing to open up and talk about their difficulties. I felt very humble by the way they confided in me and shared their burdens. It always struck me as people came to the altar week after week to receive communion from my hands that nearly everybody was putting on a front to the outside world. In so many cases the public persona was very different from the private person I got to know. We all wear masks.

And, of course, I have to include myself especially in this. Clergy are not morally better or superior to anyone else or immune from everyday trauma – I am certainly not. When in London we had found that we couldn't have children and the fault was mine. The psychological pain of childlessness still weighed heavily on us, especially Denise.

Male infertility was and still is an under-researched area. Expensive consultants in Harley Street didn't have much wisdom to offer other than telling me not to wear tight jeans and to bathe my balls in very cold water. The pain for the woman is more acute and felt more heavily. Even if it is the man who is 'the problem', the medical interventions nearly always fall on the woman. It was especially painful within a pastoral role for both of us – the large number of baptisms were painful, so was the group for Mothers and Toddlers. I was forever having to bill and coo over newborn babies, and there were endless questions about when you are going to have children. I think, indeed I know, that living with the knowledge of infertility inflicts a psychological scar long after the practicalities of whether to adopt or to try medical interventions have been decided or discarded. Somewhere deep inside there is always a sense of failure or incompleteness that unrecognised (or, indeed, recognised) can keep reappearing. I do think my 'stiff upper lip' education which taught me to carry on in the hope that things would get better, or at least you would get used to it, was of no help whatsoever. There remains for a man (for this man) a feeling of failure in manliness that recurs every time an enthusiastic message is received from friends who tell you that they are having children. Their lives and lifestyles changed and ours did not.

The experience of infertility and the fragility of some marriages made me very hesitant to embrace the family-centeredness of much church life. I hate Mothering Sunday which excludes, and possibly even actively hurts, a large proportion (if you add it up it might even sometimes be the majority) of the congregation. It hadn't been an issue in student chaplaincy, but it was in Ayr. I always tried to play it down and to speak as someone who was childless. I am always very careful not to assume that people have children as I know how hurtful that assumption can be to someone who has been desperate to be a parent.

I am painfully coming to the realisation that when you let the mask slip and expose some of that pain publicly through sermons, prayers or in conversation, then the pastoral response increases enormously. People often feel that if you are 'wounded' then they too can talk of their wounds. It is daring to do this that is so hard. Carl Jung has written powerfully about 'the wounded healer'– I wish I had read him earlier in my life – and I guess I have learnt the lesson far too slowly.[65] I hope that I now seem sufficiently flawed and broken to be approachable.

The other 'unorthodox' pastoral tip that I would always pass on to people is to disband prayer groups! In Ayr, I dutifully went along to the monthly prayer group and afterwards immediately set about shutting it down. I remember, sometime before in London, confiding in a local priest about some personal difficulties only to find that this confidential talk had been taken to the parish prayer group and, under the saintly pretence of holding these hurts before God, my secrets had been publicised throughout the parish via chains of prayer. In Ayr, the prayerful intentions that my fellow clergy and pastoral leaders shared at the monthly prayer group seemed to me to be secrets that shouldn't be shared. I closed it down. Prayer groups shouldn't be an excuse for sanctified gossip.

One of the most uncomfortable moments in Ayr involved a key parish family. Their son had become a member of an Anglican religious order. He was gay and lived and worked in Glasgow attached to a church. One evening there was a knock on the front door and a policewoman came in. Could I go with her to the house of this young monk's mother in Ayr as she broke the news that her son had been brutally murdered earlier that night? It was a horrible task and news that no frail elderly widow should have to hear. The funeral, after identifying the body and all the other gruesome necessities had been completed, was held in Ayr. As the coffin was brought into church led by the Bishop a cry went up from a member of the congregation of 'Alleluia! Praise the Lord.' It was an awful and inappropriate cry of a strongly evangelical Christian expressing his belief in the resurrection. It seemed to me that on this sad, sad occasion that contained nothing but tears and sorrow that it was totally out of place. I felt at that moment all the careful pastoral care and sensitivity we in the parish had tried to show to the grieving friends and family was thrown away.

It brought to mind a lecture I remember listening to at Queen's just before my ordination which was entitled 'why are Christians such ghastly people' – here was proof of at least one man's ghastliness.

Outwardly, things were successful in Ayr. The church became the most attended in the diocese and through a campaign we managed to improve the financial health of the church. We had a black South African curate who was studying at the University of Glasgow part-time and working in the parish, Bethlehem Nopece. He seemed a wonderful liberal priest, a friend and supporter of Desmond Tutu, so I was surprised and a little shocked to see that shortly after returning to South Africa he became a Bishop (that wasn't so surprising) but I was shocked to learn that he became the leading figure in South Africa of those who want to realign the worldwide Anglican church (GAFCON) and halt the liberal influences especially in regard to homosexuality – and that was surprising.

Exorcism was surprising too! A young couple came to see me at the church office one morning. They were perturbed because in their new home things had started flying around – kitchen utensils including knives, things from the bathroom cabinet and so on. I listened to these very young parents with their newborn child as they gradually confided in me. It was a textbook poltergeist situation. I listened and heard about the tensions and difficulties in their lives coping with new home, new baby, and very little money and the young woman's sense of being trapped. The listening and the little bit of advice seemed to help for when they returned the disturbances had ceased and they seemed happier and more supportive of each other. I chalked it up as a victory of reason and common sense. That, I thought, was that.

I hadn't taken account of their new neighbour, a regular attender of séances and the Spiritualist church. As she got to know them, they told her about their disturbances. This, she said was due to a murder that had taken place in their home and there was, she sensed, a palpable sense of evil in the home. Well, unsurprisingly the disturbances came back. They came to see me again and we went through the same process. Calm was re-established until they had another visit from their neighbour and the whole thing was hyped up again. The neighbour was going to arrange for an exorcism by a specialist in the Spiritualist church.

I didn't want this to escalate and further psychological damage to be done to the young couple, especially the young woman who was clearly struggling to cope. I told them that there was no need for an exorcist to come into their home and I assured them that I would come and make their house safe and free from these disturbances.

I rang my Bishop, Derek Rawcliffe, a man who frankly was inclined to see demon possession lurking behind every ailment and twist of fate. Because of this, he had given dire warnings to all his clergy to only use the Diocesan Exorcist when dealing with demon possession. I gave him a potted history and said I didn't think that there was a need for an exorcism and that I would simply bless the house. He was itching to have the priest designated as Diocesan Exorcist take over the case but luckily the man was ill at the time and I was given the go-ahead to bless the house.

I didn't want to get into any spooky exorcism language so I thought I would simply bless each room in the house. On the other hand, I wanted to give the couple the impression that my 'magic' was powerful and would be effective. Therefore, I dressed up in every bit of clerical garb I could find – cope, chasuble – in fact everything to heighten the sense of theatre. I took water and a sizeable twig of rosemary to help with the sprinkling of holy water and set off in the car to the young couple's home. I explained that I was going to bless the house and this would give them a home that was calm and dedicated to the God who was love.

I sprinkled holy water liberally all over the place with a rosemary twig, praying and blessing each room in turn with the young couple in tow. They thanked me for the prayers and blessing and after a short talk and cup of tea I left hoping that their neighbour would not visit and declare my ceremony null and void.

I was surprised to get a visit from the couple the very next morning. They told me that they heard this loud noise in the middle of the night and that they heard heavy steps that went down the stairs and the 'being' opened the front door, slammed it shut and went out into the night. They told me that since then a tremendous sense of peace had enveloped their house.

Carried away by my prowess as an exorcist, a few years later I was visiting a woman who told me she was possessed, again it was a question of someone, a so-called friend, telling her that she was possessed. She was a lesbian and her friend, a very fundamentalist Christian, had told her that she was possessed by the Devil and she needed the spirit of lesbianism to be cast out of her. No amount of reassurance and acceptance convinced her that she wasn't going to hell. She came to the church and I blessed her and prayed with her. I was not trying to do any miracle but just to reassure her that there was nothing devilish about her sexual orientation. It didn't work and I did what I ought to have done in the first place and arranged for her to meet a good secular woman counsellor which after a while gave her the courage to come out to her friends and family.

I am always perturbed about the blurring of the line between pastoral care and counselling. I believe that clergy can and should provide unconditional acceptance and a listening ear. That listening ear should be attuned to know enough of when to suggest to someone that they visit a counsellor. There is a danger in the rather scant training that we were given in the 1970s about pastoral counselling. Just enough knowledge, I fear, for some clergy to think they could take on the role of counsellor. Unless we have been trained and are fully accredited, that is not our skill or our role – of that I am convinced.

The Bishop of Glasgow, Derek Rawcliffe, was inclined to think that prayer and the laying on of hands was all that was needed pastorally. He was very enthusiastic about spiritual healing and if he made a visit to a local church he always added to the communion service a healing element. As you approached the communion rail, he asked you if there was anything physical that required healing by the laying of his hands on the ailment. One spirited elderly woman in Ayr, who somewhat disapproved of the Bishop, when she was asked, simply said 'cystitis' and the Bishop moved hastily on.

The people of Ayr – Shirley, Anne, John, Jean, Doreen, Douglas, et al. – taught me about grounding my faith and ministry in the every day. There are always in every parish people who are more spiritual, more intelligent and more experienced in matters of faith and ministry than whoever happens to be their priest or minister at any one time. With any luck a priest coming into a parish or church can bring a bit of new energy, new insights and fresh approach and ways of thinking. Not that their way is going to be better or should naturally be adopted but it should enter the melting pot of ideas and hopes for that church community.

The primary skill that a priest or minister brings to a parish or wherever he or she is ministering should be theological expertise. This is what we have been trained to do. We are not counsellors – there are other specific people trained in those skills; we are not social workers again those are professional skills that involve careful and specific training; we are not politicians, again locally and nationally there are people elected to political posts. We are theologians. The Church of Scotland used to think of their ministers as theologians in the parish. I rather regret the passing of that tradition.

If I reflect on what I learnt during my time in Ayr, it owes a great deal to the Church of Scotland minister, Ian Fraser. Ian had been a pioneer industrial chaplain working in Scottish dockyards, he had been a politically active missionary and worked for the World Council of Churches. His ministry was very much influenced by the base communities of Latin America. These communities were formed by priests and ministers who formed small communities in poor areas where they listened to and got to know and share the life of these often peasant communities. They would not follow the dictates of their church but listen to the needs and then find resources from the Bible and their tradition that would bring meaning and hope to the community. The key point was to define their real questions and real problems and to see what help the Christian faith and perspective could provide. Inevitably the solutions involved the overcoming of political corruption and despotic regimes which, in parts of Latin America, were often tacitly supported by the Roman Catholic church. These communities were responsible for the emergence of Liberation Theology. Their reverberation was even felt in Europe and was a key factor in the Church of England's *Faith in the City* report. The phrase 'God's bias to the poor' became a rallying cry for those who wanted social and political change – this was the era of Thatcher and Reagan where the bias certainly seemed to be against the poor who were often derided as 'scroungers' or told to 'get on their bike' and look for work. The key to this approach of faith was to listen to the people and through their concerns and anxieties to read the 'signs of the times'.

Contextual theology became increasingly important and theologies emerged from groups that felt shut out from decision-making and power. This grew into important movements by women, black and Asian Christians, gay and lesbian groups, and the urban poor. Quite simply, it changed theology from being something delivered from on high by a clearly defined 'male' hierarchy to something that was local, active and generating appropriate and positive action.

Ian Fraser was a key theologian in Scotland encouraging contextual theology and the study and use of base communities. I spent a weekend at Dunblane listening and talking to him. I was impressed and I invited him to lead a study day in Troon in Ayrshire for local churches on 'doing theology'. A good crowd came and rather than lecture to us he asked us in groups to outline the political and social problems of our areas. Having spent the morning doing that, we were then encouraged to find stories and ideas from the Bible or Christian tradition that would throw new light on these problems. A number of examples were chosen and the passages read in the context of some of the problems, and new hope and possibilities began to emerge. We were doing theology – even Liberation Theology.

The key task of a clergyperson is to learn the context – to listen and to learn everything there is to know about the community – not just the few who come to your church or the other churches in the area but the social, cultural, political life of the whole community. And then to ensure that the church is responding with its resources and instincts honed by theological skills to the needs of the community. Sometimes that response might be a challenge, sometimes an offer of support.

Ian died in 2019, he was 100 years old and was still writing every day and as angry as ever about injustice. His masterclass in contextual theology confirmed what I had learnt from university chaplaincy, that a priest or minister must be alert to what is really going on in the community and then shape the mission of the church in response to that knowledge. The problem for many clergy is that they have to contend with the wider church family – the diocese or the national church – who are only too eager to impose endless programmes of mission and evangelism on all churches. The problem with these desperate attempts to halt the decline in church numbers is that they frequently take very little notice of local context or of local and national political and social ills. They simply don't listen and instead dictate what are frequently inappropriate responses.

Ian Fraser's way of 'doing theology' came to mind when debating two fairly typical parochial questions: the role of children in church and the wider question of whether you needed to be confirmed to receive communion in church. This was an issue especially for Bethlehem Nopece and his family. In South Africa, before they came to the UK, his children were allowed to receive the wafer and the wine at communion as soon as they could walk and talk. They were considered, as baptised Christians, to be full members of the church, there were no barriers. As they settled in this white community in Scotland the first message that the children received from the church was that they were not welcome to participate fully. They had to wait until they became adults to be welcomed into full membership – which probably on reflection meant that they would then give money to the church. Bethlehem was not pleased and saw it as a racial slur. Taking the Fraser method, we explored the gospels for some light to be thrown on the subject.

What we found was remarkable. For we envision the stories of Jesus and children wrongly and often through a prism of Victorian schmaltz. There is nothing sentimental about them at all. Jesus gets angry when the disciples exclude children.[66] The scholar, John Dominic Crossan, suggests that Jesus' blessing of the children is not a slushy sentimental desire to 'suffer the little children' but mirrors the symbolic act required to adopt a child in first-century Judaism. Crossan encourages us to think of Third World street children often in gangs or begging, which is common to most oppressed and impoverished countries even today – and of Jesus including them in his community. This feels right and fits with all the other 'nuisances and nobodies' – Crossan's provocative phrase – that make up the Jesus movement.[67]

In Jesus' community of followers, and therefore presumably for us, there was to be no exclusion of children, however much the grown-ups might protest. We felt that we had the moral high ground on this but the church would still not budge and move to inclusion. So, Bethlehem and I did it anyway when we were at the altar.

Much the same was true of adults who happened upon the church. Officially, unless they were baptised and confirmed members in good standing with another church, they should not be allowed to receive communion. Studying the tradition, we found an attitude of open commensality by Jesus. Commensality is defined by Crossan as meaning:

> the rules of tabling and eating as miniature models for the rules of association and socialisation. In the gospels Jesus' critics call him a glutton and a drunkard who eats and drinks with tax collectors, sinners and whores. Jesus practices a radical egalitarianism of the open table ... that denies any discrimination between them and negates the necessity of any hierarchy among them.[68]

Purity or repentance is not required – the table is open, inclusive. In Mark's gospel and the other synoptic gospels Jesus always accepts (breaks bread with) sinners and outcasts before they express repentance or amendment of life.[69] Jesus' table is not hedged round with rules, in

Scotland (1987–1996)

contrast to the typical practice of churches down the ages, and so our 'table' and community should be open as well. These were just first moves in seeking to reorientate the church community to look out at the equivalent of street children and those excluded from society.

My four years in Ayr convinced me that it was possible for a liberal church to thrive and even to be a little more concerned with local and national political questions. I was, I felt, ready for a different challenge and I accepted the offer to become Provost (Dean) of St Mary's Cathedral in Glasgow.

Ayr was comfortable and enjoyable. I had begun to broadcast on the BBC, which was hardly an earth-shattering breakthrough, but 'god-slots' like *Prayer for the Day* on BBC Radio 4, *Thought for the Day* on BBC Radio Scotland and occasionally a bit for the World Service and other Scottish religious programmes, including a regular Sunday morning slot. Most of this was Glasgow-based. Sometimes, when I broadcast a *Thought for the Day* or spoke in my Sunday slot, I received a note from a man in the Outer Hebrides that always said the same thing – 'F**k off, you Sassenach bastard!' It was always scrawled on a torn off piece of paper and posted in a brown envelope. They continued for some months and then stopped so I wondered if I had simply become so bland that no one took any notice.

Sassenach! At that time, Englishness was difficult to defend in Scotland. I partly blame Margaret Thatcher who had a devastating effect on Scottish regard for the English. She had treated Scotland with disdain as she tried to foist the poll tax on a reluctant nation who were not pleased at being treated as guinea pigs for this unpopular reform. In the West of Scotland, my accent marked me out as English and, what is worse, posh. Not that the Scottish National Party have ever been other than welcoming and keen to count as Scottish all who lived in Scotland regardless of where they were from. Nevertheless, there were places in Glasgow where I would very carefully keep my mouth shut. I remember going to see Mel Gibson's bloodthirsty 1995 film, *Braveheart,* in which he directed and starred as William Wallace. The film tells the story of the first great war of Scottish independence in the thirteenth century and the final scenes show the defeat of the English at the Battle of Bannockburn. Sitting in a packed Odeon cinema in Renfield Street in Glasgow, every time an Englishman was killed (that was most of the time as far as I remember) there was cheering and stamping of feet with exuberant approval. Slinking out of the cinema at the end, I didn't dare open my mouth for fear of being lynched. That was one of the occasions that I realised that I didn't quite belong in Scotland.

Towards the end of my time in Ayr I had also started to be involved in diocesan and wider church committees and groups. These extra-parochial tasks consumed my time and energy and I spent most weekdays commuting backwards and forwards from Ayr to Glasgow, as did Denise who was now doing a theology degree at the University of Glasgow. Therefore, the move to the cathedral was a relief in some ways and certainly made her daily commute and my diocesan jobs easier.

The move to St Mary's Cathedral, Glasgow was freeing intellectually. The University of Glasgow's Anglican chaplaincy was run from the cathedral, members of the theology faculty at the University of Glasgow were members or frequent visitors, as were Presbyterian (Church of Scotland) theologians and ministers, like Kathy Galloway and John Bell of the Iona Community. All of this, together with challenging and progressive colleagues, gave a sense of freedom and encouraged thought and debate rather than just parochial concerns. In this atmosphere, I found that my theology was changing or more truthfully, I started to think about what I actually believed and what on earth I was doing.

At the start of my time at the cathedral, it wasn't so much my theological views that caused disruption in the congregation, as how I conducted the services. I was aware that the cathedral congregation were quite particular about how things should be done. I am not musical, uninterested in ecclesiastical ceremony and totally unconcerned about who precedes who in processions or the how, why and what of genuflexion. I like things done well, but only as a vehicle to proclaim a message, not as an end in themselves. My predecessor was a stickler for good order and precision so I thought that on my first Sunday I would play it safe and follow the very detailed instructions he had left about how things should be done. It seemed to go well so I was surprised when on the following Thursday a small delegation came to our house to ask me if I was aware that I had made 42 changes to the liturgy. I couldn't believe it – how could a group of people sit there and count mistakes. Was that worship? It was also irksome because I hadn't yet made any changes but knew that there were plenty I intended to make. The thought patterns of those who think that exactly how one celebrates the Eucharist has a bearing on salvation and the efficaciousness of the sacrament is not something I find it easy to understand or to sympathise with. Surely, behind such an attitude there must be a mindset that believes there is one orthodox position in theology and only one way of expressing that in liturgy. It is the absolute antithesis of what I believe.

I think and hope that in four and a half years I relaxed the cathedral services from being very controlled to something that was more joyous and felt like a community celebrating. I tried to take away the emphasis on the priest as central and as the mediator between God and the congregation. I always brought two members of the congregation to share with me or whoever was the celebrant, in saying the Eucharistic prayer – this also meant that there was always at least one woman leading the service. The gospel reading, usually the preserve of the priest, was read by a member of the congregation. I tried to create an altar that seemed to be in the midst of the congregation surrounded by people. I wanted to find hymns with words that didn't just express the outmoded worldview of pre-Victorian and Victorian Christianity. The struggle was always to find hymns with good music and words that reflected contemporary political, social and theological concerns and were not tied to Victorian theology and attitudes. The blandness and the banality of so many Christian contemporary choruses were not what I was searching for, but I wanted to find serious hymnology with grown-up contemporary theology. With a lot of help from Sal McDougall, we were able to choose carefully and on diocesan occasions would try to impress visitors from elsewhere in the diocese with hymns they could take back and start to use in their worship.

The various changes by and large worked and the congregation grew, overtaking Ayr as the largest congregation (I obviously had an unhealthy desire to be top dog). People were drawn by the quality of the music, by what I hope was good preaching – I certainly had some terrific colleagues who were gifted communicators – and the friendliness of the congregation.

Evensong on Sunday evening became a very popular service with a young and growing congregation. We played it absolutely straight out of the Prayer Book with its seventeenth-century language and the theologically dubious, but wonderful poetic resonance of its prayers. It was beautifully done. It caused another little traditionalist delegation to make a complaint to me specifically about Evensong. I expressed my surprise as I thought it was the one thing that would be pitch perfect for them. 'What was the problem?' I enquired. The answer came back, 'There were just too many people!'

Not that everything was well attended. There was an early morning Eucharist each day. As you can imagine, early on a cold February morning in Glasgow, this was not the most popular of services. I found myself alone with a woman in her sixties who was a regular attender. The service took place in a side chapel but she didn't come into the chapel and instead sat in the nave of the cathedral probably some 20 yards from the altar where I was and hidden from my view by the organ console. She didn't like the modern language service that we used each day. As I said the modern service, she mumbled along somewhere in the distance using the old seventeenth-century language. Nor did she like the exchange of the peace that is now a common part of modern liturgies, so she always shunned my advances and knelt down praying to avoid any unnecessary contact. The service would continue to the giving of the bread and wine and then she would hurry forward, receive, and turn on her heels and leave the building as I concluded alone with the final prayers and dismissal.

98

I often wondered what the hell I was doing and how extraordinarily weird all of this was.

There were great joys in being part of cathedral life although the experience has totally spoilt attendances at almost all churches since then. In many churches the liturgy is often conducted extremely badly with virtually no integration of the different aspects of the service. In particular, choirs frequently set themselves an almost impossible task as they try to ape cathedral choirs, usually with excruciating results. Why can't congregations tailor what they do to the skills and needs of their congregation? They should be more authentic and not try to mimic cathedrals.

Being a cathedral, it was easy to invite well-known, good speakers and preachers. When Cardinal Winning, the Roman Catholic Archbishop of Glasgow (1975–2001), visited the Anglican cathedral in Glasgow to preach at Evensong, he arrived early and joined me in welcoming a group of gay black South African miners. He couldn't have been more welcoming, approachable and loving to them. He shared with them something of his own background as the son of a Scottish miner and spoke about the tensions, ambiguities and hardships he had faced at home in his childhood. He shared his context, and he listened to and empathised with their context. Consequently, we were all looking forward to his sermon which was part of a series on *Why I believe*.

We were all disappointed as Cardinal Winning's sermon was straight down the line Catholic teaching, full of quotations from the Pope, the Catechism and recent papal pronouncements. It was hardline and unbending in tone. There was no evidence of his personality or the empathy that had been so apparent 40 minutes earlier. It struck me then and has done often since, that the main difference between orthodox Roman Catholic teaching and other more liberal interpretations of Christianity is the difference between Roman Law and English Law. Roman Law states the statute and English law is based on precedent. In simplistic language, one is from on high and the other is from below. The same is true in church matters if you contrast Roman

Catholicism or high Anglicanism with liberal Anglicanism. One will state the law or doctrine and the other will work pastorally from day-to-day experience. Of course, conscience and pastoral practice on a one-to-one basis can soften the 'law' for Catholics, just as passing motions in Synod and other church governing bodies can blunt the pastoral empathy within Anglicanism. This can be seen most painfully in the matter of divorce where the only option (until Pope Francis recently intervened) was annulment with divorced people refused the sacrament. Of course, there were plenty of Catholic priests who through pastoral concern would flout the rule (Pope Francis' emphasis on 'mercy' strongly recommends that they do). In all matters of faith there is going to be a good deal of ethical and doctrinal relativity whether this is recognised or not.

It was the genius of Anglicanism to have very soft edges rather than hard walls so that people can easily approach and enter. Its theology is frequently shaped by its pastoral concerns and that allows it the potential to be more welcoming. In Scotland both Cardinal Winning's brand of Catholicism and the biblical hardness of much Presbyterianism (although by no means all) made the Scottish Episcopal Church seem less forbidding and easier to approach. St Mary's Cathedral worked hard at being a welcoming, affirming and inclusive church.

All this was stimulating as was my increasing role in the life of the Scottish Episcopal Church. The cathedral gave me a higher profile in Scottish church life and I became the Scottish Episcopal Church's representative on the Anglican Peace and Justice Network and in May 1996 I attended their meeting in New York and Washington, DC. It was a fascinating experience and I shared a room in a hotel in Times Square with Jae Joung Lee from South Korea (Dean of the cathedral in Seoul). His stories were appalling and humbling. He told me of the period he spent in prison and of his fear as those in neighbouring cells were tortured and beaten. He spoke of how the noise got louder as the torturers gradually got nearer to his cell – the cries of others and the anticipation was almost worse than the pain of torture. It was humbling too to listen to Bishop Pie Ntukamazina from Burundi talk about the devastating effect of the genocide in Rwanda and Burundi on his family and congregations and the ongoing unease in the region. Alan Saw U had to be smuggled out of Myanmar to attend this meeting, Naim Ateek, founder of Sabeel Liberation Theology Centre in Jerusalem, spoke of his constant struggle as a Palestinian Christian – even as he spoke at events around this meeting, it was obvious he was carefully being monitored by US security. All of this made me feel as though I enjoyed a very comfortable and cosseted position in Scotland and an overwhelming realisation that peace and justice is at the heart of the Christian gospel and not the margins.

The meeting began in New York with meetings in and around the United Nations. We were then moved to Washington, DC where the group held meetings with the IMF and the World Bank as well as on Capitol Hill. It was a rather privileged view of the USA and even included a visit to the White House where some of us got almost uncontrollable giggles when, having been shown portraits of previous Presidents, including James Polk, I exclaimed in a rather too loud stage whisper, 'I didn't know they had a Poke!' An innocent remark but to those of us raised on smutty 'Carry On' films caused hopeless giggles. We were swiftly approached by security and told to show proper deference or we would be escorted out.

At our joint meeting with the International Monetary Fund and World Bank, we delegates met and listened to the legendary Gustavo Gutiérrez, a Peruvian priest and theologian, whose seminal work *A Theology of Liberation*, was first published in 1971. The book, and the movement it represented, caused a seismic shift in theology with its emphasis on the gospel of, and for, the poor. His book helped to bring about the birth of contextual theology with its emphasis on the importance of the social, political and economic realities of each neighbourhood and situation. The influence of Liberation Theology was immense and here was its high priest speaking to our small gathering at the World Bank – an institution that was the antithesis of what Gustavo Gutiérrez believed in. He spoke, I remember, about the word 'Pharaoh' as meaning those who live in 'big houses'. Houses

101

couldn't get much bigger than the World Bank and the IMF, and the message to Pharaoh remained the same, 'Let my people go!'

My London experience with the St Hilda Community had taught me a great deal about the struggle of women within the Anglican church, my experience in Glasgow taught me a great deal about the struggle of gay people within the church. The cathedral was in the West End of Glasgow near the university and a sizeable proportion of the congregation were gay. One of my colleagues at the cathedral, John Turner, was a university chaplain and he was living openly as a gay man – there was no pretence to salve the worries of the church. He had never pretended to bishops and his bosses in the church that he was anything other. He was a remarkable pastorally gifted priest and a witty and profound preacher.

He was gifted pastorally because he was vulnerable. He was vulnerable as a gay man in the church because of his honesty. Vulnerable because his strict Brethren background tortured his early years of coming out. But his vulnerability and his honesty led people to trust him instinctively and talk to him in depth. An Australian member of the cathedral congregation with Antipodean subtlety, said of John: 'this screwed up little man held all our lives together'. Of course, the mean-minded could, and sometimes did attack him, for what he was or what he said but for most people, and for me, he was a valued counsellor – a genuine wounded healer.

John told the cathedral congregation about the hostility that gays and lesbians face especially within the church. In a remarkable sermon at the cathedral in 1993, he spelt out the reality of growing up and living as gay:

> Gay men and lesbians can arouse extraordinary reactions of fear blame and envy. To be called a 'poof' or a 'dyke' in the school playground is about the worst insult of them all, and how many of us utterly outgrow the school playground in our lives? I think the heart of the matter is fear, a fear that can cast out love. The heterosexual world feels uncomfortably challenged by the presence in its midst of women who don't really need men at all, thank you very much.

And behind the need to deride and attack gay men is the fact of our fluid and sometimes ambivalent sexuality. To be an acceptable man in much of our society is still to be aggressive and heterosexual. So, the gentle and homosexual elements in a young man's personality are often deeply suppressed and denied so that he can fit in with his mates. In an ordinary male environment with more or less of a premium on machismo, an overtly homosexual individual becomes both the object of scapegoating and furtive fascination. He is living out possibilities which his colleagues unconsciously fear and repress in themselves; he is a visible reminder of what they are denied shunned, at least in public.[70]

When John spoke in 1993 it was in the wake of fears about AIDS. Nowadays there is greater acceptance of gay people in churches. If that is true (and it is quite a large 'if') then it is due to the courage of John and other Christian gays and lesbians whose example and ability to be courageously 'out' and to speak and write about it that society has become more tolerant – at least officially. John's influence meant that a large number of gay Christians started attending – we were a 'safe' church and a meeting place for people who were gay and Christian. Blessing of gay partnerships was commonplace but usually done discreetly in the couple's home or quietly, almost privately in the cathedral.

The congregation were, for the most part, extremely welcoming of new gay members. However, someone did leave the congregation because she saw two men kissing in the cathedral porch on Easter Sunday. When John left to be the priest at St George's, Berlin it was not surprising that he was succeeded by another remarkable gay priest, Donald Reid.

I began to listen to the Bible through the gay community. I found that all the proof texts (or 'the bashing texts' as the gay community sometimes referred to them) that evangelicals threw at gay people to consign them to sinfulness were not clear cut at all. There is in the gospel of Matthew a story of Jesus curing the gay lover of a Roman centurion.[71] I am grateful for this interpretation which I learnt from my friend and New Testament scholar, Alan Cadwallader. He suggests that the Greek word 'pais' used in Matthew can mean lover or companion and that the study of the Roman army suggests centurions often had male lovers,[72] and sometimes these 'lovers' were slaves. Gay relationships were common in the Roman army, probably inevitable in long periods away from home. The Roman historian, Tacitus, notes that in veteran colonies in Italy the 'soldiers were not in the habit of marrying or bearing children'.[73] Homosexuality was common not only in the army but in Roman society as a whole.[74] Whether or not there was an actual healing of a centurion's gay lover is beside the point. It is a scandalous story that a gospel writer would not employ in their narrative unless it was an important part of Jesus' ministry of inclusion.

John Turner, whose ministry was so valued at the cathedral, was equally loved in his new post at St George's, Berlin. On the face of it, it didn't seem a natural fit and he had a torrid start to his ministry there – I remember long phone calls but his pastoral skill and humour won through. It was an extraordinary transformation for a church that had been the spiritual base of the British diplomatic community and the armed forces in Berlin. John won them over. Tragically on Boxing Day 1996, he was walking to take a service and have a meal with a Franciscan community in Berlin when a car skidded on the ice, veered on to the pavement and hit him. He died the next day; he was only 42 years old. I remember remarking to a friend and colleague that this absurd sad death of our friend showed how haphazard and transitory life is and it should be lived to the full without compromise. On three separate occasions we spoke about life after death over about seven years. Each time he came up with the same evocative phrase to explain his view: 'God is the ocean and I am a wave.' There is a continual ebb and flow and we will always be part of it.

For me, John's sudden death meant making decisions about my life, my marriage, my faith and my job. In reality, I was worn down by too much work, not only with the cathedral, but diocesan and national church matters. There was, for instance, six months when I didn't have a single evening free.

104

I have a strong sense of duty. I think it was because I was often called lazy when I was a child and teenager, probably with some justification. I always seem to do too much work. I feel both obliged and guilty to work long hours and this is detrimental to family and friends. I wish I could repent of it.

During my time at the cathedral, my theology was getting more overtly 'liberal' and this was causing tensions within the congregation. A small group wanted me to meet them to talk about my theology (although it was put rather more aggressively – frankly I was summoned and made to understand by some that if my answers were not acceptable they would take further formal measures). It became a quasi-heresy trial. They demanded to know my answer to central tenets of their faith – Did I accept Jesus as my Lord and Saviour? Did I believe in life after death and the resurrection of the body? I answered truthfully but frankly hid behind careful language and selective quotations from the New Testament. These tenets aren't exactly 'yes' or 'no' questions. I survived the meeting but the complaints about my theology continued not only from them but from a member of the cathedral Chapter.

The main focus of complaint was an Easter sermon and a subsequent piece in the cathedral magazine that questioned an understanding of the resurrection that implied that Jesus just got up out of the grave after three days, brushed off the dust and walked about again. That would give us no hope, I argued, because if you open any grave you will see a decaying body and bones. I referred to Paul in Corinthians speaking about 'a spiritual body' rather than a physical body and of Paul experiencing the risen Christ as a vision, not as a physical risen body. Although biblical, this didn't go down well and I regret to say that it hurt a recently bereaved member of the congregation – or to be more accurate – a few people were hurt on her behalf. It confirmed a view that I had been trying to resist that many churchgoers are in the pews very largely because it gave an answer to death: if you worshipped this God, you would be safe in the afterlife – you would be in heaven.

105

My sense of dis-ease was brought about and magnified partly by a rare spiritual 'epiphany' I had in 1995 when I was marooned at Crewe station (almost literally – flooded line) on a journey from Cheltenham to Glasgow. This experience changed my theological understanding. God for me had always been difficult to define. My focus had always been on Jesus. The Crewe encounter helped to alter and define everything I believed about God. Strangely, it was so vivid that it was almost as though God whispered in my ear. I was re-reading a book by John Robinson called *Exploration Into God* that I had picked up in a second-hand book shop for 25p. Suddenly some words jumped out at me, startling me with their truth. They seem almost commonplace and banal now for they simply said: 'The conception of God as a being, a Person – like ourselves – will, I believe, come to be seen as a human projection. (Most people already recognise this in the case of the Devil.)'[75]

I read Robinson's words over and over again as I waited for the non-existent train to Glasgow to materialise; it was for me a moment of profound insight. A blazing light of obvious truth. It was freedom. Sometimes I revisit the same spot at Crewe station, Platform 11, which remains for me a place of pilgrimage. Weird that departing from a traditional understanding of God should feel like a genuine religious and spiritual experience.

The incident brought back and confirmed a very powerful feeling I had at the National Theatre a year or two earlier watching David Hare's play on the Church of England, *Racing Demon*. The play begins with a speech by an inner-city London vicar professing his doubts. At the very start of the play, he is alone on the stage speaking to God:

> God. Where are you? I wish you would talk to me. God. It isn't just me. There's a general feeling. This is what people are saying in the parish. They want to know where you are. The joke wears thin. You must see that. You never say anything. All right, people expect that, it's understood. But people also think, I didn't realise when he said nothing, he really did mean absolutely nothing at all. You see, I tell you, it's this perpetual absence – yes? – this not being here – it's that

– I mean, let's be honest – it's just beginning to get some of us down.
You know? Is that unreasonable? There are an awful lot of people
in a very bad way. And they need something besides silence. God.
Do you understand?[76]

Whether Hare meant this as a theological statement or simply to show
the care-worn life of a socially engaged London vicar is hard to tell. I
do know that he did a lot of homework for the play and spoke to many
clergy. It certainly was getting to be a 'general feeling'. It dramatised
what I had thought and was still rumbling around my mind when I
took the train from Crewe to Glasgow, by which time I had bought a
copy of the play and could even recite the speech.

I had begun to understand that religious language doesn't have
to be so anthropomorphised. I began to read and think hard about my
understanding of God. The books of British philosopher of religion,
Don Cupitt, had been my constant companion since Hagley. Cupitt
argues that all thinking is internalised speech and therefore all our
thought depends on language. Language is something that human
beings invented. Everything is defined and exists only because we
have named it, spoken it. From that invention evolved all the symbols
and the vocabulary of religion and morality. Through our language we
construct ourselves and the world we live in, 'Our language imposes
an agreed common shape on the raw flux of experience.'[77] Truth is
not out there waiting to be uncovered, waiting to be revealed, truth
is made not found, claims the American philosopher, Richard Rorty:
'To say that truth is not out there is simply to say that where there are
no sentences there is no truth, that sentences are elements of human
languages, and that human languages are human creations.'[78]

What do I make of God? Well to be honest, I began to find enormous
sense in Paul Tillich's way of understanding God as 'being' rather than
'a being'. I can't think of any more beautiful way to describe God than
in his famous passage about God as the ground and depth of all being:

… depth is what the word God means. And if that word has not
much meaning for you, translate it, and speak of the depths of your
life, of the source of your being, of your ultimate concern, of what

you take seriously without any reservation. Perhaps in order to do so you must forget everything traditional you have ever learnt about God, perhaps even the word itself. For if you know that God means depth, you know much about him. You cannot then call yourself an atheist or unbeliever ... The one who knows about depth knows about God.[79]

Don Cupitt, I found, put it slightly differently and offers this definition of God: 'God is the sum of our values, representing to us their ideal unity, their claims upon us and their creative power.'[80] That is a position that Cupitt describes as a postmodernist version of the older existentialist understanding of people like Tillich.[81] But, for me, Cupitt's definition holds within it something that could drive our living action – successfully or unsuccessfully as we try to live by our ideals. I find it strange though that many, perhaps even most, liberals agree with Tillich's 'ground of all being' but Cupitt's framing of his definition divides people maybe because it is couched in the language of philosophy, and, indeed, the philosophy of language, it appears less palatable. I find it the reverse. In reality, of course, Tillich's 'ultimate concern', and 'what you take seriously without any reservation' are not very different from Cupitt's 'sum of our values'.

A criticism of Cupitt's non-realism is that it makes God too relative – the sum of my values will be different from the sum of your values. Will that not lead to moral chaos? Hundreds of thousands of people doing what their God allows. Frame it in a slightly different way – think of our better selves, the person we think we could be – and it becomes more palatable.

To many people seeing God as a human projection is no big deal but for me it was. I was, for God's sake, a Very Reverend, which means I was in charge of a cathedral. Surely God should be more real to me than that. But at that very moment God seemed more real to me than ever before. That theological understanding sometimes clashed with the cathedral's formality and tradition and certainly with the ever-present coterie of traditional believers. I was still living on a precarious border between faith and doubt.

Scotland (1987–1996)

I began to think that if I said what I believed, even what was taught in some theological faculties and seminaries, then it was going to be increasingly hard to remain in a position of pastoral and parochial oversight. Alongside this I quite suddenly lost all sense of ambition. I had been appointed to the cathedral at quite a young age and I had roles of some importance and standing in the wider church, but I suddenly felt that the last thing I wanted to do was to become a bishop or move on and up in any way. I had worked quite closely with the Bishop of Glasgow, John Taylor who had succeeded Derek Rawcliffe, as we traipsed around the diocese trying to drum up a sense of mission and speak to clergy and congregations about their communities – or, frankly we were just desperate to get individual churches to do something other than worry over their own survival. We had agonised over what to do with hopeless or recalcitrant priests. I was offered an important role in the Scottish Episcopal Church for the next year and as I thought about it I realised that I really, really didn't want to do it.

I had also suffered a mini breakdown – frankly, I was tired. My marriage was in a mess. A small proportion of the congregation hated me – one even threatening to physically hurt me, and in one drunken late-night phone message to kill me. I collapsed one day in Sainsbury's, which ended up being surprisingly reassuring, as after a medical check-up I was passed as fit and well. The problem was psychological and stress-related so I had counselling and the doctor gave me some little blue pills to deal with panic attacks, which were beginning to happen more and more frequently. When I moved from Glasgow, my new doctor told me that these wonder drugs that I popped at all sorts of times and that had helped me through feelings of stress were actually a placebo!

To recover and to rest for a week I went to a library in North Wales that was founded by Prime Minister William Ewart Gladstone and strangely enough had 26 bedrooms. I loved its quirkiness and thought then that it could be a really important place for church and society if it only updated and relaxed itself and stopped trying to be an Oxbridge college. The week I spent there gave me space to think and reflect on my life and on my faith. It is a rare treat to go to a place where a train of thought doesn't last a few moments or hours but can be followed through for days. On the last day I was there I had gone to a service of morning prayer in the Library's chapel. We were asked to say the Apostles' Creed together and I found myself utterly unable to parrot its clauses:

> I believe in God, the Father almighty,
> creator of heaven and earth.
> I believe in Jesus Christ, his only Son, our Lord,
> who was conceived by the Holy Spirit,
> born of the Virgin Mary,
> suffered under Pontius Pilate,
> was crucified, died, and was buried;
> he descended to the dead.
> On the third day he rose again;
> he ascended into heaven,
> he is seated at the right hand of the Father,
> and he will come to judge the living and the dead.
> I believe in the Holy Spirit
> the holy catholic church,
> the communion of saints,
> the forgiveness of sins,
> the resurrection of the body,
> and the life everlasting.

The reason it is important to be able to say the Apostles' Creed (CE c.180) with at least a modicum of sincerity is that it is traditionally regarded as a summary of the apostles' teaching and has been widely considered a test of orthodox belief. Indeed, the Church of England's Thirty-Nine Articles, which all those who are ordained into that church assent to, state that it ought 'thoroughly to be received and believed'. I can only unequivocally affirm two out of its clauses – the two historical statements – 'suffered under Pontius Pilate' and, 'was crucified, died and was buried'. A low 'score' on this creed poses a problem for Anglican clergy who have to affirm and declare their belief by taking an oath in 'the faith set forth in the catholic creeds'. Of course, we get around it by saying that we see it as a 'community song', or we say that we might not believe every clause, but this pulls together the views of the gathered believers. It provides, you might say, the Christian agenda. Or, we might waffle a meaningless retort saying that we believe in the spirit in which it was composed (except that we probably don't as it was defining who was included and excluded in the camp of Christian orthodoxy – and we all need to know that had as much to do with geopolitical decisions as it had to do with theology). I have trotted out most of those excuses at one time or another. Nobody seems to recite it with much enthusiasm or sincerity, it certainly does not sound like a ringing endorsement of something that matters deeply to those present, it sounds like a mumbled duty that is given scant thought.

If the Apostles' Creed is one test of orthodoxy then the Vincentian canon of the fifth century framed by Bishop Vincent of Lérins is another. It states that orthodoxy is 'that which is believed everywhere, always and by all' but it simply does not stand the test of time. Doctrine evolves and understandings of what is truth change with new discoveries and in various contexts. How can it be unchanging as we, through the painstaking work of biblical critics, archaeologists, literary critics, historians of the ancient world and Judaic scholars, now know more about the cultural context of Jesus' time than former generations? We certainly know more about what Jesus actually said and did than Vincent of Lérins ever knew.

There, sitting upstairs in the gallery of the Library's reading room, I wrote a 'non credo'. It felt liberating and an important turning point in my life. It felt as though I was crossing a line, not necessarily from belief into unbelief, but into a faith that I could fully believe in. This is what I wrote:

> I can't with any confidence call God 'the Father' or 'the Almighty' – for both, to my mind, are increasingly unhelpful as God has no gender and the 'Almighty' tag makes God supernatural and all powerful – a sort of good wizard. Put the two words together and

you have a fearful and overbearing father. I would be more inclined to say that God is not a being at all, but God is being – not a noun but a verb.

Because I do not see God as 'a being' I do not think that there is a divinity, a mind or a 'something' controlling the beginning of the world, its history and its final end. I don't believe a God has set in motion the orbits of literally billions and billions of planets for our sake. It seems far too parochial!

I do not believe that Jesus was God's only Son. I feel it is not helpful to think of a divine family 'up there' in heaven. For me, God is the sum of my ideals and Jesus is for me an exemplar of those ideals. I am happier calling Jesus 'a son of God' in the sense that we are all part of one human family – brothers and sisters to Jesus, sons and daughters of God – metaphorically speaking.

I do not believe in the virgin birth, which is a story to try to explain the importance of the life of Jesus as part of a plan of a god for his chosen people. Jesus isn't God 'veiled in flesh' and born supernaturally, whatever our Christmas hymns tells us. Our world and our history simply doesn't work like that. Jesus is a human being – nothing more, nothing less.

I do not believe that Jesus descended into hell after his death to preach to the 'imprisoned spirits' (1 Peter 3:19–20) – that seems like complete nonsense. I think it belongs to a first-century worldview that is no longer fully relevant.

I do not believe that his body came to life again 'on the third day', except in the minds, hearts and memories of his followers. I believe that it was most likely that he was thrown into a common grave, never to be seen as a physical being again.

I do not believe that Jesus will 'come again' in any physical sense except in us and through us as we try to live as Jesus lived – following his way, his ethic. Believers are expected to be the body of Christ and that is how the second coming happens – it's us.

For the rest of the creed's clauses there is a smidgen of equivocation on my part: I do not believe in the Holy Spirit in any conventional sense but only as the inspiration that calls for the imitation of the mission of Jesus, action as the body of Christ and to the sharpening of our consciences as we read, listen to and try to live the story of Jesus.

I do believe we need communities of believers (churches etc.) to support, protect, uphold each other in living the Christian way but I wouldn't think of them as necessarily 'holy'. I cannot accept the word 'catholic' in either of its two meanings. If it means universal, I do not think there can be universal truths – truth needs to be contextualised. If it means a defined orthodoxy or unity of belief, order and practice then that to me is dangerous and can lead to authoritarianism.

I do believe that there are women and men who are sages, prophets and activists of many faiths and none, who have advanced humanity by their thoughts, words and actions, and that it is good to know about and important to retell their stories. If Jesus is for me the primary exemplar of my faith then these sages, prophets and activists are also exemplars. Is that what is meant by the communion of saints? I doubt it, but it is good enough for me.

I believe that in Jesus we see grace in action, usually through unconditional acceptance and love of all people, regardless of who they are or what they have done. That seems to me a more powerful idea rather than 'the forgiveness of sin' that is somehow won or bought for us on, and by, the cross of Jesus.

I believe I will live on only in the minds and hearts of my family and friends or people who might happen upon something I have written or created. My body will not be raised after death nor will I live with God or indeed with my dead loved ones in heaven (or in hell). Death will be the end except that my atoms will live on forever and feed the chemistry of this fragile earth.

What I do believe and am passionate about is the active life of the historical Jesus of Nazareth, which doesn't appear in the creed at all. For me, therefore the traditional creeds are not fit for purpose.

I have always enjoyed reading plays and when I lived and worked in London I went to the theatre a great deal. I miss that, so reading plays is the next best thing. During my week's stay at the Library in North Wales I read Tom Stoppard's 1972 play *Jumpers*, which I had never seen. I read it the night after my decision not to utter the Apostles' Creed and to write my own non credo. There is a particular speech in that play that chimed with my train of thought. In it Dotty, a prematurely retired musical comedy actress is exasperated with her husband George, a professor of Moral Philosophy. She rants at him for his old-fashioned worldview:

> Well, it's all over now, not only are we no longer the still centre of God's universe, we're not even uniquely graced by his footprint in man's image … Man is on the moon, his feet on solid ground, and he has seen us whole, all in one go, little – local … and all our absolutes, the thou-shalts and the thou shalt-nots that seemed to be the very condition of our existence, how did they look to two moon-men with a single neck to save between them? Like the local customs of another place. When the thought drips through to the bottom, people won't just carry on. There is going to be such … breakage, such gnashing of unclean meats, such coveting of neighbours' oxen and knowing of neighbours' wives, such dishonouring of mothers and fathers, and bowing and scrapings to images graven and incarnate, such killing of goldfish and maybe more – Because the truths that have been taken on trust, they've never had edges before, there was no vantage point to stand on and see where they stopped.[82]

In my small single bedroom at the Library, I thought about Dotty's sense of 'breakage', how the church's belief system was broken and how all the absolutes have gone and truths are no longer taken on trust. We are in the new world, scientific and analytic, which Dotty refers to in *Jumpers*. For the argument goes that when that contemporary worldview becomes widespread and widely accepted '… when the thought drips through to the bottom, people won't just carry on. There is going to be such … breakage.'

114

The 'breakage' is only too apparent, it was then, and it is even more marked now: mainstream credal churches in the Western world are losing adherents very rapidly; the number of clergy in training is declining; retreat houses are closing; religious orders are declining and ageing; Sunday schools are in steep decline … and now, over 50% of the British public have indicated that they have 'no religion'.

The catalogue of decline is not encouraging. I am sure that it is not the main factor, but couldn't a contributing factor to this 'breakage' be the lack of a believable message presented as though it was actually believed by clergy? There is a problem as the Christian Church can too often be a place where the words we say are not what we believe and certainly not the words we live our life by. There is a debate to be had about integrity – institutional and personal. Why do so many clergy wait until they retire to 'come out' with not only who they really are (gay or bisexual), but what they really believe? Here I am penning these thoughts in my sixties – I am just as bad, we probably all have an eye on our pension! I have spoken to and listened to a lot of clergy talking about what they do or don't believe. For many, orthodoxy is a complete sham – they have worked it out for themselves and they cannot, like me, tick many of the credal boxes.

The nonsense that we clergy all too easily babble hit me the other day when I attended the funeral of a friend – he was a regular-ish churchgoer, but I know from conversations that he did not believe in life after death and thought that death would be the end for him, just as it had been for his wife a few years earlier. And yet, the vicar's homily claimed that my friend believed in life after death and uttered assurances from the pulpit that my friend would be reunited with his wife in heaven. The prayers and the readings that were said by the vicar all implied that there was life after death – rather in the sense that come the last trumpet we would all be miraculously and bodily alive again. The upsetting thing about all of this is that I know the vicar and he doesn't think that there is life after death either in that literal and bodily sense.

I tell that story because it is indicative, I think, of credal churches and the apparent compulsion to adhere to orthodoxy. The history of Christianity has shown through the sad testimony of martyrs that orthodoxy 'can be violent and deadly'.[83] Shouldn't we be suggesting a future that allows and encourages religious freedom? In fact, it is time to do as the apostle Paul recommends 'to work out our own salvation in fear and trembling'.[84] In a published conversation at Great St Mary's in Cambridge which I first read on my short visit to North Wales, Don Cupitt makes much the same point to John A T Robinson. The passage is basically telling Christians to grow up.

> The New Testament Epistles often make a contrast between two kinds of religion. There is a religion of the letter and a religion of the spirit. There is a religion of milk fed to babes in Christ and there is a religion of meat for adults who are old enough to think and act for themselves. There is a religion for schoolchildren who are under the discipline of an external authority, and there is a religion for those who have come of age.[85]

Tradition tells us that we should love God with all our heart, mind and strength. We often forget that we should grow up and use our brains as well. Doubts and deviations from orthodoxy that I have are mirrored by many people in congregations as they think about their faith. And those who haven't these doubts are usually only too eager to tell you where you have got it wrong (admittedly they sometimes tell the church authorities as well).

If there is an annoyance when doubts or ideas that seem contrary to orthodoxy are aired from the pulpit then the annoyance is often that no one has expressed these doubts and deviations from the pulpit before.

Stepping aside and spending just a week of reflection was enormously helpful to me. Why hang on to a traditional Christian faith? Am I wasting my life just going through the motions of ritual and belief? My answer, then and now, is that despite it all there is something that won't let me go, namely the historical ministry of Jesus. Just before coming to North Wales for the week, we had invited David Jenkins, the former Bishop of Durham, to preach at the cathedral and spend an evening discussing his views with members of the congregation. Afterwards in my house over a glass or two of whisky before bed, he said 'As I get older I find I believe less and less, but what I believe, I believe more and more strongly.' I can affirm that same thought unequivocally.

I was now on the border between faith and doubt. I realise I had been for some time but my sojourn at Gladstone's Library and the careful listing of what I didn't believe confirmed that for me. I had given myself a little space to think and reflect and the answer now seemed that I could not with any inner credibility still be in parochial ministry or in charge of a cathedral. Not that I want to say categorically that I was a non-believer; Jesus remained a very powerful figure and icon in my life but not, absolutely not, someone who died for our sins. And God seemed just a word I used to carry my worldview. Prayer seemed to be a stilling of the mind, a silence through which some insight did sometimes come. Praying for others, as I was frequently asked to do, was a conscious focusing of thought on a person and their situation rather like Quakers who sometimes talk of holding someone in the light. Nothing magical, nothing supernatural. Silence.

I felt I needed to shed the obligations that tore me in two. I was obliged to recite liturgy that I didn't believe, and had to reassure members of the congregation of God's love, mercy and forgiveness when I didn't believe there was anyone up there who was going to make any difference to their lives. It was time to leave and to find an honest borderland.

It was in this spirit that I reluctantly left North Wales refreshed and thankful to Gladstone's Library for the space to recover, to think and to find some resolution to a restless tussle between faith and doubt, belief and dis-belief. Sitting in a local pub with a fellow guest from the Library, a psychiatrist from Manchester, I knew that if the job of Warden of Gladstone's Library ever came up that I would apply. It was and I did.

PART II

THE GLADSTONE YEARS

CHAPTER 5
LIVING IN A LIBRARY
(1997–2021)

… If librarians were honest,
they would say, 'No one
spends time here without being
changed.'
Joseph Mills – 'If Librarians Were Honest'

I had been in the West of Scotland just short of 10 years. I had learnt a lot about pastoral work. It is possible that the endless campaigning of the London chaplaincy has made believe that it was causes that mattered most. Well, in Scotland I learnt that yes, causes mattered but my faith needed to be grounded in everyday parochial concerns. The congregation were my primary pastoral concern – their hurts, grudges, depressions, deaths and sadness as well as moments of celebration of birth, love and laughter and those terrifying Scottish ceilidhs where I always tried to time a visit to the bar or the loo as a dance began. In Ayr and Glasgow, I was still concerned with the least, last and lost but they were basically the least, last and lost of the congregations I was serving. Real problems that needed to be listened to and offered real support, not with a march and a waving of a banner, but some practical down to earth help. And now, lesson learnt about grounding my faith in the everyday world, I headed back to institutional life of a kind and to what has proved to be a sort of chaplaincy for grown-ups.

The selection process was thorough and I was clearly not the preferred candidate to be Warden of Gladstone's Library. My predecessor as Warden, Peter Jagger, more or less told me that I was only there to make up the numbers and he boasted that a well-known highly respected Anglican theologian and priest was almost certainly going to get the post. He and the senior staff couldn't have been more disdainful of my candidature. I went into the interview unashamedly speaking about the need for change.

Despite the opposition, I had absolute confidence that I would be appointed – was that God or just cocky arrogance? A few minutes after I had driven home to Glasgow, the Chairman of the Trustees, Sir William Gladstone, great-grandson of the Prime Minister, rang to offer me the post. Some six months later, I headed for Hawarden and the Library at the beginning of January 1997.

This belief that God wants me to do something or be something is a strange sensation. Of course, it isn't God at all. It is just what I strongly feel that I want to do or be – sometimes it is a conscious longing and sometimes subconscious yearning and both manifest in a sudden moment of clarity. In each instance of my so-called 'spiritual experiences' – be it a sudden feeling of reassurance at a time of threatened nuclear war, or a sense of vocation coming out of the blue, or a revelation on Crewe station, or now this calling to a new and quite different ministry at Gladstone's Library – there is simply an inner articulation and clarity of what I want to do (or, conversely, don't want to do). Those of us who are religious deify these senses into being something that is demanded of us by God, which removes it from any normal discourse, perhaps it is just an unconscious sly move by us.

Gladstone's Library had already played a significant role in my life. It had been a catalyst to change, leading to a sense of recovery and clarification which added to its attraction for me. I valued it and felt I owed it my very best shot. Gladstone's Library seemed as though it could be my home. I liked the idea of a 'liberal' place. I liked the idea of being free to work out my faith and perhaps write and lecture a little bit. It felt like freedom. I wanted to get out of Glasgow, my marriage and a ministry at the cathedral that was both uncomfortable and that I felt I wasn't particularly suited to. I like to be liked and I wasn't. I don't think I even liked myself very much.

Life as an Anglican clergyperson in a parish can be pressurised; a clergyperson might well be looking after several churches, have a diocesan role and be involved in their local community. There is not much time, if any, for theological reflection and so the weekly demand for a sermon inevitably means a rather hastily put together mixture of theology learnt some time ago mingled with pastoral and local needs. There is not the time or the energy for wrestling with theological concepts. Clergy cannot fulfil their role of being the theologian in the parish. So, engrossed by the life of their church and parish they are also frequently out of touch with contemporary culture.

The move to Hawarden in North Wales, a mile from the English border, also meant change in my personal circumstances. My wife, Denise, stayed in Glasgow to finish her PhD as I headed to North Wales. In fact, shortly afterwards we separated and divorced. I suppose my principal feeling was one of sadness, pain and loss. We were both now free. Denise was in a new relationship. I was free to start a new life too. My childlessness which had so blighted my first marriage was also unbeknown to me about to end. For I remarried some four years after arriving at the Library to Helen. We have a daughter, Lucy. Lucy is herself now married to Phil, and they have a son, Rupert, who delights us all. All of this gives me a happiness and completeness I never dreamt was going to be possible. That is the major transformation of my long period at Gladstone's Library. I am happy.

The move from Glasgow to the village of Hawarden in North Wales, the personal changes to my life, the opting out of normal parochial ministry perhaps provided a moment to pause and reflect on what I had achieved in life and what I wanted to achieve for the rest of my life and ministry. Looking back, I could see that my clerical career had been consumed with issues of inclusion and exclusion. From a privileged start in life through privileged education I had been trained to divide the world into us and them. This dominated my childhood – who was I encouraged to play with and who was I not. The Birmingham experience changed me, not enough, but it at least opened my eyes to the least, the last and the lost in society. My church career gave me the opportunity of living alongside the people of the parish and learning from them through involvement in key moments of their lives, and just listening and learning. My theological instinct taught me to focus on injustice and everyday life – a theology from below rather than from above.

The Library at Hawarden is on the border between Wales and England. Border living suited me – it was an expression of my relationship with the institutional church as well as trying to straddle the secular and religious worlds.

When I arrived at Gladstone's Library it was proudly old fashioned, somewhat right of centre in politics, stuffily high church in its theology and liturgy with dwindling numbers of visitors and struggling to make money, in fact it was losing considerable sums each year. I longed to change it – indeed, I had been appointed to change it by the Trustees because it was clear to most of them that unless there was change it would soon disappear. It was not so much what it was, but what it could be, that intrigued me. Its ethos was very closed and you had to get two references before you were allowed to stay at the Library. The local public were not allowed in unless they paid to become day readers, which also required two references. Inclusive it was not, and somewhat prided itself on its exclusivity and seriousness. It needed widening.

Gladstone's Library is unique. It has 200,000 books at one end of the building and 26 bedrooms at the other. In 1997 most of those who stayed were clergy (in fact about 80%) with a smattering of other researchers and readers. It had been founded by Gladstone to house his 30,000 books, of which he had read over 22,000 and about half of those he annotated, often creating his own index at the back of the book.

My most famous predecessor was Alec Vidler, the noted radical liberal theologian, who was Warden during the years of the Second World War (1939–1948). He instinctively understood Gladstone's purpose in setting up the Library – to live on the border between the secular intellectual world and the world of theology and the Church. He came close to achieving Gladstone's vision. He was an intellectual heavyweight (he became Fellow and Dean of King's College, Cambridge) who was sent by Archbishop William Temple and with the agreement of the Library Trustees to invite theologians and other scholars to consider why Britain had failed to see and understand the growth of fascism both on the continent and in this country and, most importantly, to explore what sort of society should be created after the war. At the same time Vidler was made editor of the journal *Theology* which would help him disseminate the fruits of these discussions.

> In those war years, the Library became a temporary home to not only British theologians and other intellectuals but also emigres and Jewish refugees from the continent. In an appreciation of Vidler, a colleague of his at the Library, G.R. Dunstan, remembers that throughout the war years, and after, Hawarden offered a home (which is more than a refuge) to a group of distinguished refugees; scholars from all over the world found themselves drawn to the Library to study, to confer, to think, to experience a mode of life and thought ... which was a product of the Vidler mind and the Gladstone intent.[86]

Vidler was in tune with Gladstone's purpose for the Library. He was almost quoting Gladstone directly in an editorial in *Theology* when he wrote:

> Christian theology cannot be achieved in isolation ... the ever-widening gulf between the actualities of modern society and the affirmations of the Christian faith, and the apparent irrelevance to what is said and done outside ... It is the function of theology to see and declare the truth about this permanent crisis, and to interpret the truth in the context of our contemporary situation.[87]

The goal for me was to, within our contemporary cultural context, recreate the vision that Gladstone had, and which Vidler lived and articulated. In 1997, the signs weren't very auspicious, bells rang to summon us to terrible meals – on a Sunday night it alternated between cold pilchards and limp lettuce or a slice of spam and limp lettuce. Every other evening meal throughout the week was always a stew. As an American visitor said to me in the pub one evening, 'everything is brown: the carpets, the curtains, the furniture, the food – even parts of the lettuce!' No alcohol was available. Grace was said before and after meals and the Warden presided, often inviting distinguished guests to eat next to him at a long table in an amateurish representation of an Oxbridge college.

Even in the late 1990s the village community and other outsiders were not allowed into the Library. You couldn't even see it from the road as a large hedge sheltered the Library from prying eyes. It had a smell vaguely reminiscent of a prep school or, as a member of the Gladstone family was overheard saying when visiting with friends, 'it smells of failure'. It relied on a small number of regular visitors who valued its old-fashioned values and the wonderful collection held within its reading rooms.

The Trustees, with one or two notable exceptions, were local gentry, a couple of bishops, and a few Gladstone relations. From the end of the Second World War it had been used by the Anglican church as a training college to help reduce the shortage of priests because of the war. Frequently people were sent to the Library for a short period of study and training to be Anglican clergy because they had been Catholic priests, Methodist ministers, teachers or lecturers of religious studies and wanted to switch to Anglicanism. It also helped to train non-stipendiary priests in England, Wales and Ireland. The training of priests which carried on into the early 1990s gave the Library an avowedly Anglican ethos. The church authorities, quite rightly, stopped its role as a training establishment as there was no longer any call for clergy to train as though they were auditioning to be a curate in a Barbara Pym novel. There had to be change.

Since the training of clergy had stopped, I sensed that the Library was looking for a new role and wasn't yet sure of what it was and who it was for. The security of having more than half of its beds filled by trainee clergy paid for by church funds had hidden the fact for many years that it was in a deep financial mess. If it continued to rely primarily on clergy for its income then it would not survive. I remember sleepless nights trying to work out how it could possibly break even and have a future.

The writer Penelope Fitzgerald visited four times between 1969 and 1974. Her description is affectionate but shows the essential

126

character of the place. In her biography of Fitzgerald, Hermione Lee wrote:

> It was a combination of research centre for Gladstone scholars and an Anglican theological college ... Fitzgerald developed an affection for it, but felt ill at ease when she arrived there on a very hot July day, wearing what she felt sure must be far too-short a dress, the only woman surrounded by eccentric elderly clerics, 'amiable lunatics' who were not spared in her letters home:

> *The dinner bell has just interrupted me – I went down five minutes late, which I thought was about right, but they were half way through dinner already, the sub-warden absurdly presiding in a gown – a new ancient deaf cleric had arrived from the Canary islands – he says that he is going back in 3 weeks – why did he come at all? – another cleric said to me 'I saw you soaking up the sun on the back lawn' – I shall sit on the front lawn tomorrow – another cleric who seems to be wearing a wig (they've all got wives but haven't brought them) has asked me if I'd like to come to the Castle tomorrow to see the interesting Temple, I shan't go, as he gives me hysterics. But the Gothic Gladstone library was wonderfully quiet, the grounds were lovely.*[88]

It was more or less like that when I arrived – the majority of those who came to stay were clergy with a few of their spouses lightening the load. It was very male and far from the bastion of liberalism that I had hoped for.

Changing the culture of institutions has always fascinated me. It has always been one of the prime motivations for seeking new jobs. The Library could, I was convinced, be an exciting institution but as with all change there are always some who resist and, in this case, it was the senior staff and a very significant (and complaining) minority of the guests.

It was a stormy beginning. My predecessor obviously had little faith in me and had ensured that his second in command stayed on to check that everything ran smoothly. Fair enough, but returning early from a short holiday I found my predecessor and his former second in command rummaging through files and papers in my office. One of the other senior members of staff seemed to think a day's work consisted of reading the newspapers and going for long walks. It was clear that it was going to be an uphill struggle.

There was also Father John Thorold to contend with who was, in his charming and eccentric way, one of the obstacles to change, although he would have hated to think that was the case. He was a permanent resident and his presence somewhat defined the place. He was an Anglican religious – a monk – who lived in the 1950s or, rather, just carried on as though he was living in the 1950s. When I arrived he was in his early eighties. He enjoyed the constant invasion of groups of clergy and found out where they were serving at present and where they had been previously by consulting *Crockford's*, the Church of England's clerical directory, which he knew almost by heart. He liked to know which school each visitor went to – school meaning public school as others didn't count – and which College at university – again, only Oxbridge as the others didn't really count. His father had been Chaplain-General and, as a family, they had lived in the Tower of London. Despite being a monk, he had expensive tastes: London was reached not by train but by taxi; in London he always stayed at his club, the Travellers, in Pall Mall; every Sunday he would have lunch at the five-star Grosvenor Hotel in Chester where he also stayed for four months when we were refurbishing the Library. These he wouldn't consider extravagances, they were quite simply the only places he knew about – it would, for instance, never occur to him that there were other hotels in Chester.

Father John had very clear views about how liturgy should be led in chapel; he very definitely wasn't a person for innovation. He quaked at the sharing of the peace. Once, an over-exuberant American priest, Father Frisby, who was apparently a relation of the man who invented the Frisbee flying disc, hugged him at the peace in a fond embrace. Later in the day, having just about recovered, Father John searched the man out and told him – 'I kissed my mother when I was a child, I once kissed my father, but I have not and will never kiss anyone else.'

On the other hand, Father John was quite liberal in ethics. He had no problem with homosexuality – 'E M Forster once sat on my knee in his rooms at King's', he told me proudly as though it was a gay pride badge he had won. I have no idea about his sexuality; he thought Joan Collins was the sexiest and most glamorous woman in the world, which doesn't prove anything one way or another! He was ridiculously forgiving, once suggesting that a member of his religious order who had been imprisoned for having sex with a teenage boy could be rehabilitated by being found a job in a boy's prep school and could I help him find a place. That, of course, encapsulates so much of what was wrong with the church's attitude to sexual abuse – care for the perpetrator and little concern for the victim. For Father John and many of his generation, there was a total lack of engagement with the real world – the church was their only world and looking after its own was the priority. You could, and probably should, dismiss Father John as an anachronism, but this out of touch cleric who knew virtually nothing beyond the church and his faith has been a spiritual advisor to bishops, archbishops, politicians and even a prominent member of the royal family. Knowing all this, and in a sense despising him for all of this, why on earth did I confide in him from time to time, especially as I knew any advice he gave to me I would almost certainly ignore?

Father John was very aware that he might be considered 'out of touch' and he would remind us that he was a parish priest at Mitcham in Surrey for 32 years and had seen life in the raw, 'I have seen murders, rapes, robberies and even smelly lifts.'

Father John was particularly devoted to the kitchen and housekeeping staff at the Library, which I think was a throw-back to his childhood as he was devoted to both his Nanny, his 'Cookie' and the family chauffeur, all of whom he seemed rather closer to than his parents (although I don't think he kissed any of them).

It is part of my own and my colleagues' 'chronic niceness' that real reform in the Library only took place after Father John moved into a nursing home. There were 'economic' reasons for our caution as he was exceedingly generous to the Library giving us well over half a million pounds in gifts during the years he was with us and perhaps that is why change waited for his departure. He also paid the full rate for his room at the Library month on month for 25 years. People still remember him with a wry smile and affection (more in retrospect than they demonstrated at the time). I was devoted to, infuriated by, despairing of and amused by Father John.

John Thorold left the Library because of ill health in 2008 and died in 2010. His death represented the end of an era for the Library. When Father John arrived in the 1980s the Library was a quiet community comprising clergy and a few academics. It was a retreat, providing a step back in time away from the hurly-burly of modern life. Father John's worldview was certainly frozen in time – firmly anchored in the 1950s with his beloved Harold Macmillan as Prime Minister. He did his best to keep us all in that same epoch.

Little by little I tried to move it forward. It had always been valuable as a quiet place to stay but the comparative few who happened upon it were not going to make it financially viable. I am fond of a saying by Jack Welch, the former CEO of General Electric, in his Annual Report in 2000: 'When the rate of change inside an institution becomes slower than the rate of change outside, the end is in sight. The only question is when.'

Welch's aphorism seemed to sum up the Library perfectly. And change it did. There were two stages, the first was to relax and update the place, open it up to the public, make it easy to join, take the terrible brownness away by refurbishing, improve the food and change the religious ethos from something almost exclusively Anglican and clerical to something broader. The rate of change was slow at first and then in the last 10 years it has accelerated.

Surprisingly, but comfortingly and appropriately, the most profound change was by going back to Gladstone and his books. Within the 21,000 books of Gladstone's that we could identify as definitely belonging to him, there were three main broad subject areas. Yes, there was a great deal of religion and spirituality, but in fact it was the smallest of the three core areas; there was a hefty amount of history and politics/current affairs, however, the largest of the three areas was literature, both classical and contemporary.

This was liberating as was the discovery that when Gladstone founded the Library he called it 'Monad', a Greek philosophical term, but after 18 months he changed the name, presumably because the name was considered too esoteric, to St Deiniol's Library, simply calling it after the neighbouring church. After he died in 1898, and the present building was built as the national memorial to him. It continued to retain the name St Deiniol's Library but was also referred to as the Gladstone Memorial Library. To simplify things, we decided in 2009 (the bicentenary of his birth) to rename it Gladstone's Library.

The Library when it was founded was dedicated by Gladstone 'for the pursuit of divine learning'. He meant not just theology but the 'divinity of learning' because for Gladstone God is truth, truth is God. This chimes with the idea of 'monad'. Gladstone took the name 'monad' from Pythagoras who held that the 'monad' is the principle point, the origin and end point of all, the unity at the beginning and end of all things, the totality of all things. For Gladstone, the monad is the Christian God, but he was well read enough in Greek philosophy to know that from ancient cultures onwards there have been different understandings of truth. For him the Christian faith provided the master key but he knew there were other keys that unlocked truths. The library that Gladstone founded was, therefore, not only for Anglican clergy and laity but all denominations, not only all denominations but all religions and ideologies.

As we became more closely allied to Gladstone's original aim and purpose, it seemed sensible to change the name to Gladstone's Library rather than honouring a Welsh saint about whom no one knew anything. Changing the name from 2010 immediately seemed to take away a sense of religious mystique, and even fear, about what sort of place the Library was. It almost immediately started to widen the range of guests. This was liberating. The capture of the Library by the Anglican church and its use as a base for training from the post-war years until the mid-1990s had actually skewed its purpose and made it a support for the church rather than Gladstone's idea of a place for exploring truth and of seeing religion in dialogue with history, politics, literature and philosophy.

Gradually we shifted the focus from almost exclusively 'religion', to embrace the other core Gladstone subject areas in the collection: history, politics, current affairs, and above all, literature. This altered our programme as well as our clientele. We started to be innovative and launched a writer-in-residence programme as well as an arts festival (Gladfest) and a democracy festival (Demfest). It helped us to find a new local clientele alongside the residential guests.

It has been the literary emphasis that has brought Gladstone's Library the greatest rewards. Reading an article in *The Sunday Times* in 2010, my colleague, Annette Lewis, became aware that Damian Barr was running a literary salon in London as well as literary house parties. We wrote to him and suggested that the Library could be used for this sort of event. He came for a weekend in 2010 and agreed. He felt we needed better food and a more comfortable ambience before we could be a destination that would attract writers. We aimed to start a writer-in-residence programme in 2012. Damian curated the first year of residencies and thereafter it has been competitive. We have been so blessed in the calibre of those we have attracted to the scheme. Nowadays we get 80 to 90 applicants each year and it is a tough job to create the shortlist, even with the enthusiasm, knowledge and assistance of my colleague, Louisa Yates, who has spearheaded the writers' programme. The shortlist is then given to a group of judges who select four to six writers to be resident for up to one month. I have loved every minute of it and our writers – novelists, poets and literary non-fiction writers have achieved considerable success.[89] In addition, we have since 2017, in co-operation with Theatr Clwyd, been host to four Welsh playwrights each year.

For me, this has been liberating and inspiring. It has taken me back to the world of literature and drama. I would have to say that I often get far more insight into our contemporary world through literature than through most books of theology. Just as literature and drama liberated me from the clutches of fundamentalist Christianity at university, so literature and drama has saved Gladstone's Library from closure.

The project has gone from strength to strength and that is due in no small part to the sponsorship of Joanna Munro, a banker with strong literary leanings, who attending an event sat next to one of our writers, the novelist and theatre maker Stella Duffy, and listened to how hard it was even for established writers to make ends meet or to find the time and space to write. Her sponsorship of our writers in residence programme provides the chosen writers with both time and space. Joanna has helped to ensure the survival of Gladstone's Library and provided the institution with a new sense of purpose and energy.

I read with fascination the authors' work and continue to follow their careers. It hasn't felt like a retreat into escapism but a very enlightening and enriching prism through which to observe contemporary society. Although very few, if any, have been active Christians, many have a religious or spiritual thread in their work. I can think of Stella Duffy, Naomi Alderman, Damian Barr, Sarah Perry, Melissa Harrison and Richard Beard, all of whom touch on the spiritual or the religious. But there is a wider interest as well; anyone writing a novel is engaged in what can be characterised an ethical enterprise. In an interview in *The Guardian*, Zadie Smith tellingly explained:

> That the novel – writing a novel, reading a novel – is an ethical enterprise, a practice place for morals where we watch, in safety, people choosing what they do, and what they lose when they choose wrongly; that is the closest possible rehearsal for the real thing, which is the most important thing of all.[90]

It is in discussion with novelists about this 'ethical' role that I have learnt so much about their inner self, be they avowedly secular or religious. I concur with Chekhov's comment, which seems to imply a quasi-prophetic role to the best of authors:

> The best of them are realistic and paint life as it is, but because every line is permeated, as with a juice, by an awareness of purpose, you

feel, beside life as it is, also life as it ought to be, and this captivates you.[91]

The 'liberal' tradition of Gladstone's Library gave me the space to explore the theological agenda that feeds me. Within the first year I travelled to Leeds for the launch and study day of a book that interested me – *Explorations in Theology and Film*.[92] Cinema had always been one of my abiding passions since childhood and theology was my day job so it seemed made for me. Clive Marsh, one of the editors, had worked with me as a pastoral assistant in chaplaincy work in London during my time at Queen Mary College, and William Telford, one of the contributors, was a regular visitor to Gladstone's Library so I felt I would enjoy the day. The result of a fascinating day was that I decided to hold a 'Film and Theology' weekend at the Library. It has been an annual event since 1998. A book was created of talks given at the course, *Cinéma Divinité*[93] and I have contributed to many academic publications on the subject, as well as speaking to varied groups of theological or religious audiences in the UK, Australia and USA.

The subject of film and theology caused for me a rerun of some old skirmishes about the nature of theology. There were areas we could all agree on like the biopics of Jesus or figures from church history but in a way these were the least interesting films and often quite awful. The most interesting films of the gospel story are to my mind *Celui qui doit mourir, Jésus of Montréal* and *Son of Man*.[94] These three films have very specific contemporary contexts, and do not strive for authenticity but capture something of the motivational, emotional and political experience of Jesus and his disciples and in the process, they seem to be more authentic than versions that strive for historical and textual accuracy.

I very soon became disillusioned with an approach to film and theology that sought out Christ figures and Christian iconography, or dwelt on examples of redemption to compare and contrast with Christian redemption. It reminded me of the arguments I had in St Andrews over the lack of theology in the plays on which I had chosen to write. I realise now that my approach to film, and previously to theatre, is based on the assumptions of contextual theology rather than traditional theological themes. I am interested in why films were made at a specific time and how they reflect that context, critique the values of that society, and express the tensions, anxieties and difficulties of the period in which they were made. Then, and only then, can a debate be had between the films' values, society's tensions and difficulties and how these relate to Christian values and vision. There is always a reason, very often greed, that makes producers and studios spend untold millions of dollars on a huge blockbuster film because they feel it cashes in on or captures a cultural moment. Smaller, independent films also spring out of their cultural context and a desire by the filmmakers to address an issue or a contemporary foible that they want to highlight. It is quite easy to guess the date of film by thinking about the issues and societal tensions that it depicts.

My line into film criticism from a practical theological point of view is to ask, why did the producers think this was a good film to make at this moment in history? I find that question opens up an interesting and valuable discussion. Film can, and does, aid Christian mission. I have little time for taking lessons of faith from short sequences in film – it is all too easy to 'baptise' films and twist them to our godly purpose. My approach is about having an inter-faith discussion with the values (shared or divergent) that the director and producer have put on the screen.

The Film and Theology course attracts a full house of participants each year and brings together Christians of all traditions who love cinema, a welcome wideness, the only common denominator being that they are 'open' in attitude and attuned to contemporary society. Indeed, I think this is the great gift of bringing together a Christian group to study contemporary film as it straddles traditions.

Not once in over 20 Film and Theology courses has there been any inter-theological nonsense between participants about being 'saved' or 'damned' or of splitting into theological camps. It is mercifully free of Christian skirmishing over the meanings of faith and focuses instead on understanding the values behind the filmmaker's art.

Film is also valuable pastorally as it enables people to discuss potentially contentious issues in a non-confrontational way. The deepest and most considered discussion I have ever experienced about abortion was the result of reflecting on the film *Vera Drake*.[95] All sides of the debate were aired and sensitively considered despite the gathering containing a Catholic anti-abortion protestor and, I subsequently found out, a woman who had had not one but two abortions. The distance that the film and its characters provided enabled a profound exploration to take place and a discussion to progress with empathy and understanding for all who were present. The focus on film and literature widened the Library's scope.

This widening circle had been a thread throughout my time as a Christian priest. It started with countering the exclusion of a pregnant teenager from the congregation, was followed by the struggle for the ordination of women, the understanding that children were full members of the church, and the full inclusion of LGBTQ people into the church. I feel, very strongly, that to be wholeheartedly inclusive is a hallmark of Jesus' ministry and part of being a Christian is, I believe, about affirming life in all its fullness for all members of society.

In 2005, another need to widen the circle became evident. During the early evening of 7 July 2005, I started to speak to a Canadian clergyperson at the Library. He looked tired and rather 'rattled' and was sipping a very large Scotch whisky. As we talked, he told me that he had landed at London Gatwick early that morning and had arrived in Central London at about 10am to find chaos. In the previous hour and a quarter, four bombs had disrupted London life. He found out that three bombs had exploded on the Underground system (three at or near Aldgate, Edgware Road and Russell Square Underground stations) and a further one on a double-decker bus in Tavistock Square. The bombs planted by Islamist extremists had killed 52 people and injured hundreds. I had emailed him some days before some simple instructions about how to cross London by Underground but they proved to be useless – the system was shut and in chaos. He decided to walk from Victoria Station to Euston Station to catch his train to Hawarden. However, that proved difficult too; there were police everywhere and Euston was closed. He, along with many others, had to shelter for some hours in the Quaker building near Euston. Eventually, duly searched and questioned by police, he got through the protective cordon and on to the train and a few hours later arrived at the haven of tranquillity that is Gladstone's Library.

The whisky made him reflective and we had a good talk, including admitting to our own scant knowledge of Islam. Such ignorance was not acceptable in these times. It was clear there was a huge amount of misinformation and disinformation about Islam and we both decided to improve our knowledge.

I don't know how he progressed with improving his knowledge of Islam, but the privilege of running a library helped me. There exists a great gulf of misunderstanding and lack of knowledge of each other's traditions and, to muddy the waters, a torrent of pernicious disinformation.

The Library managed to find enough money to convert a suitable room that was adjacent to the Library's reading rooms; it was decorated and shelving was bought and, with the help of a number of scholars who suggested books we should add, we managed to create a balanced English language collection. We filled the room with about 2,000 books which makes it a good and valuable collection – much larger than many universities who boast a strong focus on Islam.

We had decided to make the Islamic Reading Room our chief contribution to the Gladstone bicentenary in 2009. I started to write about it, speak about it and even preach about it. A number of events made me realise that this was an essential thing to do. I was preaching at the neighbouring church in September 2008, a service arranged by the Library which we held once a year. The Oxford theologian Keith Ward had to pull out as guest preacher so I had to step in at the last minute. In the sermon, I remarked that when the author of John's gospel was inspired to put the words of John 14:6 into Jesus' mouth, he was writing in a context starkly different to our own. I said:

To hold on to the words from John's gospel, – 'I am the way, the truth, and the life. No one comes to the Father except by me' – as though they were actually said by Jesus and are eternally binding, is unhelpful in our diverse world. Those who hold to this mindset are not going to promote dialogue and understanding between the world's major religions but are in danger of encouraging hostility and suspicion against other faith traditions.[96]

I believed then, and still believe, that fundamentally Christianity and Islam are both committed to social justice, equality and compassion. To harness that combined commitment really would be a significant force for good in our communities and in our world.

As I finished the sermon and was leaving the church, the rector of the church was waiting for me at the back and subsequently told me that I was not welcome to preach in his church again. The rector's remark simply heralded further condemnation of our Islamic Reading Room by him and others. The rector has now left and I have occasionally preached there, but whenever I do, there is often a small rump of his supporters who are quick to write to the bishop and complain about my lack of orthodoxy.

It seemed such a simple and good project: the new reading room provided the opportunity for Christians and others to have a greater understanding of Islam. It contains material to inform Christians and others about Islam – just as the Library's present collection provides an opportunity for Muslims and others to learn about Christianity and other world faiths. This widening of the Library's focus parallels the shift in universities from Christian Theology to Religious Studies. As someone committed to divine learning, I claimed that Gladstone would understand and approve this change in Gladstone's Library's collection policy.

Surely Gladstone, I argued, if he were alive today would be active in promoting understanding between Islam and Christianity. As a person of faith and as a politician he would work to counter the ignorance and suspicion of each other's faith traditions that is one of the contributory causes of so much national and international tension.

Living in a Library (1997–2021)

This does not mean that Gladstone, or those of us who work to keep his inclusive vision alive, would wish to suggest some sort of merging of the two world faiths – that would get us nowhere. However, it is impossible, when you spend time with people of other faiths, not to recognise a shared religious sensibility. I don't want to say that we are all the same and that differences don't matter but I do want to say that God and religious sensibility are revealed in and through many faith traditions. The life of a holy person in a different tradition is not markedly different to a holy person in my own tradition. For instance, I would not want to claim that my Anglican Christian tradition contains the whole truth about Christianity, there is always much to learn from different Christian traditions and denominations. The same can be said of other world religions: to spend time with Buddhists is to become aware that in prayer and meditation the average Christian is splashing about in the shallow end of the pool of spirituality; to spend time with Muslims is to be aware how ill disciplined, individualistic and unstructured much of our religious practice appears.

A flood of hatred cascaded down on the Library after an interview on BBC Radio 4's *Today* programme. Their researchers had uncovered what they thought was a Gladstone quote. Gladstone holding up a copy of the Qur'an in the House of Commons allegedly said: 'As long as a copy of this accursed book survives there can be no justice in the world.' This quote subsequently appeared in comments online in the *Daily Mail*, *The Sun* and the *Daily Telegraph*. The quote is entirely fictitious and only started to appear in the 1950s. Throughout Gladstone's attack on the barbarity of the Ottoman Turks in Bulgaria and Armenia, he was at pains to distinguish between the Ottoman regime, whose cruelty he detests, and Islam, whose prophet and its ethics and spirituality he admired.

Following this, and the vitriol of many of those blogs, the Library suffered some vandalism – windows in the chapel were broken and a certain amount of damage was caused. It was minor damage but nevertheless disturbing and the police were keen that we reviewed our security.

In both church and academy, the neglect of other faith traditions is wilful. Within Anglicanism, those discontented with the liberal trend in Western Anglican churches cite inter-faith dialogue as a 'compromise' to be confronted with other liberal trends like divorced clergy, women's leadership, gay clergy and same-sex marriage. They criticise the promotion of dialogue, especially dialogue with Islam, as denying both the uniqueness of Christianity and a perceived gospel imperative to evangelise all non-Christians. Demands for such exclusive and excluding Christian evangelism can only be made on the basis of a quasi-literalist reading of Scripture. They are not made through any desire to heal wounds in our communities, or to help heal the perceived breach between the Christian West and Islam.

We called the Islamic Reading Room the 'House of Wisdom' or, in Arabic, 'Bayt al-Hikma', after the library in Baghdad that between the ninth and thirteenth centuries helped classical culture to survive while Europe was in the so-called Dark Ages. In the Baghdad library, Jewish and Christian scholars worked alongside Islamic scholars to study science, mathematics, philosophy and medicine. The House of Wisdom was largely responsible for preserving the wisdom of the Greeks and laid the foundations for what would become the European Renaissance. We are so quick to think of Europe as the cradle of civilisation and forget that without the openness and commitment of Islamic scholars there would have been no Renaissance or European Enlightenment. It is one of those untold and hidden stories of history that deserve to be better known. It was Chris Hewer, one of the chief consultants for the project, who told me the story of Bayt al-Hikma, which to my shame I knew next to nothing about. It is a story like that of Cordoba under Moorish rule, which also became a centre of great learning and influence throughout Christian Europe. These stories are easily, or deliberately, forgotten as today the West thinks of itself as more advanced, educated and sophisticated than Muslim countries. It is lazy thinking and bad history to dismiss Islam as uncivilised and primitive in terms of scholarship.

Living in a Library (1997–2021)

I find the dialogue with Islam fascinating. On one hand, I am amazed how much we have in common and affirm our shared objective to make the world a better place. I was deeply moved that on one Sunday I presided at a Eucharist in the Library's chapel for a congregation of Christians and Muslims, which was followed immediately by the Muslim call to prayer and morning prayers, with the Imam standing in the very place where just moments before I had shared bread and wine to remember Jesus Christ. It seemed natural and right and above all hopeful. Perhaps we could live and create a new 'we' together. On the other hand, I was appalled that at this otherwise hopeful and encouraging act of worship the Muslim women were made to sit at the back separate from the men. I find the Muslim gender segregation in mosques, and more often than not at meetings, appalling. If you simply changed the word 'women' for 'black people' what they suggest would be illegal and understood as morally wrong. It is morally wrong to segregate women in this way. I have been equally appalled too at the lack of inclusion of gays by Muslims. As an institution with an avowed inclusive ethos, this has sometimes prevented us from working more fully together with the local Muslim community.

During this period (February 2011), there was an attack in the neighbouring community of Shotton on a property that the Muslim community had arranged to use as an education centre. Muslims in the area were a tiny minority but their numbers had outgrown the small hall where they met for Friday prayers and education. The new premises, an old working men's club in Shotton which was now vacant, was to give them more room. A march by the English Defence League stirred up a good deal of anti-Islamic feeling and a week later the premises were burnt down. The Library tried to help the Muslim community who suddenly, after years of peaceful co-existence, found themselves in a community where attitudes had almost overnight become sharply polarised. The police blamed it on local youths, but the fact that the English Defence League held a march – something of a celebration a few weeks later – seemed to confirm our suspicions.

Local churches and others supported the local Muslims in any way we could and this was appreciated by the community who subsequently wanted to hold a meal to thank us in the local 'Indian' restaurant, in addition to sending grateful letters of thanks for our support. We were delighted to be invited and many of us turned up. Three Muslim men were there – all associated with the restaurant. No women and no other member of the local Islamic community. In many ways, it was understandable, but nevertheless disappointing. Our hopes to start an Islamic women's group at the Library also foundered.

It is a sad thing to reflect that those who are most open to Islam are those who are also most likely to be disdained by Muslims because of their views on the full inclusion of women and the LGBTQ community.

There is also a theological difference to reckon with. I have yet to meet a practising Muslim who doesn't believe, well at least in public, that the words of the Qur'an were delivered directly by God to the prophet Muhammad. This is impossible to believe in any literal sense; it is supernatural nonsense just as surely as it is to think Moses was somehow dictated the Ten Commandments or Jesus turned water into wine. I cannot understand the widespread lack of acceptance by Islamic scholars of the skills of textual criticism to which the Christian Bible has been subjected. This leads to inevitable Muslim fundamentalism – yes, there are differences of interpretation and often an acceptance of cultural relativity and the consequent need for interpretation, but basically the text remains the untarnished word of God.

It is sad that a religion, whose intellectualism led to a great flowering of education and whose influence ended Europe's Dark Ages and led to the Renaissance, should become dominated by conservative theologians who opposed innovation and saw 'reform and modernisation as something inherently anti-religious'.[97]

To Christians who have been schooled in textual criticism and find that it both alters and strengthens their understanding of faith, this reluctance by Islam to engage with these skills is disappointing. Indeed, there can be no real inter-faith dialogue unless the life of Muhammad and the text of the Qur'an is critically examined in the same way as the life of Jesus and the New Testament has been. Without that willingness, there will be no real progress and no emancipation for women or LGBTQ people in Islam.

Fascinating and infuriating as the attempted dialogue is, it is something we cannot give up on. It remains one of the most important (if not the most important) tasks facing religion and society in this century. From the 1990s onwards, the controversial Roman Catholic scholar, Hans Kung, has consistently maintained this essential mantra:

> No peace among the nations without peace among the religions. No peace among the religions without dialogue between the religions. No dialogue between the religions without investigation of the foundation of the religions.[98]

Contemporary society struggles with the disinformation and misinformation between the Christian (or post-Christian) West and the Islamic world which has led to bloodshed and terrorism and threatened the freedoms that we all enjoy. That doesn't even begin to look at the root causes of the rise of populism in the West, much of which is fuelled by Islamophobia. Not that all of the blame can be aimed at the West, it is just that I am aware that I and my fellow clergy have often been complicit in fanning those flames of hatred, or at least ignoring this particular burning fire. There is comparatively little dialogue between Christianity and Islam.

The 'circle of us' must continue to widen. During the 2020s, and for the first time in my lifetime, the widening of the circle of us has ceased and even started to contract. The reasons for this are many but the rise of populism in the West and the increasingly 'drawbridge up' mentality of shutting people out and providing a secure and pure citadel has taken over from a drawbridge down mentality of welcome and hospitality to those different from ourselves. This can be seen underpinning the Trump administration in the USA and the vote for Brexit in the UK.

Countering the optimism of the widening circle is in part due to the large number of people who feel left behind and whose life choices are severely limited. At the top, the same is true – the privately educated still dominate – for instance, within the last decade the Archbishop of Canterbury, the Prime Minister (two of the last three) and the Mayor of London all went to Eton. Only 7% of the population go to private schools but 74% of judges, 71% of military offices, 61% of top doctors, 80% of newspaper and magazine editors and 54% of journalists went to fee-paying schools. Considering boarding school fees for the top schools range between £30,000 and £40,000 per year it is not surprising that they are rapidly becoming the preserve of the super-rich.[99] The UK is one of the most unequal countries in the world (seventh) and only Estonia (fifth in the world) is more unequal than the UK in Europe.[100] I am a product of this unequal society and I am to some extent part of the privileged elite. That is a fact that sits uncomfortably with my Christian belief.

Christianity, certainly as far as the gospel evidence for Jesus is concerned, is about inclusion. Not simply wishing and praying for a more equitable world (no more 'We' and 'They') but calling for action on the side of the oppressed, it demands radical inclusion. All that is safe to say from a pulpit, even commonplace. In reality, the church seems very much on the side of the status quo. I remember a letter to the press from Donald Coggan, the former Archbishop of Canterbury complaining about the sidelining of Christian perspectives in government and what made this plea so ridiculous, was that the letter's address was the House of Lords. When I was a curate in Hagley at the start of my life as a clergyperson, we were living in the small curate's house adjacent to the church. There was a general election in May 1979 and I was asked by the local Labour Party to put up a poster in the garden. I agreed – this was the election that first brought Margaret Thatcher to power. It hadn't been up longer than a couple of hours when my boss explained to me that as clergy we had to remain politically neutral – apolitical. I couldn't show my support for the Labour Party. I reluctantly understood and dutifully took the poster down. About a week later, there was a knock on the door and a member of the local Conservative Party stood there, he was a leading member of the congregation, the treasurer in fact. Could I display their poster as they had always had one in the curate's garden in the past? That perhaps is the Establishment's understanding of what being 'apolitical' means. The Church of England was still considered to be the Tory party at prayer. It took Robert Runcie's 1985 report, *Faith in the City*, during the turbulent Thatcher years to change that perception.

The assumption during my time as a university chaplain, as rector in Ayr and at the cathedral in Glasgow was that clergy were left of centre. The catalyst for that shift was undoubtedly the extremes of the Thatcher government and the supremacy of neo-liberal economics. Coming to Gladstone's Library presented a different problem, Gladstone started his political career as a Tory but became the leading Liberal of the nineteenth century. I found that despite being a charity (and, therefore, apolitical) it was quite possible to cite Gladstone by finding speeches and other writings that could throw light on contemporary political events. Indeed, whether it was Ireland, the Balkans, Afghanistan, the Wars on Terror, devolution in the UK, Brexit or Trump – there was plenty of scope for Gladstonian rhetoric.

In 2016 Gladstone's Library was involved in an argument with UKIP. During the Welsh Assembly elections, UKIP, the far-right anti-European party in the UK, used a picture of Gladstone's Library in their manifesto. We quite naturally were furious as Gladstone was very much a European and internationalist. UKIP's policies seemed the antithesis of Gladstone's liberal values. I wrote a reply on our website and we started to send out comments on Twitter and Facebook. Our supporters were peeved with UKIP and we were soon trending on Twitter and Facebook as they harangued UKIP. Of course, UKIP fought back. As this was during the Welsh Assembly elections, UKIP complained to the Charity Commission that we were electioneering and that we should have our charitable status revoked. We entered into discussions with the Charity Commission, I had to amend my short statement on the website and we stopped tweeting. Our supporters did not, of course, and the tirade of tweets went backwards and forwards for several days. The Charity Commission were firm but understanding for we had fallen into a UKIP trap which they exploited to try and ruin us. It was a much needed warning and we have been less naïve when people and organisations try to draw us into party political battles.

Nowadays, whenever I speak publicly or respond to political issues in the media or online I am careful to talk about Gladstone's liberal values (with a small 'l' rather than a capital 'L') and to cite accurately Gladstone's own words. The UKIP episode does not mean that I, or my colleagues, are going to stop speaking out when Gladstone's values are challenged by contemporary political issues. Is this tirade against UKIP a lack of inclusion on my behalf? I don't believe it is. It was simply an attempt to define an attitude that is welcoming of all – a drawbridge down mentality – rather than one that is clearly defensive, anti-immigration and has a drawbridge up mentality.

I have always been surprised that those who have fought for inclusion, whether of women or LGBTQ people or, for instance, Islam, fail to see a connection between all these liberations. I often refer to it as an automatic reflex for liberation and inclusion that wants to make the circle of us ever wider. And, of course, there has to be a corresponding and active distaste for those who would exclude and desire to constrict the circle to only 'people like us'. It was the novelist Naomi Alderman who wrote of a widening circle of us when she became Gladstone's Library's first writer in residence in 2012.

> When Gladstone was born, his father made money from the slave-trade, and the circle of 'real human beings' extended no further than adult Christian white men with property. Slowly we've moved that circle outward, expanding it liberally. Not just men with property, but all men. Not just white men but black men. Not just men but women. Not just Christians but also all faiths and none. Not just able-bodied, but also those who are disabled. Not just straight but also gay. Not just cis-gendered but also transgendered. That is what it means to be liberal. To open up the doors of power and influence. To make sure that we invite people in, because we know that our humanity is damaged when we start seeing other people as less than people.[101]

The widening circle that Naomi outlines is about building inclusive institutions and communities. It is such an important task not only for an institution like the Library but for our contemporary world. It is the opposite of narrow intolerance. Asked to name 'evil', Kofi Annan admitted he was queasy about calling anything 'evil' but if pushed he said:

> Let us name it as intolerance. Let us name it as exclusion. Let us name it as the false assumption that we have nothing to learn from beliefs and traditions different from our own. That I believe is the true evil of our time, and I urge you all to join forces against it.[102]

How do we approach those who choose to exclude others? I am uneasy about the idea of simply giving 'no platform' to those who would want a narrower and exclusive society, or who attack the idea of a more inclusive society. I believe that we need to engage and debate with all views. We should protest but never stop listening and arguing. I am not, of course, talking about hate speech or incitement to violence as those are subject to the law. I am asking for a little more faith in reason and justice. Those who want a more inclusive world must practice what they preach. Openness, inclusion and debate is at the heart of this institution just as it was for the Library's founder.

CHAPTER 6
GLADSTONE
A TOPPLED HERO?

Immortal Wm. Ewart Gladstone! I must conclude my muse,
And to write in praise of thee my pen does not refuse–
To tell the world, fearlessly, without the least dismay,
You were the greatest politician in your day!
William McGonagall – 'The Burial of Mr Gladstone'

I was sitting in Christ Church Cathedral, Oxford, in May 1998 at a service to give thanks for the life of William Ewart Gladstone on the centenary of his death. The sermon was given by Robert Runcie, former Archbishop of Canterbury, in which he claimed without a shred of hesitation or qualification that to stand amidst the books in Gladstone's Library 'is an intimidating experience, for it is an encounter with the restless, brooding intelligence that was William Ewart Gladstone'. A bold assertion since Runcie had never visited the Library.

Gladstone not only bestrides the nineteenth century, he was born in its first decade and died in its last, but he shapes and defines liberalism and the politics of the twentieth century. His ideas permeate virtually all UK political parties: Margaret Thatcher, George Osborne and the present Chancellor of the Exchequer, Rishi Sunak, admire his thrifty economics and free trade stance; one of the Founders of the Labour Party, and its first leader, Keir Hardie admired his commitment to social justice and his support for the poor; New Labour's Tony Blair and Gordon Brown both compared their third way to Gladstonian Liberalism; David Cameron's idea of the 'Big Society' also owes much to Gladstone's liberalism; it goes without saying his influence and ideas still reverberate in Liberal Democratic circles. Nor is his influence confined to British politics: the European Union was built on Gladstone's idea for peace and trade within Europe and US President Woodrow Wilson used those same ideas to draft his idea of the League of Nations.

Gladstone: A Toppled Hero?

For me, it was Gladstone's human rights record that was particularly impressive – be it his attempt to gain Home Rule for Ireland, his defence of Italian political prisoners, his support of both Bulgaria and Armenia against further atrocities by the Ottoman Empire, or his advocacy, at some personal cost, for prostitutes in London and other cities. Here was a thinking, principled Christian leader who was prepared to take a stance in the name of justice even if it was not always particularly politically expedient to do so.

People often ask, 'who do you support, Gladstone or Disraeli?', his political nemesis, and I unequivocally answer, 'Gladstone'. It is strange that depictions in novels and films usually show Disraeli in a positive light as witty, wise and popular whereas Gladstone, if he is shown at all, is regarded as a scheming politician. This is very clear in John Madden's 1997 film *Mrs Brown* where Gladstone is shown in an unfavourable light as a shadowy figure plotting politically. In fact, Gladstone was principled, popular (referred to as 'The People's William') and an impressive orator with a strong Christian social conscience.

Naomi Alderman told me an anecdote when she was a writer in residence at Gladstone's Library that her father, the renowned Jewish historian Geoffrey Alderman, had found evidence that Disraeli owned a financial share in a brothel in, I think, Southend. Naomi thought she might write a story in which a prostitute escaped from Disraeli's brothel and was rescued in London by Gladstone. The anecdote shows, she thought, the distinction between these two great politicians of the Victorian era.

I have always thought of Gladstone's Library as an inclusive and liberal institution taking its lead from the humanitarian example of its founder. Over the 20-something years that I have been here as Warden and Director, William Gladstone has become for me, if not exactly a hero, someone I greatly admire and who inspires me. I was not quite hero-worshipping in the same manner as McGonagall's doggerel (at the head of the chapter) but I was a definite apologist and enthusiast. This admiration was, I admit, based on a very selective reading of

Gladstone and focuses primarily on his humanitarian liberalism, as well as reflecting my empathy for someone who shifts, politically and religiously, from a conservative background and grounding to a liberal and radical standpoint.

As a Gladstone fan, I was a little put out when, after staying at the Library for an extended period, a North American crime writer, who was writing her latest North Wales-based comedy thriller, came up to me and said just before she was leaving that I was the murderer in her whodunnit. As she parted, she left me a draft of the book. Kindly, she had changed my name from Peter Francis to Francis Peters. I was still Warden of the Library and a scene began with me looking out of my study window at the statue of Gladstone and despising the man. It then goes on to state that Francis Peters had got the job by lying on his CV. I stopped reading and quickly sent her an email saying the book was in the hands of the Library's lawyers and I wanted several changes both to the setting and to the very thinly veiled use of my name. Thankfully, she amended the text. However, in June 2020 I wryly remembered that image of Francis Peters looking out of my study window at the statue of Gladstone because something happened that caused me to question my enthusiasm for Gladstone.

On Sunday 7 June a statue of the slave trader Edward Colston was toppled and thrown into the harbour in Bristol. This was part of the Black Lives Matter unrest following the killing of an African American, George Floyd, by a white police officer on 25 May in Minneapolis. The horrific killing, which was filmed by a bystander, sparked a wave of protest across the world. The Black Lives Matter movement and protests in the wake of Floyd's killing began to erupt in Britain: Colston fell, there were calls for the statue of Cecil Rhodes in Oxford to be taken down and a list of targeted statues of 'racists' was published on an Antifa website. Gladstone's statue at the Library was cited as one of 20 that needed to be toppled and a date and time, 5:30pm on 16 June, was advertised. About 50 people gathered at the appointed time. It transpired they were all locals determined to defend the statue. There were also about the same number of police visibly making their presence felt both on the ground and in vehicles nearby. As I mingled with the crowd there seemed to be a consensus that indeed, John Gladstone, William's father, was a plantation owner and the man who received the most compensation from the government at the time of abolition, but William Gladstone was a great reformer and a leading liberal who shouldn't be blamed for the sins of his father. They were proud of William Gladstone and wanted to defend the statue. The truth was somewhat more nuanced than that.

The 23-year-old William Gladstone entered politics in 1832 as the Tory MP for Newark, 'the rising hope of stern unbending Tories' in Macaulay's famous phrase. His father, John Gladstone, was a Tory, and William in his early years as an MP was also a Tory and remained very much the dutiful son until his father's death. John was a slave owner with plantations that relied on slave labour in the Caribbean and South America. A Gladstone plantation in Demerara had been the scene of an infamous slave rebellion in August 1823, which ended when hundreds of slaves were shot by British troops as the slaves sought to negotiate a surrender. We do not know whether William was even aware of the Demerara rebellion, he would have been only 14 at the time. However, we do clearly see the parental influence in William's first speech in Parliament (June 1833) when William, aged just 24, spoke in favour of compensation to slave owners for the abolition of slavery. He supported the compensation clause, and it is impossible not to feel slightly queasy when we find out that John received the highest amount of compensation of all slave owners – over £93,526 for 2,039 slaves (that is estimated at over £8.9 million at today's values). He was not the only recipient of compensation in the Gladstone family: one of William's brothers received compensation of £21,011 (about £2 million today) as well as £9,225 each to an uncle and three cousins (over £900,000 today). William, himself, was not a slave owner although he received the gift of a sugar plantation from his father in 1839, which he swiftly sold. He, and all of John Gladstone's sons, received very generous allowances from their father. William found his wealth worrisome. He wrote in his diary: 'This increased wealth so much beyond my needs, with its attendant responsibilities is burdensome.'[103]

William found it difficult to come to terms with the fact that his own prosperity, his education and half of the cost of his Parliamentary seat of Newark was paid for by his father's income and we know that a considerable amount of that income derived from the plantations and from slave labour. However, William continued to be the dutiful son using his influence to defend his father's interests and protect his father's wealth. When in 1838 there was a move to abolish apprenticeships in the plantations, which some rightly saw as simply slavery by another name, William spoke against the move. His intervention caused much inner turmoil. He wrote in his diary that he prayed for the success of his intervention on behalf of slave owners (forever the dutiful son), but considered it 'a blasphemous prayer, for support in pleading the cause of injustice'.[104]

Biographers, especially S G Checkland,[105] paint a vivid picture of John as an overbearing father and of a mother, Anne, whose strongly evangelical outlook dominated the household. It is not surprising with this background of Christian obligation that William felt ties of filial duty (it is one of the Ten Commandments after all) which was in conflict with his increasingly liberal stance. All of this goes some way to explain how, as he was canvassing to become Conservative MP for Newark, he was able to remark that slavery was not 'necessarily sinful'[106] (after all, it was not condemned and even possibly condoned in the Bible) and why he was able to stand on his feet in the House of Commons and urge vast sums of compensation be paid to slave owners including and pre-eminently to his father.

The primary difficulty that many people have with William Gladstone is the financial benefit he gained indirectly from his father's plantations in Jamaica and Demerara. This is what caused the Antifa complaint. S G Checkland's biography *The Gladstones* details the dispersal of Sir John Gladstone's estate after his death in 1851 and agrees with William's own estimate that he inherited about £120,000 (worth about £17 million today)[107] from the estate. Is it fair that the sins of the father are visited upon subsequent generations? The answer, of course, depends on what they do with their lives thereafter.

After the death of his parents (mother in 1835 and father in 1851) William Gladstone becomes a very different person, you could almost say that he is set free from filial duty and the Christian evangelical constraints which demanded honour to parents as part of God's law. John Morley, his friend, colleague and biographer, talking to Gladstone in 1891 on a trip to Biarritz, elicited this reflective response:

> *Morley:* You know the saying that nobody is worth much who has not been a bit of a radical in his youth, and a bit of a Tory in his fuller age.
> *Gladstone:* I can put the change that has come into my politics into a sentence; I was brought up to distrust and dislike liberty, I learned to believe in it. That is the key to all my changes.[108]

The distrust and dislike of liberty is a common hallmark of a particular kind of conservative evangelicalism that was pervasive in the Gladstone household. In 1865, Gladstone acknowledges both his quasi-fundamentalist upbringing and his present position having shed that straitjacket:

> I do not believe that God's mercies are restricted to a small portion of the human family ... I was myself brought up to believe that salvation depended absolutely upon the reception of a very narrow creed. But long, long, have I cast those weeds behind me.[109]

After this change in attitude Gladstone reflects on his first speech in Parliament that supported compensation to slave owners. His speech was not something that he was proud of after he had left the Tory party. Reflecting on the speech to Morley, he wrote, 'I can now see plainly enough, the sad defects, the real illiberalism of my opinions on that subject.'[110]

By 1850, William Gladstone was becoming independent of his father, and speaking in the House of Commons he is very clear about his abhorrence of the slave trade.

I can find no words sufficiently strong to characterise its enormous iniquity. I believe the slave trade to be by far the foulest crime that taints the history of mankind in any Christian or pagan country.[111]

Later in his life in a review of a book about a slave owner in a Southern state in America, he wrote what could almost be a description of his own journey towards abhorrence of slavery and a realisation of his weakness in not condemning slave ownership more wholeheartedly earlier in his political career:

We are not to judge individuals hastily on account of social mischiefs that may be due to them as a body, through their holding of a position inherited from their forefathers, the nature of which they have not had strength and depth of wisdom to detect.[112]

A profound change had slowly taken place in Gladstone's thought, values and political allegiance. A love of liberty can be seen by his passionate espousal of liberal and humanitarian causes from the 1850s onwards. From this time forward, Gladstone finds his friends, and those with whom he feels most sympathy on the benches of Parliament were liberal in attitude and humanitarian in spirit. The early 1850s see the start of his move to Liberalism.

Gladstone's moral and political trajectory toward liberalism and humanitarianism was the story I told myself and often recited to others and it proved not to be totally true. For Gladstone maintained what we would rightly regard as racist and unacceptable views even in his Liberal years. For instance, he compares the treatment of Bulgarians and other subject peoples by the Turks to that of 'negro slavery'.

In some respects it is less bad than negro slavery, and in other respects a great deal worse. It is worse in this respect, that in the case of negro slavery, at any rate, it was a race of higher capacities ruling over a race of lower capacities; but in the case of this system, it is unfortunately a race of lower capacities which rules over a race of higher capacities.[113]

To Gladstone, black people were less developed and had lower capacities than white people. To the twenty-first-century mind that should be iniquitous but in the nineteenth, it was a view that was widely held. The superiority of white people, and the British in particular, was assumed by the majority of the British ruling class.

As I write, Westminster Abbey is considering placing a plaque near Gladstone's tomb to explain his links with slavery. Elsewhere, William Gladstone's name has recently been removed from student accommodation in Liverpool, primarily for his father's slave-owning role; in Newark the William Gladstone Primary School has removed his name and in the London Borough of Brent they are contemplating renaming Gladstone Park. The taint on William Gladstone seems to focus on his speech supporting compensation for slave owners at the time of abolition and the undoubted financial privileges and security that came to him from his father, with little regard for the contribution that he made to British, European and world politics.

What should I, writing this now at Gladstone's Library, think about his now tainted reputation? Does the same taint of slavery besmirch the Library's reputation? The Library was after all completed using Gladstone family money about 10 years after his death? On the face of it the money had no association with slavery. The library wing of the building was paid for by voluntary donations – public subscription – and the Gladstone family finished the project a few years later by paying for the accommodation wing themselves with money raised from the success of John Morley's biography of Gladstone – in which case any direct link with slavery is very tenuous indeed.

Some might say that the money is tainted anyway because among the British public who gave money to the Library as the national memorial to Gladstone, there were undoubtedly, probably a majority, who thought that black people were less developed, less evolved than white people. Systemic racism was even more prevalent in Victorian times than it is in contemporary Britain. Most buildings and monuments erected in Victorian times are tainted by slave money. I do not want to excuse Gladstone's views but there is an element of scapegoating when, in fact, it is a national repentance of racist views and attitudes that needs to be faced up to. That repentance although it clearly includes the nineteenth century would also pre-date it and post-date it and most importantly include today's world.

William Gladstone's views on race, while unacceptable today, were nevertheless commonplace even among intellectuals in Victorian Britain. The default view in those times was that the white *man* was superior to the indigenous inhabitants of our Empire, where foreign flesh was treated as inferior and of less value. Britain wasn't alone in such thinking; in America the writers of the American constitution calculated that a slave was less than half of a human being. On both sides of the Atlantic, the prevailing view was that black lives don't really matter, or certainly don't matter as much as white lives. To pick out Gladstone as the scapegoat for these views would be wrong. Once again, virtually all our forebears shared these attitudes. I know that their defenders may well retort that we should not judge the people of the nineteenth century by our own values. Some may well go on to ask whether we should allow the good our forebears did to be cast away with the slur of being racists. I think those arguments are excusable for a Victorian when it comes to understanding something like biological sciences but they certainly do not hold any credibility when it comes to defending making money out of the misery of our fellow human beings.

I have to admit that as I researched William Gladstone's links with slavery, I felt defeated. This was when I thought the North American crime writer might have been somewhat prophetic. Should I have fought so hard to change the name of the Library from St Deiniol's to Gladstone's Library? Should I have invested so much time and energy in writing and talking about my enthusiasm for Gladstone? Does such a flaw nullify the good he did? Is the name, the brand, forever tainted? Is there a case for the defence?

It is clear that Gladstone came to abhor slavery and considered it a shameful chapter of history which was a blemish on the whole British Establishment and he doesn't exclude himself. Does that remove the taint?

Gladstone: A Toppled Hero?

Should we dismiss Gladstone as a relic of the Victorian age and an example of the sins of our forebears? Can we judge the attitudes of Victorian society from the standpoint of today's woke culture? Two astute political commentators, John Micklethwaite and Adrian Wooldridge clearly do not think so and see Gladstone as a prototype of the great moral and pragmatic leader that the West is crying out for today. They write of Gladstone:

> The erstwhile Tory broke with his party over free trade, apologised for his father and turned into one of the more radical social reformers ever to hold office … As chancellor of the exchequer and four-time prime minister, he masterminded an astonishing range of reforms, opening civil service jobs and Oxbridge fellowships to competition, inventing the modern company, abolishing the purchase of army commissions and much else besides.

> The People's William was a passionate defender of the poor and advocate of equal opportunity – publicly, he gave ever more men the vote and introduced a national curriculum; privately, he devoted his evenings to trying to rescue fallen women.[114]

Micklethwaite and Wooldridge's positive understanding of Gladstone was more or less the version I choose to tell myself.[115] Mine was a sanitised version with the bad bits glossed over. As regards slavery: yes, I used to say, he spoke in favour of compensation but that helped to end slavery more quickly than in the USA; yes, he was apologetic about his views and became a friend of Wilberforce, even visiting him on his deathbed; yes, all of that was when he was a right-wing Tory, but he converted to being a Liberal and a great humanitarian. Can I still point to the statue standing proudly in the grounds of the Library as a monument to change, or refer to Gladstone's political and humanitarian change and think of him as redeemed? Gladstone after all was very much against jingoism and grandiose boasting of the greatness of the British Empire. Consider this eulogy for rights of all human beings across the globe, as he spoke to stop war in Afghanistan:

Remember the rights of the savage, as we call him. Remember that the happiness of his humble home, remember that the sanctity of life in the hill villages of Afghanistan among the winter snows, is as inviolable in the eye of Almighty God as can be your own. Remember that He who has united you together as human beings in the same flesh and blood, has bound you by the law of mutual love; that that mutual love is not limited by the shores of this island, is not limited by the boundaries of Christian civilization; that it passes over the whole surface of the earth, and embraces the meanest along with the greatest in its unmeasured scope.[116]

These are not the words of an unthinking Empire loyalist but of a humanitarian.

There are also times when Gladstone seems way ahead of his time. For instance, the Black Lives Matter movement is critical of the loot from wars of Empire that are displayed in British museums and seeks their repatriation. This is nothing new and it was Gladstone in Parliament on 30 June 1871 who lamented the looting of artefacts that were meaningless to us but had symbolic and religious importance for those from whom they were seized by the British. He urged their return to their rightful home. Gladstone deeply lamented looting by the British army and officials and the subsequent hoarding of such loot by British museums.

It was Gladstone's government in the 1860s who considered the idea of separation from the colonies, and of the unwinding of Empire and suggested 'a friendly relaxation of the relationship'.[117] Gladstone was a very different man from his father, whose first instinct was to make money regardless of ethical concerns, and also very different from his great rival Disraeli who in 1877 made Queen Victoria Empress of India, which was a move to make the British public more interested in and supportive of the Empire. In 1878 Disraeli's compulsively pro-Empire stance led to the word 'jingoism' being invented. I don't hear the call for statues of Disraeli to be toppled, yet in terms of support and promotion of the Empire and its racist values, he was certainly far more tainted than Gladstone.

Gladstone: A Toppled Hero?

Isn't Gladstone's trajectory a reminder to all of us that we can all change our mind, alter our perspective and realign our sympathies in the light of new evidence, the company we keep (or no longer keep), the books we read or the influences that we are exposed to? Isn't it a reminder too that we are often very different from our parents in our social, moral and political attitudes.

The Welsh government commissioned an audit of commemoration to review all statues, street names and other monuments associated with the slave trade and the British Empire. The report believes that Gladstone remains an acceptable figure to be memorialised:

> At the time of his maiden speech, he represented West Indian interests, speaking in favour of compensation for owners such as his father. He cautioned 'a safe and gradual emancipation' to achieve 'the utter extinction of slavery'. After abolition, he sought to end slavery in other countries by supporting an anti-slavery expedition up the river Niger and arguing for duties on sugar in exception to his own free-trade philosophy to counter slave-based production.

> Gladstone left the Tory faction to join the Liberals and went on to be one of Britain's most progressive reforming politicians.[118]

The Christian religion with its belief that 'in Christ there is no difference between slave or free'[119] was a truth that was ignored when it came to ruling the British Empire. Gladstone forgot that truth, but rather less often than many of his countrymen and women. The plight of oppressed Bulgarians, Armenians, Italians, the Irish or women prostitutes in British cities, or those working in appalling conditions in the mill towns of Britain, touched him perhaps more deeply than the plight of slaves or those forced into indentured labour. He cared about liberty and the plight of the oppressed, including the enslaved, but in common with the clear majority view of the times he believed and clearly stated in Parliamentary debate (1873), as Roland Quinault[120] reminds us, that whites were 'the superior race', and the negroes were 'the less developed race'.[121]

The Widening Circle of Us

The Gladstone statue in the Library's grounds, stands in all its grandness as a statement of pride in our nation's history and those who shaped that history. And Gladstone, let's be honest, shaped nineteenth-century politics more than anybody else. Gladstone's influence provided a beacon of liberal thought and action. That interpretation has been found wanting in the light of a more 'woke' culture. The statue is a monument that needs reinterpreting. Today, the statue stands as a reminder of the imperfection, racism and arrogance of the British Establishment in the nineteenth century. Should it be toppled? No, it should be displayed, explained and contextualised. We need to face up to the truth. Our nineteenth-century predecessors, even progressives like Gladstone, were tinged with racist views and perceptions. But to isolate a few culprits and to shift the focus on to their views is perhaps to deflect from the reality of racism today and ignore the prejudice that black people still face. It is not a question of blotting out unacceptable chunks of our history but rather owning up to them, examining them and giving credit or criticism where it is due.

Then and now, racial superiority wasn't and isn't confined to the ruling class in Britain. In Victorian days it was assumed by a large proportion of the population. Today it remains a taint that has not gone away and race riots and racial tensions still exist as the Brexit campaign and the scandal of Windrush have all too clearly demonstrated. Systemic racism pervades the UK's cultural, social and political groupings which inevitably leads to disparities of wealth, justice, employment, health care, housing and education.

A way of edging towards a remedy is to give agency and voice to people of colour. And there is a need for liberal elites to listen to that voice and respond with more than tokenism. The black US activist and intellectual Keeanga-Yamahtta Taylor speaking on the *London Review of Books* podcast says of the Black Lives Matter bandwagon that so much of it is mere window dressing by institutions, corporations and individuals:

> And you can say to every corporation that is talking about Black Lives Matter, people taking the knee and all of this empty hollow

bullshit doesn't actually cost them anything ... We have to listen to people. We have to understand what their struggles are.[122]

The task of a 'liberal' individual or institution is to listen to authentic voices to learn and to respond appropriately. The real task is not to resort to tokenism, not to topple our statues or write people out of history. Yes, by all means counter the glorious Empire version of history and write some other voices and experiences into that history. 'The whitesplaining of history is over,' writes the historian Priya Satia. She believes, 'the inclusion of scholars of diverse backgrounds has transformed our knowledge of race, gender and culture, undermining the narratives that underpinned empire and other forms of racial inequality'. Satia goes on to say that other voices and perspectives will draw attention to a different take on our Empire history. It is possible to learn something other than what we have been taught in our classrooms and history books. In truth, the Empire demonstrated an 'abysmal history of looting and pillage, policy-driven famines, brutal crushing of rebellion, torture, concentration camps, aerial policing, and everyday racism and humiliation'.[123]

The Black Lives Matter movement highlights the need for the circle of us to continue to widen. The circle of us should not be an echo chamber of liberal self-congratulation but a challenge to continue to ensure that every individual is included and treated with respect and dignity.

The hard work, the real work, is to address today's problems and begin to listen to voices outside of our own comfortable self-congratulatory circles. That, of course, is a role for somewhere like Gladstone's Library. Gladstone was a detailed researcher, humanitarian and someone eager for debate and change, and that is not a bad template for an institution bearing his name.

Can I offer an honest assessment of Gladstone rather than a sanitised tale of a political hero? If there is to be reckoning then Gladstone's many accomplishments should not be overlooked. There is much to celebrate about Gladstone but there is some repentance required as well. His views on race are detestable but they were not views out of kilter with the mainstream views of the Victorian era. I can believe that if alive today he would be at the forefront of those demanding justice for the victims of our colonial history and be a strong advocate of the view that black lives do matter. He would be as horrified by the death of George Floyd as any of us. I came to the conclusion that is something we cannot prove but those who have some responsibility for what is done in Gladstone's name, or in the name of liberalism, have an obligation to do him justice.

The radical Liberal, John Stuart Mill, who was a man who strongly opposed slavery and anything that oppressed human beings, spoke warmly and strongly in favour of Gladstone in 1862. Clearly the taint of Gladstone's indirect involvement with slavery is forgiven and forgotten by Mill for how else could he eulogise Gladstone so enthusiastically to the Westminster Reform meeting:

> Respecting Mr. Gladstone (Cheers) … Every year of his official life had been marked by a succession of measures – no year being without them – some great, some small, but all aiming at the public good – to the good of the people of this country, and especially of the poorer classes. These measures were not even suggested to him: they were the offspring of his own mind, will and purpose – the free gift from him to his countrymen, unprompted, unsuggested. (Loud cheers) … Mr. Gladstone seemed to be the first statesman who has come up to the idea of a great modern statesman: … If we do not stand by him …we shall not easily find another to serve us in the same way. (Loud cheers).[124]

Mill's and the crowd's adulation are echoed by many from the nineteenth century onwards. Here is a striking testimony of Gladstone's influence from Rabbi Julia Neuberger who visited the Library just a few years ago; I was showing her round and pointed out a golden wreath with a silver crossband that hangs from the first-floor gallery of the main reading room. I told her that it was given to the Gladstone family by the Bulgarian government on the centenary of William Gladstone's birth in 1909. The inscription reads 'To the great William Gladstone from a grateful Bulgarian nation.' It was placed on his tomb in Westminster Abbey prior to a service of remembrance the following morning and guarded by 21 policemen overnight. Julia Neuberger told me that in the Second World War when the Nazis were trying to deport Jews from Bulgaria to the extermination camps, the Bulgarian political leaders, along with the monarchy, would not let this happen. They stood in front of the trains and the Nazis backed down. In a sense, I thought, they were standing up for the Jews just as Gladstone stood up for them. For Bulgarians, and also the Armenians whom Gladstone had also defended against Ottoman atrocities, the example of Gladstone still lives on as an example to be followed. The current President of Armenia, Armen Sarkissian, in conversation with me referred to Gladstone as 'the man who saved our country'. As I listened to the Rabbi's remarks and reflected on President Sarkissian's admiration of Gladstone, I thought that although Gladstone was not quite the hero he once was to me, he was basically a man whose life and example when weighed in its totality contributed to the general good of humankind. We should not topple his statue or try to write him out of our history books.

I remain an enthusiastic supporter of Gladstone as a humanitarian and politician – despite a brief wobble in the summer of 2020.

There are very few human beings whose life could stand such detailed scrutiny of what they, and their siblings or parents, said and did throughout their life. It is time to turn my attention to someone, Jesus, who seems genuinely untainted and whose life expanded the circle of us and demanded a commitment to inclusion – although horrendous actions undertaken in his name throughout the centuries eclipse any accusation levelled at Gladstone.

CHAPTER 7
YESHUA

He's my firmament
I hang on every word,
lassoed by considering the lilies,
by camels and needle-eyes,
bread of life and light of the world.
Robert Hamberger – 'Gethsemane Nude'

I came to Gladstone's Library to try to rescue an institution that I felt could be a useful creative centre of liberal values, and, from a personal point of view, I wanted to explore my Christian faith. In Christian ministry, there is little time for reading and pondering theological or scriptural truths or untruths. The demand for a weekly sermon, funeral orations and articles in parish magazines means that most of a clergyperson's writing, or indeed thinking time, is rightly taken up with fulfilling these obligations. There is an oft repeated quip, and it is not too far from the truth, that you can tell the date a clergyperson was ordained by the date of the latest theology book on her or his bookshelf. It is possible, of course, to read a bit, take a few journals and talk to clergy and possibly academics, but the daily round of ministry is disrespectful of the need to think and even argue about theology. Coming to Gladstone's Library was liberating for my theological thought. By speaking on, and participating in, courses on liberal Christianity I had to think and be challenged about the foundations of my faith. The focus of my interest, reading and enthusiasm was the person of Jesus. Find your Christology, your understanding of Christ, and the rest of your theology falls into place.

There has been very little about Jesus in these chapters except in relation to controversies in the church. Study of the historical Jesus, and the subsequent forming of a Christology, are perilous tasks and scholars have rightly observed that authors tend to create Jesus in their own image as the feminist theologian, Rosemary Radford Ruether bluntly articulates:

> Those who claim to give us the fully objective and finally scientific portrait of Jesus only illustrate once again the close similarity between their Jesus and their own conscious or unconscious self-portraits. This does not mean that historical method cannot provide real parameters and limits about what we can say and cannot say about Jesus, and these have grown more precise through the labours of many generations of scholars.[125]

We all latch on to a reading of Jesus that seems appropriate to our personal and political situation. Yet, I want to argue, there is something more 'spiritual' happening as well. The figure of Jesus we paint is idealised and compelling and yes, we have been selective in the aspects of the Jesus story we have chosen to focus upon but they can, if we dare, encourage us to reach beyond ourselves and act bravely, inclusively and humanely. Ruether might suggest that theologians end up portraying a Jesus that was in sync with our own ideas and values but the point is that the Jesus we have cobbled together, although subjective, offers an icon of someone who is always better than our better selves and inspires our living and dying.

This is a memoir and on the face of it this chapter is an interlude – a biblical digression – but in reality, if Ruether is to be believed, it reveals more about the writer than almost any other chapter.

At Gladstone's Library I have had the time, the resources and the will to study and reflect on who Jesus is for me and whether that Jesus can be legitimately considered to be anything like the real Jesus. I have been free of constraints like the weekly round of sermons required in parochial life, and I haven't been constrained by a church lectionary indicating what parts of the Bible I should preach and teach week by week. At Gladstone's Library, I have also had the privilege to talk to a great many famous theologians and church leaders of all denominations as well as ordinary clergy and church workers about their faith and doubts. I suppose I am a safe sounding board for liberal leaning clergy as I am not now actively part of any formal ecclesiastical structure and yet I know how the system works. I have been surprised and heartened by the number who have a humanistic Christian belief but often disheartened by the fact that they feel obliged to keep on telling the old story so as not frighten congregations. But that old story with its creeds is something that they (and probably a large percentage of their congregations) do not believe in. You could say that this is rather late on my part to examine the central figure of my faith and you would be right, for I too have lived with the same constraint – being cautious in what I said from the pulpit and how I said it. I wonder if we were right to be cautious – isn't half-belief very easy to see through?

Here then is my, no doubt subjective, life of Jesus: the essential kernel of (my) Christian faith and values. In my lived experience as a Christian minister, I have seen that Christianity can be seen to be about inclusion and that this goes to the heart of what we know of Jesus' ministry and, more surprisingly, of the writings of Paul. Both Jesus and Paul have been misunderstood but both presented, in their contrasting styles, the same message of radical inclusion. Both have had their 'truth' warped and made to serve exclusive and excluding institutions. Between them they laid down the framework for modern secular liberal values. They provide, whether you are a Christian or not, the basis of secular humanism. Dig deep into movements of secular feminism and gay liberation and their origin can be found in Galilee. That is a big claim and I have to try to substantiate it.

This is my attempt to describe what I feel we can say with a degree of certainty about the historical Jesus. I started my renewed quest by reading the work of the Jesus Seminar which had been set up in 1985 by the American biblical scholar Robert Funk to renew the search for the historical Jesus. Some 80 scholars worked to find a consensus to determine which were the authentic words and actions of Jesus. They argued, they voted and they reached a consensus and the results were published in *The Five Gospels*. Of course, this was contentious and anathema to those who were religiously conservative. I found it compelling and persuasive and the Jesus that emerged from their scrutiny I found challenging and believable. In reality, their results were rather more positive and conservative than many major theologians – two very respected recent theologians, E P Sanders and Edward Schillebeeckx, had been far more cautious in their respective assessments of the actual sayings of Jesus – both believed that there were fewer than five genuine Jesus sayings. What is certain is that there is more in the gospels that was never said and done by Jesus than the material that we think is likely to be genuine.

The New Testament scholars at the Westar Institute's Jesus Seminar agreed by consensus that of the 1,330 recorded sayings of Jesus in the gospels, only 29 are likely to be authentic – from John's gospel 0; Mark's gospel 1; Matthew's 11; Luke 14; Thomas 3.[126] The number of sayings increases considerably if you include those sayings that Jesus possibly said, or said something very similar: Mark 18; Matthew 36; Luke 50; John 1; Thomas 36. For an historical figure who lived two thousand years ago that is, in fact, quite a lot of justifiable information. For those who believe the Bible is the divinely inspired word of God, such a process of sifting and studying is almost devilish!

The work of the Jesus Seminar seemed to me a bold and important development in its implications for those of us who wanted to get back to the historical Jesus. Their work is an invaluable tool. However, it is possible to widen the selection of gospel material by the inclusion of some carefully selected secondary material. For instance, the stories of the woman caught in adultery (John 8) or the healing of the centurion's gay lover (Matthew 8). These stories, although not necessarily historical, show something about the character and nature not only of Jesus' ministry but of the early Christian community.

My interest in the historical Jesus had started when I was a student at St Andrews where I read Hans Küng's determined defence of a modern Christian faith in his book *On Being a Christian*. Küng believed that after over 200 years of intensive New Testament study we are able to see a clear and recognisable outline of Jesus and of his message about the reign of God.[127] At the time Küng boasted that we know more about the historical Jesus than those living at the start of the second century of our common era.

The difference between the period when Küng wrote, 50 years ago, and the Jesus Seminar is the scholarly study of and the subsequent inclusion of the Gospel of Thomas, which although it was available, was rarely studied in Küng's day. It contains some original sayings of Jesus and should be considered alongside the four canonical gospels (Matthew, Mark, Luke and John). This has given a new impetus to those of us who seek to get back to the historical Jesus.

What can we say about this historical figure of Jesus? Again, I owe an enormous debt to the scholars of the Jesus Seminar for their two books on the gospels about what Jesus said, *The Five Gospels*,[128] and what Jesus did, *The Acts of Jesus*.[129] I am not sure they told me anything new or surprising, it was just confirmation of my own views of and about Jesus. I have tried, below, to give a brief outline of the life of Jesus. It might seem minimal and my selection and criteria betray my bias but everything within these few pages of biography is justifiable, defendable and, I would say, as historical as we can get.

Jesus, or more correctly Yeshua, was most likely to have been born in Nazareth, which was part of the Roman province of Judea, in the reign of Herod the Great (37–34 BCE) and probably towards the end of his reign. Herod was a puppet king whose task was to support and in return be supported by Rome.

Jesus' mother was called Mary but knowing who his father was is a more difficult case. Joseph who becomes the spouse of Mary was not Jesus' biological father. Jesus was almost certainly illegitimate, although interesting speculation that Mary was the victim of rape or other possible scenarios is mere conjecture.[130] The truth will never be known but stories of a miraculous virgin birth (only in the gospels of Matthew and Luke) have been designed to camouflage that truth. We don't know who the sperm belonged to, but we can be absolutely sure that it was human sperm and no outside supernatural agency had anything to do with it.

We know nothing of Jesus' early life in Nazareth. Joseph was possibly a builder, more of a stonemason than a carpenter, if the reports that this was Joseph's trade are accurate. Jesus would, therefore, have been middle class, certainly not poverty stricken (I am grateful to the late Ian Fraser for this insight) as his father was probably involved in the reconstruction of Nazareth's neighbouring town, Sepphoris. He had brothers and sisters. He lived in Galilee, which was often scorned as being almost semi-pagan and open to Greek and other foreign influences. Jesus spoke in Aramaic and possibly also Greek, as Sepphoris had a Greek-speaking population. We do not know whether he could read or write – it is unlikely as it is estimated that 95% of the population were illiterate.[131]

We first become aware of Jesus as an adult human being when he goes to the wilderness near the Jordan river and was baptised by John the Baptist. It is possible to date that to CE 28–29. Jesus became a follower of John, who was reminiscent of a prophet from the Hebrew Bible, baptising and preaching hard-hitting moral sermons demanding justice and a moral and spiritual transformation of life. John baptised converts as a symbol of cleansing in readiness for the coming of the Messiah and the overturning of the present world order. It was a crusade of preparedness for the coming change. John was a devout Jew but antagonistic to much of the contemporary practice of Judaism by compromised temple authorities, who collaborated with their Roman overlords to survive. John's understanding of faith didn't require this tainted priestly caste to act as intermediaries between believers and God. John's faith was open to all. As well as the baptism, John's followers ate a communal meal at which they believed that the Messiah who would bring in this new age was somehow spiritually present.

John attracted huge crowds to the Jordan river. These crowds were hostile to both Herod and Rome. John's message of hope was considered treason by the client king, Herod Antipas (4 BCE–39 CE). John's message, although couched in spiritual terms, was nationalistic. It was almost inevitable that Herod Antipas would have had John executed.

Jesus leaves John's movement before the arrest of John. He starts a rival movement that doesn't draw people out into the wilderness but goes to them, travelling around the villages and towns of Galilee preaching and teaching in local synagogues and in the open air. Jesus inherited from John the un-brokered religious approach (no need for priests or ritual) and the same message of God's coming kingdom. John's movement and Jesus' movement were competitors. This rivalry between the two movements continued beyond the death of John and Jesus.

The similarity between the two groups headed by John and Jesus is symbolised by the fictitious story early in Luke's gospel of the pregnant Mary visiting her cousin Elizabeth who was pregnant with John. Jesus and John were not related, the story is there to play up the similarity between John and Jesus and heal the rivalry between the two groups after the death of the two leaders although, of course, the gospels always gave the superior role to Jesus.

Jesus became a popular wandering preacher and gathered followers who followed him through Galilee. There was no actual sermon on the mount, that is an artificial construction by the author of Matthew's gospel to accentuate the parallel with Moses on Mount Sinai and to showcase Jesus' teaching but with a carefully Jewish twist – Jesus is the new Moses setting out new commandments that do not nullify the old but complete them. The idea of 12 disciples is also almost certainly a concoction of the gospel writers to symbolise the 12 tribes of Israel, although some of the names probably do refer to his closest followers.

It seems that amongst his followers were orphans (a sort of first century equivalent of street children), people of diverse backgrounds, nationalities and religions. His followers included people who had colluded with the occupying power and those who had actively fought against them. It was an inclusive and diverse group – a wide circle.

Jesus became known as a healer but his healing power seems to be primarily about communicating worth to those whom society excludes, calls unclean or vilifies: a man with severe skin disease, a woman with constant menstrual bleeding, an adulteress, a prostitute, a crooked tax collector. He gave people hope and something to live for, an acceptance that nobody else gave them.[132] He was criticised for consorting and eating with sinners and he ignored, and even denounced, kosher rules. He was not an ascetic which is in sharp contrast to John the Baptist. When Jesus comes up against the beliefs and institutions of Judaism, he is invariably against them.

In what is an inconvenience for modern day family-centred Christian churches, Jesus seems to have been indifferent to his family and claimed that his followers were his real family. His followers are drawn from different regions, even perhaps different nationalities. Certainly, different allegiances and ties of geography or kinship seem to count little with him. In terms of ethnicity, if the texts can be trusted, all ethnicities seemed to be welcomed amongst Jesus' followers: Samaritan, Syrophoenician, Roman. His close band of followers included Peter, James and John, although some of the other names vary in the gospel accounts. Possibly uniquely, for first century Judaism, his followers included women. Women, as has already been stated, had a leading role in the movement, although this has been largely obscured by the gospel writers but in the Gospel of Mary, parts of which might be a very early source but other parts can be probably be dismissed as a second-century gnostic document, Mary of Magdala is seen to be pre-eminent within the group of disciples.

Jesus shunned signs and wonders. He preached in short sayings and parables using ideas and metaphors that ordinary people could understand. His message was of the nearness of God's kingdom which will not come by watching for it. Jesus spoke of the kingdom as being here amongst us. 'It will not be said, "Look here!" or "Look there!" God's kingdom is spread out on the earth and people don't see it.'[133]

Jesus' message was popular, especially amongst the common people, the people of the land – 'am ha-aretz'. These people were largely uneducated and unobservant Jews who were too busy trying to survive rather than adhere to all the prerequisites of religious observance. They had a hard life living off the land. Grandiose building schemes of the Herods added to the enormous tax burden exacted by the Roman occupiers and then by the Temple authorities.

Many families were forced to sell themselves into slavery when debts became unpayable. Bribery, corruption, prostitution and begging were all commonplace. That there must be something better than this was a persistent hope. It was to these poor people of Galilee that Jesus preached, taught and healed while proclaiming and revealing hope for the building of a better world. It wasn't pie in the sky, it was life here and now if only we just lived it. Don Cupitt sums up the nature of Jesus' ethical teaching like this:

> Turn the other cheek; When sued for your coat, give your cloak too; Go the second mile; Love your enemies ... These all teach excessive, supererogatory, absurd love, and attack popular ideas of justice.[134]

As with John the Baptist, Jesus found that popularity carried with it real danger. A movement such as Jesus' was always likely to be crushed, for it threatened the status quo. When Jesus went to Jerusalem, he was arrested on the orders of the high priest because of something that upset the temple authorities. He was handed to Pilate, the Roman governor (26–36 CE) who, without a moment's hesitation, had him flogged and crucified.

After the crucifixion, there was no miraculous empty tomb; Jesus' body like the majority (many thousands of victims) of those who were crucified in Roman Palestine would have been left to rot on the cross and then been buried in a shallow pit for birds, dogs and rats to scavenge.

A striking piece of liturgical poetry by the Roman Catholic theologian, Edward Schillebeeckx, is refreshingly free of theological jargon, exudes the humanism that distinguished Jesus' life and summarises his life-enhancing ministry:

> We remember that
> wherever Jesus came
> people rediscovered their humanity,
> and so were filled with new riches,
> so that they could give one another
> new courage in their lives.

We remember,
how he spoke to people,
about a lost coin,
a sheep that had strayed, a lost son:
of all those who no longer count,
out of sight, out of mind; the weak and the poor,
all those who are captive, unknown, unloved.

We recall that
he went to search for all who were lost,
for those who are saddened and out in the cold,
and how he always took their side,
without forgetting the others.

And that cost him his life
because the mighty of the earth would not tolerate it …[135]

When Jesus was arrested and crucified for being a public nuisance (literally thousands of people who threatened the status quo in Roman Palestine suffered the same fate) his male followers fled and his death was (and this may be historical – although an element of wishful thinking on my part might be at work here) watched by a small group of women followers, including Mary of Magdala. She along with Peter (one of Jesus' original followers and, possibly, a Galilean fisherman), James who was the brother of Jesus (we don't know whether he was kith or kin) and, a few short years later, Paul appear to have been the key figures in the early Christian community. It was Paul who started to define what we now refer to as Christianity. Before that title was conferred on them they were simply followers of the 'way'.

Can we say that this man, Jesus/Yeshua, died for our sins? Of course not. We can say that he died because of human sin, the sin of totalitarianism, of fear, and repression, of cold-blooded tyranny. We can say that Jesus, knowing the consequences, was prepared to live and die in the service of his fellow oppressed women and men. We believe his message was of the utter worth of each and every human being, however wretched and whatever their 'sin', nationality or moral turpitude. This message was worth dying for. And that is remarkable and inspiring.

We can say that Jesus/Yeshua was true to his name. It is not just a scholarly affectation to call the man we know as 'Jesus' by his Hebrew name 'Yeshua' – for this name is derived from the Hebrew word for salvation. The Hebrew concept of 'salvation' has nothing to do with gaining a ticket for the next world, and is firmly this-worldly. The word 'salvation' has often been used in Christian parlance to exclude and define whereas originally it meant something that was liberating. The Hebrew word for 'to save' is 'yasha' – which means to be wide, spacious, and ample and is perhaps best captured by the word 'liberation'. The noun 'yeshua' means salvation – the state of being wide and spacious, of being liberated and free. This understanding of salvation reclaims an important word of faith. Salvation is no longer about asking people 'Are you saved?' and then winning them to a particular viewpoint, often through playing on their sense of guilt. This Hebrew concept is wonderfully broad – yes, it embraces freedom from guilt and sin but it also includes down to earth examples of people simply having enough food or living without fear. It is about having the space and freedom for people to achieve their potential and to be the person they feel God has created them to be. The forces stopping ordinary people from having the room to be themselves can be political and economic (taxes, oppressive landlords, virtual slavery), personal (illness and depression) or even religious (the inability to live religious lives because of daily pressures, remoteness and the irrelevance of the temple and synagogue worship, as well as the burdensome religious taxes). The opposite to salvation is the Hebrew word 'sara' which means to be narrow, hemmed in, oppressed, stultified or suffocated – not able to achieve full human potential.

This is how, I imagine, Jesus would have understood salvation. The name Jesus/Yeshua (the word for salvation) was a popular name for Jews. It was especially popular at the time of Roman occupation into which Jesus was born because it carried with it a nationalist hope of liberation, with its memories of the great leader Joshua (another anglicised variation of the same name as Jesus) who in the Hebrew Bible is said to have led the chosen people into the promised land after the death of Moses. In the dark times of Roman occupation, the name 'Jesus' was common and expressed a hope for a better world just as Joshua had won for their forebears.

What went wrong? What turned this broad, life-affirming concept of salvation into something that has become a narrow concentration on saving souls from hell? For some, the work of Jesus is seen less as a call for social justice and the building of a better world than about a man who saves us sinful folk from eternal damnation. The answer for this other-worldly interpretation partly lies in the translation of the Hebrew word 'yasha' into the Greek word 'soteria'. Philip Potter, the former General Secretary of the World Council of Churches, has written that for the Greeks, 'soteria' spoke more, but not exclusively, of 'the deliverance from bodily life, rescue from the burden of material existence'.[136] This came to be the primary theological understanding of salvation when Christianity was subsumed into the Roman Empire. This is quite contrary to the Hebrew (and Jesus') understanding of salvation as being for this world rather than from the world (and Jesus' mission underwent a similar change from being a movement to make the world a better place to a promise for true disciples of a place in heaven when they die). The Greek philosophical framework behind this shift in meaning of the doctrine of salvation has had a lasting influence on Western Christianity with believers' thoughts being channelled to thinking about the afterlife – escaping the world ('Am I saved?' 'Will I go to heaven?') rather than affirming life in this present world. In other words, life before death rather than life after death.

The central motif of Jesus' teaching was the idea of the rule of God which is 'spread out on the earth and people don't see it'.[137] Living Jesus' life-affirming ethic was bound to conflict with the strict control of Roman rule. Jesus' way was thoroughly this-worldly, rooted in the place and moment. When love and life are affirmed, salvation is realised. Under God's rule justice and love reign. Under Caesar's rule there is oppression, taxes and death. Salvation, and its hoped-for realisation as the Kingdom of God, is not about a ticket to the other world but living an ethic of justice and love now in this world.

The whole point of being a Christian is not primarily to worship and to give thanks for being saved from hellfire, but to live the Christian way, to try within our capabilities to live the same values and belief that inspired Jesus – liberation based on the absolute worth of each and every human being. That was and still is the basis of my faith. It is the core that I get excited about. This outline has formed the basis of my preaching and thinking for most of my ministry, but it will always be necessarily fragmentary and often called out as being counter to the orthodoxy of the historical creeds of the church.

The Jesus story profoundly motivates our living and acting; in that sense Jesus does live on. Dorothee Sölle, a radical German Liberation theologian and poet, expresses that motivation well in her poem *Credo*:

I believe in Jesus Christ
who was right when he
like each of us
just another individual who couldn't beat city hall
worked to change the status quo
and was destroyed
looking at him I see
how our intelligence is crippled
our imagination stifled
our efforts wasted
because we do not live as he did
every day I am afraid
that he died in vain
because he is buried in our churches
because we have betrayed his revolution
in our obedience to authority
and our fear of it.[138]

However, the story of Christianity does not finish with the death of Jesus. The success of early Christianity owes a great deal to the first-century Christian convert, Paul of Tarsus. There are those who believe that the real founder of Christianity is Paul and certainly his letters comprise a significant chunk of the New Testament. Paul's genuine writings pre-date the gospel accounts but not, of course, any oral and other accounts that pre-date the actual composition of the gospels. Any understanding of Christianity has to come to terms with this man Paul, whose role in shaping and founding what became a recognisable faith is pivotal, but somewhat distinct and separate from the faith of Jesus. However, to my comparatively recent surprise, closer study shows that there was less of a distinction between the messages of Jesus and Paul.

I had always been antipathetic to the writings of Paul. They have been quoted so often to put down the causes and concerns that I espoused throughout my ministry. They have been used against women wanting a leadership role in the Christian Church and are still used to condemn LGBTQ people. They have been used to decry a theology of good works or theologies concerned with action to make the world a better place. Paul's theology is often presented as focused on sin and has been used to support views of the atonement that save us from sin and eternal damnation. In short, they revolted me for in my life as a Christian it is quotations from Paul that have been used, often enough, to slap me round the face.

That the story of early Christianity continues with Paul cannot be ignored. For many people, he is central to an orthodox understanding of the Christian mythos: Jesus is risen and so the story does not end in death. I have already indicated that the biblical evidence for the event we know as the resurrection is very scant and unconvincing. Nevertheless, we have to realise that if the story ended with crucifixion then the life of Jesus would have remained obscure and confined to the footnotes of history as yet another failed Messiah figure.

The success of the early Christian community after the death of Jesus is due in large part to the skill of Paul. We think we know Paul, and liberals like me often dismiss him as a woman-hater, maybe a closet gay and as someone who takes the simple message of Jesus and turns it into something that is sin obsessed and concerned more about the 'other world', rather than this world. Paul, too, needs a radical reappraisal. He turns the message of an itinerant Palestinian preacher into the Christ of faith and a rag-bag group of wandering nuisances and nobodies into something capable of being a world religion.

As far as we know, prior to his conversion to 'the way', Paul was a zealous Pharisaic Jew concerned with stamping out revisionists like Jesus. But Paul suddenly and dramatically underwent a transformation that turned him from persecutor of Jesus' followers to a leader of the new movement with a commitment that was tested by imprisonment and finally, we are told (with scant evidence) to his death at the hands of Roman persecutors.

Paul was not from a backwater like Jesus' more humble beginnings in rural Galilee but an educated and academic man. However, we need to be careful about ascribing all the letters that say they are written by Paul to his authorship. Through analysing style and theological content, it is possible to say that only the following letters were written by him and even those have parts that were almost certainly not written by him but later additions. These are considered the genuine letters of Paul: the first letter to the Thessalonians, Galatians, the bulk of the Corinthian correspondence, Philemon, Philippians, and most of Romans. That means a number of letters purported to be written by him are later additions with different theologies and in almost all cases a desire to conform to social structures and the conventions of the Roman Empire. The original Paul is much more in tune with the radical spirit of Jesus. It is this same message that Jesus proclaimed that inspires Paul. As a Pauline scholar, Arthur Dewey, suggests:

> We can see Paul as a man who joins in the cultural debate of his time over what constitutes the value and meaning of humanity. This is a man who can imagine those considered outsiders as equals, a man who has found freedom and meaning in the rag-tag communities of nobodies.[139]

The revolutionary nature of Paul's message is emphasised by the cultural historian, Larry Siedentop, who sees early Christian equality and inclusion as defining for secular Western liberal democracies (although this is more than a little unfair to the Jewish prophetic tradition). Siedentop points out that this equality and inclusive message is the basis for all our demands for equality of opportunity and of all those movements of liberation – feminism, slavery, gay, racism, as well as disability and equality.[140] Christian equality as practised by the early followers provides the unrecognised moral bedrock behind all Western secular liberalism. When Paul, echoing the teaching of Jesus, states that there is no longer any distinction between 'Jew or Greek, slave or free, male or female',[141] he is saying something revolutionary and liberating for those who are on the wrong side of those binaries of entitlement. Paul's reciting of those words is, some suggest, echoing something that was perhaps an early Christian baptismal formula or perhaps a well-known hymn of the early Christian community in Galatia.[142] The understanding of inclusion and equality were of utmost importance (even defining) to the early Christians. I think we are inclined to forget that in such a hierarchical world as the Roman Empire or, indeed, first-century Judaism, a group of people who declared that amongst them there is no distinction to be made on the basis of gender, wealth, religion, nationality or economic status was bound to be lauded by those who were without power and viewed with suspicion and hostility by the powers that be.

This is the same message (although more philosophically presented and nuanced by Paul) that was felt by the poor of Galilee, received through the teaching and example of Jesus, who taught that they were as important to God (and each other) as those of the highest social, political or religious standing. There is absolute equality – all are children of God and equally prized.[143] If there was a bias in Jesus' mission then it was to those who were oppressed, the poor, women, those discarded as unproductive or labelled as unclean or irreligious,[144] to those who needed to be lifted up. This is the truth that the educated Paul was blind to and to which he suddenly woke up, saw and understood.

It is this powerful message of equality and liberation that remains after the death of Jesus. In a sense, therefore, it is a 'bodily' resurrection for in his first letter to the community of believers in Corinth, Paul coins the phrase 'the body of Christ' to refer to the followers of Jesus. He expects believers to be the walking, talking body of Christ, so much so, that in real and tangible sense Jesus lives. John D Davies, a priest who courageously fought against apartheid in South Africa, underlines the functional and operative importance of the phrase 'the body of Christ'.

> A body is, first and foremost, a person's functioning, and its soundness has to be measured in functional terms. A body is truly a body if it communicates, operates, experiences, and registers sense perceptions efficiently. The Body of Christ is validated as such not by its qualifications but by its operational effectiveness. The Body of Christ is the Body of Christ if it enables the word of Jesus to be heard, the activity of Jesus to be performed, and the experience of Jesus to be suffered. If it doesn't, it may perhaps be a mystical body – whatever that may be, and if the phrase is not a contradiction in terms – but it will not be what a body is primarily supposed to be, namely a functional body.[145]

'Christ has no body now on earth but ours; no hands but ours; no feet but ours' is a phrase sometimes ascribed to Teresa of Avila in the sixteenth century but emphasises the same point. The body of Jesus lives, there is 'bodily' resurrection wherever and whenever people try to live as Jesus encouraged.

This not only answers questions about the bodily resurrection and spread of Christianity, but also takes the message of Jesus' second coming away from being a quasi-historical happening at the end of the world (as a literalistic reading of the final book of the Christian Bible, Revelation, might suggest), to a realisation that Jesus comes again when his way of life is followed and lived by each believer. We, believers in Jesus, are the so-called second coming.

Many say that this interpretation ignores the role of the Holy Spirit. I have deliberately left out the detail of the emergence of the post-resurrection church, the story of Pentecost and the coming of the Holy

Spirit contained in the Acts of the Apostles. Luke, the probable author, in creating the stories of the Ascension and Pentecost at the start of Acts is carefully paralleling the post-resurrection story with the Jewish lectionary. I don't want this to lessen the importance in any way of the early followers who felt inspired by the way and words of Jesus and who were able to lead a mission throughout the Roman Empire in spite of appalling persecution by the authorities. They felt a sense of 'profound motivation' to be Christ's body on earth with a radical and important message. As I understand it, that sense of 'profound motivation' is what is meant by the spirit and, indeed spirituality. It is an idea that the Scottish theologian, Kathy Galloway, borrows from the Latin American Jesuit Jon Sobrino and by this she means 'those instincts, intuitions, longings and desires – both of nature and culture – that move us, inspire us (literally, 'breathe through us'), and shape, inform and fill our decisions and actions'.[146]

The distinctions between the teachings of Jesus and Paul are less stark than we assume. The followers of Jesus were known in the first years after his death as 'followers of the way'. It is a thoroughly worldly movement.

The story of Jesus and the 'true' writings of Paul encapsulate a spiritual and political worldview that I find inspiring and relevant to our strange political times. For me it is the mainspring, the values against which I measure the movements, foibles and morals of our present world and my own living.

Is this portrait in any sense an objective consideration of the person of Jesus and of early Christianity? Probably not, but it does offer Jesus as an iconic human being to look up to and try to follow. Jesus demonstrates an orientation of life and living which challenges our cossetted world and its flabby values. The Jesus I want to portray presents values that are still easily understandable today and poses questions of inclusion and diversity that even in the twenty-first century we have not fully addressed. He proffers a way of commitment and inclusion that challenges our world.

CHAPTER 8
PRESENT-ING JESUS

For he does not wish that men should love him more than anything
Because he died; he only wishes they would hear him sing.
Stevie Smith – 'The Airy Christ'

A key obligation on clergy and others who lead communal Christian worship is to reiterate what Jesus said and did, so that it can inspire action in the world. It will be clear from the preceding chapter that I do not believe that means a wholesale acceptance of what is written in the gospels but a scholarly attempt to present to the best of our ability the historical Jesus. It is intellectual laziness that accepts at face value the infallible historicity and accuracy of the gospels. Faith does not exclude using your brain and the brains of scholars. Faith requires a commitment of the mind as much as that of the heart. It is a manipulative con to believe those who say we must accept what the Bible says or a particular church's teaching to be a Christian. Christian orthodoxy or membership of a church isn't going to win a place in heaven (that is not what it is about), it is about making the world a better place. John Lennon was right when he sang 'Imagine there's no heaven, it's easy if you try./No hell below us, above us only sky.'[147] Christianity is not a reward system for good behaviour.

When it comes to private prayer or meditation, the task is somewhat different. It is about seeking direction or inspiration. It is not about asking God or Jesus to do something or to answer requests. It is very personal, and rightly so, for it is about personal commitment and motivation. For me it is about making the way and words of Jesus present, here and now, and of reflecting on them in relation to my own life choices and decisions. I am not looking for miracles or divine intervention but I am, I think, looking for clarity.

I want to write a little bit about what private prayer and meditation have come to mean for me and how they feed this understanding of Christianity. I start by finding a short gospel reading and a poem or secular reading that I think corresponds to it in some way. I am careful to choose what I think is a genuine saying or event in Jesus' life for the gospel reading. I read them through several times and then I like to sit still and simply be silent, consciously breathing deeply until the rhythm of my breathing becomes natural, unobserved and my jumbled, shouting mind gradually quietens. Meditation can induce that receptive and perceptive moment that we know from the borderlands of sleep. It is in that almost semi-conscious trippy moment (the technical word is 'hypnagogia') that I find an idea, a person, or a situation comes to mind in a clearer and fresh way. Thoughts come, thoughts of a different dimension to the usual clutter of the mind.

Gradually and naturally, after a while, I come back to the real moment and the day begins. This isn't magic, I think of it as prayer but I don't address anyone or ask for intervention. I just know when I don't do it, I feel the loss of something precious.

The Quakers talk of holding people or a situation 'in the light' but this is not necessarily looking for divine intervention, rather space to think. This to me is prayer and it allows for, as Mary Oliver has written 'a silence in which another voice may speak'.[148] That other voice, I believe, is my own inner thoughts, others might choose to call it the spirit or even God.

This form of meditation is not just for the religiously inclined. In *the little book of humanism*, a suggestion is made, devoid of religious language, about a very basic meditation technique:

sit somewhere comfortable and close your eyes.

Try and sit like that for a few minutes.

Congratulations – you have just meditated. Meditation has been practised in religious and non-religious ways for thousands of years. You don't have to be a dedicated student of meditation to enjoy some of its benefits.

People tend to find they feel better and can think more clearly as a result of having these little moments of quiet.[149]

Although the authors' instructions in *the little book of humanism* are devoid of a religious element, mine are not and I carry in my thoughts the short gospel passage and a poem so that these tangentially fill and shape my thoughts, as do of course the events of the coming day at work or the personal joys and worries of home and family. Those are all part of the clutter. Sometimes that discordant clutter is overwhelming and I need an aid to help me relax and start a 'journey' into a state of receptive silence – for instance, a lighted candle, or the haunting sound of a Tibetan singing bowl. At other times, to be honest, the necessary receptive peace of mind simply eludes me.

On the following page of *the little book of humanism* the value of this quietness is heralded by a quotation from Bertrand Russell: 'If we spent half an hour every day in silent immobility, I am convinced that we should conduct all our affairs, personal, national and international, far more sanely than we do at present.'[150] What Russell and others claim for a period of meditative silence is that it is the most valuable and important part of each day, more valuable than Bible reading, hymn singing or any other religious observance. Do this and you will live better lives. Talkative Christianity can sometimes eschew silence, which is strange as the gospels refer to Jesus seeking solitude to be quiet and to reorientate himself.

Gone for me is the discipline that Anglican clergy are supposed to follow of saying the Daily Office – Morning Prayer and Evening Prayer – with set readings from the Bible. In its place is this period of silent reflection. It is followed at the Library by a morning service – a communal event rather than private practice.

Communal worship that reflects the inclusive nature of Jesus and is composed for an inclusive community needs to reflect this in the language that is used. The language of public prayer and praise wars (I use the word advisedly as the traditional language is powerful, male and hierarchical) against my 'reading' of faith – what language can be found that expresses faith and the mission of Jesus?

The problem begins with how to address God without resorting to hierarchical adjectives. For instance, I always recoil at the use of the word 'Lord'. It has particular problems for those of us who live in the UK because of the House of Lords in our Parliament which is an institution that needs reform or abolition. The word seems feudal, aristocratic and hierarchical, none of which apply to an itinerant preacher in first-century Palestine or to how I would address my concept of God. Nor am I going to talk about God using primarily male images of power (King, Lord, Ruler, Judge, Almighty, etc.). Nor do I think that 'Father' is desirable as it sounds rather austere and somewhat Victorian – not many use the word 'Father' as a term of address nowadays, it is almost as outmoded as a form of address as 'Pater' and, of course, ties God to being male. Jesus, we believe, addressed God as 'Abba' – a childish word (male I admit), but among the first a baby might utter – mama, dada, abba – which takes away its taint of masculine power. I noticed the other day that my baby grandson who is just beginning to form a few words said 'Dada' and went straight to the outstretched arms of his Mummy. Baby words like 'Abba' are not strongly gender specific. However, in most contexts, I wonder if the gender neutral word 'God' should simply suffice? It does not force an anthropomorphic image into prayer and worship. Most of the time as I write liturgy, I refer to God simply as 'God', perhaps with an appropriate adjective appended. I am, I confess, drawn to the word 'Yahweh' which is an ancient Hebrew word for God and notoriously difficult to translate: it can mean 'I am that I am' or 'I will be what I will be' and resonates with many people's theology today who understand God not as a being but being itself.

I like, but do not often use, the tendency to write the word God as G-d with the vowel missing. This emerged from the Jewish custom of not pronouncing the name of God. I like that tradition as it too takes away the personal aspect of God as a being and moves in in my mind to being itself – something that is not too pronounced let alone anthropomorphised. The use of G-d, Yahweh and Abba all help to remind us that our tradition stems from Judaism and is born of a culture and time very different from our own.

In public worship, I generally avoid the use of the word 'Yahweh' for God or 'Yeshua' for Jesus as both seem rather superior and exclusive – an intellectual affectation. However, in my private prayer I do use both those names as they remind me that Jesus and the first followers of the way were Jewish and both words carry real theological heft.

If the word 'God' poses a problem then the Christian concept of the 'Kingdom of God' which is central to Jesus' message poses just as big a headache. The Greek word that is often translated kingdom is 'basileia'. The word basileia is used in many ways in Greek – 'commonwealth', 'empire' or even 'royal palace' – all to my mind creating contemporary problems and intimations of power and territory. The Aramaic word behind the Greek translation which Jesus is more than likely to have used is 'malkut', which refers to the rule, the exercise of sovereign power. Therefore, the phrase 'Kingdom of God' should more correctly be translated as 'the rule of God'. Does that suffice? It is certainly more 'alive' than the Greek options but I would go a little bit further and try to find a word that carries that dynamism, but is more descriptive of Jesus' actual community which was inclusive and without a hint of hierarchy. Therefore, I am attracted to the concept that has emerged in feminist circles and I use the word 'kin-dom' which implies something far more inclusive. It suggests not only all those I am related to in various ways but brings to mind the phrase 'kith and kin' which widens the understanding to friends and acquaintances. Kin-dom does not have the hierarchical and patriarchal connotations of kingdom which indicates that there is a distinction between rulers and ruled and from which people can be excluded because of ethnicity, or for religious, political, sexual or social reasons on the whim of the ruler. Kin-dom is less defined and seems to describe Jesus' rag-bag community of followers better than a word that brings to mind regimented power and status.

'Kin-dom' does, in the Library's liturgy, replace 'kingdom' in the Lord's Prayer. The occasional complaint is that we are messing with a tradition although many (even the present Pope) are not happy with the versions of Jesus' prayer handed down to us. Isn't it a sign of following Jesus to ensure that religious traditions are made for men, women and children, and that men, women and children are not made to bend to unhelpful traditions?[151]

Communal worship at Gladstone's Library includes selected short extracts from the Bible – always one of the designated genuine readings from the gospels (Matthew, Mark, Luke, John and Thomas) and frequently readings from the Hebrew Bible or the Letters of Paul – again the genuine letters rather than accepting the traditional ascription. Listening and reading is how we hear of the radical nature of Jesus and the early Christian followers of the way and their commitment to diversity and justice.

The language is sparse and understandable rather than weighted with theological terms and phrases. The service uses the Christian tradition of the Eucharist (Holy Communion, Mass, call it what you will) with its structure of taking, blessing, breaking and sharing; it is a symbolic demonstration of how we could and should spend our days if we are following Jesus' way.

It is not primarily language that defines the inclusiveness of a community, it is a question of who attends and, even more importantly who is excluded. Any reform of worship would fall down if people were excluded because they don't belong to a particular Christian denomination or, indeed, call themselves Christian. It has to be properly inclusive just as Jesus' community was inclusive. The celebrant at Gladstone's Library worship is always a minister of religion but can be drawn from any and almost every Christian denomination from Roman Catholic to Unitarian. Nobody is excluded from attending and participating fully regardless of whether they have been baptised, confirmed or any of the other human rules that hedge our church lives. This open table is an important symbol of the kin-dom. It reflects Jesus' open table in the gospels with no barrier of age, ethnicity, religious affiliation, gender or sexual orientation. I am proud to say that Jews, Muslims and virtually all Christian denominations, as well as atheists and agnostics have all participated fully. This 'no barriers' policy is something essential to my understanding of worship and faith, it is a hallmark of the kin-dom.

There are practical measures needed to ensure a service is inclusive. Above all it needs to be easy to follow so that people don't feel alienated or are unsure what they are meant to be doing or saying. There mustn't be some people in the know about what to do and say and those who haven't a clue and remain anxious and confused throughout. There should always be a service sheet that not only leads people through the service but can be taken away and perhaps pondered over, discussed and agreed or disagreed with.

A standard outline of the service is printed below. Of course, I write the service to be inclusive of all comers both in language and in being easy to follow. The language is not hierarchical, excessively male, or full of power images. I try to keep theological jargon to a minimum. I write different versions of the Thanksgiving Prayer to suit various occasions, the one below is general and typical. The service is well within the traditions and understandings of most Christians and I hope it is accessible to others who drop in who may be from other faiths or none. Here is the outline (I have excluded any poems, reading or seasonal variations). It is the template from which I create the Library's daily services:

A poem or a short reading presenting the theme of the service

Prayer of Preparation.[152]

God of peace, keep our minds
on what is true and commands respect,
what is just, pure and kind,
whatever is excellent and commendable.
Let these fill our hearts
and guide our actions in Jesus' name.
Amen.

Absolution and Confession[153]

God forgives you
Forgive others

Forgive yourself

In the gospels forgiveness always precedes repentance.
In Christ, no matter what we have said or done,
we are forgiven, accepted, loved and welcomed to the feast.
In response to such grace let us confess our sins:

We need your healing, merciful God:
give us true repentance.
Some sins are plain to us,
some escape us,
some we cannot face.
Forgive us:
set us free to hear your word to us;
set us free to serve you. Amen.

A Song of Praise[154]

Goodness is stronger than evil;
love is stronger than hate;
light is stronger than darkness;
life is stronger than death;
victory is ours through the One who loved us.

Collect of The Day
A short prayer on the theme of the day.

A Reading
from the Hebrew Bible, the New Testament, a poem or some other
appropriate writing.

A brief silence is kept after the reading

The Gospel

Please stand as the Gospel is announced.

Listen to the Gospel of Christ according to ...
Glory to you, O Christ.

At the conclusion of the Gospel:

This is the Gospel of Christ

Praise to you, O Christ.

The Intercession

Please sit and if you feel inclined please come forward and light a candle for a person, a situation or for yourself. This can be done in silence or with a very short spoken intention, 'I light this candle for...'

The candles are left burning as we sit in silence until the celebrant concludes with an appropriate prayer to gather these thoughts, hopes and prayers together.

The Peace[155]

Please stand

We, Angels and Mortals, Believers and Non-Believers,
look heavenward and speak the word aloud.
Peace. We look at our world and speak the word aloud.
Peace. We look at each other, then into ourselves
and we say without shyness or apology or hesitation

Peace, My Brother.
Peace, My Sister.
Peace, My Soul.

The Thanksgiving Prayer

God be with you.
And also with you.

Lift up your hearts.
We lift them to God.

Let us give thanks to God.
It is right to give our thanks and praise.

Holy God, whom we hear in the sheer silence of your presence,
and whose hope for humanity is etched in the life and way of Jesus.
Your kingdom breaks through in acts of goodness, love and justice.
Inspire us by your Spirit

and kindle in us the fire of your love
to keep us alive and bring warmth to the world.

Holy, holy, holy, God of love and majesty,
the whole universe speaks of your glory.
Hosanna in the highest.

Blessed is the one who comes in the name of our God.
Hosanna in the highest.

We remember that on the night of desertion and betrayal,
the day before his torture and death,
as Jesus had supper with his friends
he took bread,
he thanked you, broke it and gave it to his friends and said,
'Take this and eat it for this is my body broken for you.
Do this to remember me.'
After supper, Jesus took the cup of wine,
He thanked you, gave it to his friends and said,
'All of you drink from this cup, it is my blood
Shed for my love of humanity and my love of God.
Do this every time you drink it to remember me.'

Christ has died.
Christ is risen.
Christ is here.

Send your spirit up on us
and upon these small gifts,
a piece of ordinary bread and a cup of ordinary wine,
may this signify for us something extraordinary
– the body and blood of Jesus.

Inspire us as we continue to follow Jesus
from whom we have learnt to be free,
free from powers which estrange us, free to do good.
In confidence and hope we pray as he taught us:

Abba,
hallowed be your name.
Your kin-dom come.

Give us bread, sufficient for our needs.
Forgive us our debts,
as we, here and now, forgive our debtors.
Do not let us succumb to temptation.
Amen.

The Invitation

The gifts of God for the people of God

The Receiving of Communion

Please gather around the altar

The Body of Christ The Blood of Christ
Amen.   **Amen.**

The Dismissal[156]
Either:
This is what is required of us, only this:
to do justice,
love kindness
and walk humbly with our God.

Shalom
Shalom.

Or:[157]
Here on the pulse of this new day
you may have the grace to look up and out
and into your sister's eyes,
and into your brother's face,
your country,
and say simply
very simply
with hope –
Good morning.

There are various key moments in this short service. Firstly, it provides an opportunity to reflect on what we have done wrong and to move on; this is what in many traditions would be referred to as an act of confession and absolution. Each weekday in the Library's chapel the leader proclaims forgiveness (absolution) before the act of repentance (confession), reversing the usual order of confession and then absolution. This 'scandal' of unearned, undeserved forgiveness, which is such a hallmark of Jesus' ministry is adhered to by reversing the order. Jesus' acceptance of people astounds with a generosity that can still be life changing. Jesus proclaims in life, and here in this liturgy, that no matter who we are or what we have done we are accepted. We can move on in life. I know this simple liturgy of acceptance works – people sometimes come to me in tears after services with a sense that a paralysis of deep guilt has been overcome. After the gift of acceptance, confession and repentance are our natural response.

Secondly, the service affirms that we should be aware and accepting of each other. This is most tellingly demonstrated by what is known as 'The Peace'. It offers a conscious moment of awareness of each other, our shared equality and our shared responsibility not only at this symbolic meal but also in life. Rather than rushing around pointlessly shaking hands, this liturgy uses part of a poem by Maya Angelou to express that oneness in what I believe is a meaningful way.

Of the key elements of the Daily Eucharist, the third is perhaps the most defining as it offers a daily re-enactment of Jesus' frequent fellowship meals with his followers and, most poignantly, a symbolic re-enactment of his last meal before his torture and death. This should be presented in stark and unflowery prose so that the full uncomfortable reality of the words does not get lost or lessened in theological language. There is something terrifying about the words uttered by Jesus over the bread and wine; he is a man who knew he was about to face death. It is easy to see how it remained a central part of re-membering him.

To participate is not just to go through the motions of a memorial or re-enactment but to re-member, which I take to mean to come together as a body and to go out and be disciples of Jesus in our contemporary world. The aim is to encourage all of us to bring to life in our daily living the hopes and motivations of the kin-dom. Christ still lives not in some spurious supernatural way but is made alive, re-membered, by our words and actions in our everyday lives – Christ has no body on earth but ours. Christ still, in effect, lives. The resurrection and the second coming of Jesus is up to us and our re-membering. Indeed, it is us.

A lot of nonsense is spoken, and many have lost their lives over the interpretation of the meaning of the bread and wine as the body and blood of Jesus. I do feel that contemporary semiotics (the signifier and the signified) can cut through much of the problem. This is simple and easy to understand without falling into endless theological debate and avoiding a tendency to think of the Eucharist as being something of a conjuring trick performed by a priest. This is not only superstitious nonsense but suggests that priests have some special gift bestowed on them.

The fourth regular element that is threaded through each daily service is the frequent use of secular poetry, usually contemporary, to illustrate a theme of the service. I like the openness of poetry and the possibility of many different readings of the text. I like, too, the possibility of a line or a phrase from these skilful wordsmiths lodging in the memory and unfolding a meaning gradually throughout the day, the week or however long it may take. There is an openness about poetry that is not at all didactic. It is more 'subtle' than that, 'T. S. Eliot wrote that a poem's meaning was just the hunk of meat that the burglar throws to the guard dog to keep it occupied while the poem works its real magic.'[158] Most poetry opens up possibilities of meaning rather than defining and closing it down. It means that some carefully crafted poetic words resonate for longer than the 20 minutes of the service.

You could argue, and I would not disagree, that there is very little evangelical drive in my understanding of the role of worship. That is because I regret the emphasis on the missionary nature of Christianity which is in sharp contrast to Judaism from which it emerged. The scholars of the Jesus Seminar do not believe that any of Jesus' post-resurrection missionary words in the gospels or the Acts of the Apostles (Acts 1) are genuine. I wonder if the missionary element blunts Christianity's message of focusing on doing justice. Do we really want to win souls for Christ by exclusive and excluding conversions? Isn't that the antithesis of what Jesus stood for? Shouldn't we rather be joining with those (from all religions and liberation movements) countering anything that diminishes human beings or abuses our planet? Doesn't that reflect more closely the mission and ministry of Jesus? Isn't that what salvation is all about? Isn't that what God requires of us?

Have I failed to widen the circle of us and instead created something tailor-made for my own theological understanding? That is debatable, I accept, but the barriers of exclusion that have been so evident against women, against LGBTQ people, against other Christian denominations or other faiths can be and have been removed, or at the very least attempted to be removed in the rarefied world of the chapel at Gladstone's Library. My attempts at presenting a liturgy that focuses on our acceptance of each other is just one, probably very inadequate, attempt to keep the circle widening rather than constricting. If a core characteristic of the founder of our faith's mission was inclusivity then, at the very least, we can ensure that when we gather in his name there are no barriers and no one is excluded.

I know that I have not got it all right. There are other expressions of faith and worship that will suit other people better and reflect their religious sensibilities and I would not wish to challenge their right to exist or their ability to feed people spiritually. The important question of how the many strands and interpretations of faith, even in a broad denomination like Anglicanism, can hold together needs to be addressed urgently. Maybe it should develop a more federal system of denominational government that would honour and celebrate diversity with just a very few core shared principles. Could Anglicanism move away from an 'empire' mode to a 'commonwealth' mode of polity? That is a debate for another time.

It is now time to write about the one subject that does not discriminate between people, religions, churches or theologies – death.

It is the one universal certainty in life. How Christians understand and respond to death will depend on their understanding of the death of Jesus.

CHAPTER 9
INEVITABLE DEATH

This is a special way of being afraid
No trick dispels. Religion used to try,
That vast, moth-eaten musical brocade
Created to pretend we never die,
Philip Larkin – 'Aubade'

It is inevitable that by the time you reach your sixties death is going to wrench parents, elderly friends and mentors away from you. I was 44 when I arrived at Gladstone's Library and I have now been there for over 25 years. I suppose it was inevitable that such a period of my life was almost bound to include the death of both my parents. My father, Richard, died aged 86 in 2003; my mother, Pauline, aged 92 in 2015; Helen's mother died in 2019, aged 83.

A great deal of sentimental nonsense is spoken about death: 'She has gone to a better place.' 'It was his time.' 'She was promoted to glory.' 'Gone fishing.' I am used to death. As a clergyperson I coped professionally and, I hope, sensitively with the death of parishioners. But closer to home it is different. My father had been ill for a long time. His active and sporty life had been cut short by the very sudden onset of rheumatoid arthritis in his seventies. It started when he complained of pain whilst playing badminton in his early seventies and then swiftly accelerated and eventually led to him being disabled and wheelchair-bound. All of this he endured with great stoicism. Towards the end of his life there were more and more visits to hospital. My mother acted as main caregiver with help from visiting nurses – she too endured all this with equal stoic resolve. It was a very touching example of loving 'for better or worse … in sickness and in health … till death us do part.' His death was neither a surprise, nor a tragedy but a natural consequence of a long debilitating and painful illness. Sad, yes, but also a relief.

Perhaps, because activity in his last years of life was necessarily curtailed, it was possible to get to know him and his vulnerabilities in a way that had not been possible before he was so incapacitated. I suppose we, my mother and all the close family, related to him in a more caring manner and he relied on us for help and support. He was very supportive and genuinely fond of Helen and Lucy and welcomed them into the family enthusiastically. It was during this period that I had some of the most meaningful discussions with him that I don't think would have been possible before his illness or indeed without the prompting of Helen. These discussions were always short and thrown matter-of-factly into the conversation often as statements, and equally quickly responded to by me I hope in a more open way, inviting discussion. This sometimes elicited another statement, but then we would move on to pleasantries perfectly pleasantly. Somehow, though, they were important markers thrown down.

My mother's illness and death was more harrowing but perhaps 'depressing' is a more appropriate word. She used to come and stay with us at the Library after my father's death for three days at a time – perhaps three or four times a year. She always said that visits should be kept to three days. 'Visitors like fish smell after three days,' she would always quip. Indeed, as with many elderly people, worries would continually surface, and questions be repeated, sometimes many times an hour. On the last of her visits to us, I took her to a matinée at the theatre in Mold, a rather terrible production of the farce *Boeing-Boeing*. We had a good pub lunch before the performance and she ate heartily – fish cakes and, her favourite, sticky toffee pudding. During the interval, I went to get her an ice cream and left her chatting happily to a talkative woman from Burnley in the next seat. When I came back just before the end of the interval the woman was still chatting to her. Mum wasn't responding. I offered her the ice cream, still no response. I touched her arm and no response. It was clear that she had suffered some sort of stroke or heart attack. I tried to break into the chatty woman's monologue as I summoned a member of staff and as the lights went down ready for Act 2 of *Boeing-Boeing*, we carried her out from the middle of our row to a waiting wheelchair. The performance that had been halted momentarily then began its farcical unwinding. The woman from Burnley was grateful for my Mum's ice cream and thanked me as I helped carry my Mum from her seat to the waiting wheelchair.

The rush of the blue-lighted ambulance took us to Wrexham Maelor Hospital and to immediate active busyness by the A & E staff. Mum regained consciousness and typically didn't want to make a fuss despite no movement in her arm and leg and very limited speech. The scan showed that it had been a major stroke. The consultant said there was a possibility of future strokes and probably she would only survive another 18 months at most and, of course, there was an immediate likelihood of another within the next 24 hours. However, he said that as my mother was otherwise very fit, he would like to offer a new treatment – an injection that would either greatly improve her chances of recovery or might, he confessed, kill her. He was going to take another scan and see if this was still viable. If it was, he would need my response immediately. As fate would have it my two sisters were both out of the country, Clare was living in Perth in Western Australia and Diana was in Singapore, a stopover on her way to visit Clare and her family. I felt that I needed to try to contact them before I made such a decision. Both proved uncontactable but I left messages. Together with Helen, who had now joined me in my vigil at the hospital, we tried to make up our minds what the answer should be to the consultant's life-deciding question. I was veering on the side of saying 'no', I think basically to give my sisters a chance to come and say goodbye when the consultant appeared and said that the damage was too great to try the procedure.

She was then condemned to over two years of deteriorating health and several more strokes. For most of this time she couldn't walk, talk with any ease, read or feed herself. She was kept alive through PEG (percutaneous endoscopic gastrostomy) feeding with a tube straight into her stomach. All sorts of antibiotics and medicine as well as nutritious substances were fed to her ensuring she was kept alive and free from infection. She survived for over two years which included bouts of MRSA and countless other bugs. She had little sense of what was happening or any idea of time. Thankfully in her nursing home, she sometimes thought she was on a cruise. For most of this time she longed to go home. It was a pitiful closure to her life and we longed for it to end. Helen and I immediately resolved to write a living will so our end would not be long, drawn out and as demeaning as this.

Helen shouldered the bulk of the visiting and was the most skilled at communicating. She was also the most at ease with the medical world and more inclined and able to demand better care for my mother than my sisters and me with our naïve belief that they – medics and carers – were doing everything they could and knew best. Helen was fantastic and deeply caring, communicating as best she could and for some strange reason coaxing me to dance for my mother. I can't dance to save my life but it seemed to amuse her, especially my weird and utterly unwonderful Egyptian dance.

When Daphne, my cousin who had been an eminent nurse with an equally eminent surgeon as husband, visited from Canada they were quite clear that Helen's view was right. Helen knew when standards had slipped and was, thank God, not diffident in saying so. My siblings and I were less good at this but attentive. Clare flew over from Australia at least every six months and Diana was a frequent visitor from London every two weeks or so. Mum would usually forget our visits as soon as we had gone which was particularly annoying after a long flight from Australia. We rued the cleverness of modern medicine with its ability to sustain human existence, it couldn't be called life, and yet it seemed to be endlessly and needlessly prolonged. The care was paltry and often condescending. This is the way our lives end 'not with a bang but a whimper'.[159] I received a kind letter from one of my brothers-in-law thanking me for the way I had looked after Mum; it was in a way totally misdirected as all the thanks should have gone to Helen. How typical of life that the man gets the credit.

It took me some time to properly grieve the death of my parents. In fact, it didn't happen until October 2017, two years after my mother's death. I had been to lunch with my sister, Diana, in London. I was then walking rather aimlessly around London's Embankment and Strand area when I had a strange experience whilst window shopping. I was passing Waterstones bookshop in the Strand and caught my reflection in the window – and it seemed as though the person whose reflection I was glimpsing was my father. I thought nothing of it but as I walked on and again glimpsed my reflection just round the corner in a restaurant window it seemed that my mother was looking back at me. Of course, I have often been aware of parental traits in my appearance and in certain of my idiosyncrasies, but this somehow seemed different, it was beyond a casual glimpse. It was different too from the image and influences of my mother I see so clearly in my sisters Diana and Clare – that always conjure up memories of her. This seemed to me of a different order and somehow provided two contrasting images: a judgemental image from my father's reflection and a quizzical smile from my mother's. I felt uncontrollable sorrow, utter gloom, and let out a whimper of anguish. I carried on my walk and sat down in Embankment Gardens, with a feeling of being overwhelmed by a profound sorrow, of not having said what I wanted to say to them. I felt that I was letting them down in some way and being a disappointment to them. Muddled up with this was a sense of my own mortality. A passing Asian man and woman asked me if I was alright and I indicated that I was. They had broken the spell and I carried on with the day's meetings. It was brief and surprising, and from first reflection to the breaking of the spell can only have been 10 or 15 minutes at most.

I was moved too when reading Seamus Heaney's translation of *Aeneid Book VI* where, towards the end, Aeneas travels to the underworld and meets his dead father and longingly says:

> 'Let me take your hand, my father, O let me, and do not
> Hold back from my embrace.' And as he spoke he wept.
> Three times he tried to reach arms around that neck.
> Three times the form, reached for in vain, escaped
> Like a breeze between his hands, a dream on wings.[160]

The passage somehow resonates with my London window experience. A longing for connection and to say things to the dead that I wish I had said when they were alive but it is, as Aeneas finds just 'a dream on wings'.

These two parental deaths and my own ageing – 'I ache in the places that I used to play'[161] as Leonard Cohen so aptly sings – have made me reconsider my understanding of death and dying. In the midst of parish life, it is very difficult for clergy to do anything other than peddle certainties (carefully nuanced for one's own integrity) about the afterlife – that is what is expected. It is only with the freedom of no regular pastoral routine that I have looked seriously and critically at what I think about the afterlife spurred on by the death of my parents.

As you will have already gathered, I have never been convinced by the New Testament evidence for life after death. The testimony of the gospel writers is a muddle and full of contradictory stories. It is impossible to try to pool all the gospel tales of resurrection appearances into a single narrative as the gospel writers were writing theology not history. In the gospel accounts, sometimes Jesus appears amongst them even when the doors are locked or indeed, he suddenly vanishes. Sometimes he appears to be flesh and blood. Thomas put his hand on the wounds of crucifixion and Jesus eats with the disciples, but some stories have him suddenly vanishing like an apparition. At other times he is unrecognisable to Mary of Magdala and to the travellers on the road to Emmaus, who realise his identity only when he breaks bread with them (almost certainly a reference to the way the early Christian community gathered for worship). If the body is resurrected (whatever that means) then obviously the writers have a body on their hands – how do they get rid of the body? To tie up the loose ends from his resurrection story in his gospel, Luke opens his sequel (the Acts of the Apostles which charts the story of the birth of the Church) with what Christians refer to as the Ascension, where Jesus literally ascends to heaven, rather like a rocket. This is, like much of the Acts of the Apostles, a fiction – the creation of the writer to mimic and indeed to trump the Elijah/Elisha stories in the Hebrew Bible.

I believe death is the end. In all the English-speaking countries the funeral service has quite rightly become a thanksgiving for the life of somebody, a celebration of their life. In fact, funerals have become memorial services. That's to say traditional beliefs about life after death – heaven or hell – have been given up. I would like to bet that you've never been to a funeral where the clergyperson told you to repent of your sins because you too will face a last judgement. That whole complex of ideas has gone. Instead, we now have a life-centred view.

The fear of death with judgement and hell as eternal punishment has all but evaporated in the UK. Hell, if people think of it at all, is seen as life without God, eternal darkness. What is the nature of heaven? It is surely not a place. What would eternal life with God be like? But if God is 'being' rather than 'a being' then life with God is rather nebulous. Death is the end and the only difficulty is coming to terms with grief.

I conducted the funeral of my mother-in-law Mary, a woman who was always welcoming and loving to me and our love for her shone through the service. Before, during and after the funeral many stories were told of her that brought smiles to the whole extended family. And yet, it was a moment when a burden on the family was also lifted and something approaching normal life could resume, most notably for Tony her husband who was freed from round-the-clock care. That is a pathway that is all too familiar. But it is when those of one's own generation die, suddenly or through incurable disease, that death chills the soul. The day before Mary's funeral, I had presided at the funeral of John, my sister Diana's husband, who died far too young. His death was sudden and unexpected. He simply woke up dead one day, which was a phrase my mother always used about how she would 'like to go'. A nice way to die but it was just 15 years too early in John's case. Mary was a committed Methodist, from a family of committed Methodists, John by contrast was not a Christian believer. He was one of the cleverest people I have ever known. He believed not in God and Jesus but was fascinated by 'consciousness' or as he frequently put it 'what am I doing in one?' He was confident 'this remained a mystery not answered by religion, philosophy or scientists such as Richard Dawkins'. John would, I think, be amused to think that I, his brother-in-law, whom he mockingly referred to as 'your Grace' or the 'Holy Father', would be presiding over his funeral and I feel so conscious that every sentence I uttered at the funeral would have been scrutinised and poked fun at by John.

John's death also taught me something about the importance of family. As soon as Diana phoned to tell me the news, I rushed down to London to be with her. By the next morning, Clare had arrived from Australia and remained for several weeks supporting Diana. I realised, like never before, that there was a strong bond between us that meant we would always support each other when it mattered and I felt I had been rather casual and indifferent to that in the past. It took John's death to bring that home to me.

John's funeral was secular. Diana and close friends spoke about him with affection. Poems were read and music that was important to him was played. There was barely a mention of God. It did not pay lip service to a religious pretence of life after death. It simply celebrated in music, in poetry, in remembrances by Diana and his friends of his life. Not that spirituality or serious contemplation of life and its meaning were missing.

Mary's funeral was conventional, as she would have wanted it. Tony delivered a beautiful eulogy that remembered the woman he had fallen in love with. Her son Richard, a Methodist minister, led the prayers, which were appropriate, personal, expressing grief, thankfulness for her life, relief for an end to suffering and hope of eternal life.

All that was meaningful and moving. I presided and joined together the meaningful family contributions with the conventional religious phrases and certainties of the funeral service. It is those certainties that I am uneasy with. John's funeral did not have those religious statements about life after death, but Mary's did.

Two people, John and Mary, who were important in my life had two very different funerals, yet both conjured up images and remembrances that brought John and Mary vividly to life. I think it is important to set down carefully and with as much detail as possible what one would like for one's own funeral service. I don't like to think of my ending being a bag of lies about what I thought or did. I would like it to be recognisably me.

I believe my role as a clergyperson in the process of helping people come to terms with death is not to peddle faith or any half-believed beliefs but to simply be there and help those that are grieving remember the life that has gone. It is easy when there is love and admiration, as was the case with John and Mary, but harder when there has been distrust and even hatred. In those cases, it also requires staying alongside someone and helping them to venture into their new situation without fear, guilt, hate or distrust.

The greater the love for the deceased, the greater the grief and the greater the desire to hold on to that grief and not let go of the memories. Helen found this passage by the novelist Matt Haig who puts these thoughts into the mind of his 400-year-old hero in his novel *How to Stop Time*:

> People you love never die … They don't die, not completely. They live in your mind, the way they always lived inside you. You keep their light alive. If you remember them well enough, they can still guide you, like the shine of long-extinguished stars could guide ships in unfamiliar waters. If you stop mourning them, and start listening to them, they still have the power to change your life. They can, in short, be salvation.[162]

Haig's writing expresses clearly how I think we can live on after death, it is nothing to do with professing a faith, and nothing some divine being can do for us, it is dependent on those left on earth and the next generations and how they remember us and the impressions that we have left. It is dependent, of course, on how we have lived, the mark we have left.

Dietrich Bonhoeffer, the German Christian martyred by the Nazis, makes much the same point about death and remembrance. In his *Letters and Papers from Prison,* he beautifully expresses the need to preserve the memory of someone close to us. He acknowledges the pain and doesn't minimise it. His words hold true for believers and non-believers.

> There is nothing that can replace the absence of someone dear to us, and one should not even attempt to do so. One must simply hold out and endure it. At first that sounds very hard, but at the same time it is also a great comfort. For to the extent the emptiness truly remains unfilled one remains connected to the other person through it. It is wrong to say that God fills the emptiness. God in no way fills it but much more leaves it precisely unfilled and thus helps us preserve – even in pain – the authentic relationship. Furthermore, the more beautiful and full the remembrances, the more difficult the separation. But gratitude transforms the torment of memory into silent joy. One bears what was lovely in the past not as a thorn but as a precious gift deep within, a hidden treasure of which one can always be certain.[163]

Bonhoeffer's understanding, despite being a Christian martyr, seems to be truthful without resorting to any sense that death is part of God's plan or judgement. It is true perhaps to his religionless Christianity. God doesn't really come into it. Death and coming to terms with death must be thoroughly this-worldly.

I am now of an age when I start to think about my death, 'The anaesthetic from which none come round', as Philip Larkin so starkly remarks in his poem 'Aubade'. After those two days of funerals for people that meant a great deal to me, I feel so strongly that I want my funeral to be more like John's. I don't want a scaffolding of religious ideas peddled as certainties enveloping my own funeral. I want it to be true to who I am and what I believe. I want it to be my funeral – recognisably mine and authentic.

However, I have to admit that there is, of course, a sense in which 'life after death' is always a reality. Not that I am suddenly going to wheel on God but take a scientific view. Bruce Frederick Cummings writing in his diary in 1920 shows the true nature of life after death. This, too, is what I believe, it is the only interpretation that is absolutely true, beyond a shadow of a doubt and for me, at least at the moment, it is enough:

> To me the honour is sufficient of belonging to the universe – such a great universe, and so great a scheme of things. Not even Death can rob me of that honour. For nothing can alter the fact that I have lived; I have been I, if for ever so short a time. And when I am dead, the matter which composes my body is indestructible – and eternal, so that come what may to my 'Soul', my dust will always be going on, each separate atom of me playing its separate part – I shall still have some sort of finger in the pie. When I am dead, you can boil me, burn me, drown me, scatter me – but you cannot destroy me: my little atoms would merely deride such heavy vengeance. Death can do no more than kill you.[164]

For me and my life I am (almost) certain that death is the end. But Cummings is right, I will live on with 'some sort of finger in the pie'. Isn't that the same positive but rational thought as my friend John Turner's belief that if God is like the ocean then we will be waves, always and forever part of the ebb and flow? Helen, who has virtually no traditional Christian faith, fascinates me as she would love to think there remained some connection after death, some inkling of living on in some way. I would like to agree but, truthfully, I can't. I can understand, objects, phrases, people and places may carry a memory for us of someone departed and enable us to hold on to a sense of presence but I can't go beyond that.

There is sadness, fear and liberation in the death of parents: sadness of losing those you loved, and who for good or evil have shaped your life; fear because we are now the generation facing decay and death; liberation because you do not have to temper your thoughts and behaviour out of respect – a final recognition of being grown up and of the maternal and paternal bond having been severed. For instance, I can have these thoughts and views about death and eternal life now because they will not now upset my parents. Unless, of course, they are sitting watching and listening from an armchair in heaven, in which case I am barking up the wrong tree.

Plate 1: (above left) Peter Francis aged three
Plate 2: (above right) Peter's mother, Pauline in the 1940s

Plate 3: Peter (second left, back row) in the Tormore First XI Cricket Team

Plate 4: St Benet's Chapel, Queen Mary University,
London E1 (courtesy of Ella Sharples)

Plate 5: The interior of St Mary's Cathedral, Glasgow
(courtesy of Abha Paulina)

Plate 6: The statue of William Ewart Gladstone at the front of Gladstone's
Library (courtesy of Rhian Waller)

Plate 7: (above) The interior of Gladstone's Library (courtesy of Rhian Waller)
Plate 8: (below) Gladstone's Library in the snow (courtesy of Helen Francis)

Plate 9: (above left) Peter's wedding to Helen
Plate 10: (above right) Peter in 2012
Plate 11: (below) Peter and Helen in Manchester in 2008

Plate 12: (above) Peter walking Lucy down the aisle
Plate 13: Lucy and Phil Kingsley's wedding in 2014

Plate 14: (above) Lucy and Phil's wedding reception at Gladstone's Library
Plate 15: (below) Lucy and Rupert in 2020

Plate 16: (left) Helen in the summer of 2020, Plate 17: (below) Rupert aged 18 months

Plate 18: (above) Peter and Rupert in 2020, Plate 19: (right) Peter and Rupert in 2021

PART III

CODA

THREE MEN, TWO WOMEN
AND A LITTLE CHAP

I am a part of all that I have met
Alfred, Lord Tennyson – 'Ulysses'

I haven't come to these conclusions on my own. They owe so much to those who have taught me and those whose books I have read. Many of those who I admire have been scorned or ridiculed by those who do not want change. The churches have been hard on outliers who are trying to express different theologies and have often sought to silence by ridiculing the liberal or radical voice. We only have to think of Mary Daly, John Robinson, Dorothee Sölle, Leonardo Boff, Daphne Hampson and Lloyd Geering, to name just a few.

I have been privileged in my ministry in London, Glasgow and Hawarden to meet and befriend some of those who have been at the forefront of challenging the conservatism of Anglicanism and supporting liberalism in society and the world of faith.

Interesting people come to Gladstone's Library, historians, theologians, clergy, novelists, poets, cineastes and they come to find the space to think and write. They come to a place that is empathetic and is not going to be a place of right-wing views, which need to be parried at every turn. It is the richness and privilege of this discourse that has helped to shape my thoughts and particularly my spirituality. However, there are three men, two women and one little chap whose presence and influence hovers over the whole of this book.

The first of these influential muses is John Shelby Spong. Jack Spong was born and brought up in the Southern States of the USA and when he was a rector in Richmond, Virginia that pastoral situation opened his eyes to the Civil Rights Movement. The growing awareness of civil rights led to meaningful involvement with the Richmond community. Later, as Bishop of Newark, he was confronted by both the issue of gay clergy and the ordination of women – and he became a leading voice in demanding change in the church to fully embrace gay members and clergy and demand the full inclusion of women in the ministry of the Episcopal church. Each of these major 'battles' was forced on him, not only by his role, but where and to whom he was ministering. Equally important was his shift from a semi-evangelical with a traditional background of belief to a more radical stance calling for a new reformation in the church and addressing the very large constituency of what he calls 'believers in exile'. He gives credit for his 'conversion' to liberal Christianity to John Robinson, the author of *Honest to God*, who became one of his most significant mentors. In 1998, he wrote a piece for the Newark Diocesan Newsletter calling for a new reformation. A friend from the USA sent me a copy and I immediately worked on inviting him to the Library. In the article Jack distilled this new reformation into 12 theses, thus deliberately imitating Martin Luther's theses hammered on to the church door in Wittenberg that started the first Reformation:

> Theism as a way of defining God is dead. So most theological God-talk is today meaningless. A new way to speak of God must be found.

> Since God can no longer be conceived in theistic terms, it becomes nonsensical to seek to understand Jesus as the incarnation of the theistic deity. So, the Christology of the ages is bankrupt.

> The Biblical story of the perfect and finished creation from which human beings fell into sin is pre-Darwinian mythology and post-Darwinian nonsense.

> The Virgin Birth understood as literal biology, makes Christ's divinity, as traditionally understood, impossible.

> The miracle stories of the New Testament can no longer be interpreted in a post-Newtonian world as supernatural events performed by an incarnate deity.

> The view of the cross as the sacrifice for the sins of the world is a barbarian idea based on primitive concepts of God and must be dismissed.

Resurrection is an action of God. Jesus was raised into the meaning of God. It therefore cannot be a physical resuscitation occurring inside human history.

The story of the Ascension assumed a three-tiered universe and is therefore not capable of being translated into the concepts of a post-Copernican space age.

There is no external, objective, revealed standard written in scripture or on tablets of stone that will govern our ethical behaviour for all time.

Prayer cannot be a request made to a theistic deity to act in human history in a particular way.

The hope for life after death must be separated forever from the behaviour control mentality of reward and punishment. The church must abandon, therefore, its reliance on guilt as a motivator of behaviour.

All human beings bear God's image and must be respected for what each person is. Therefore, no external description of one's being, whether based on race, ethnicity, gender or sexual orientation can properly be used as the basis for either rejection or discrimination.[165]

In the same year, 1998, Spong developed these 12 theses in his book, *Why Christianity Must Change or Die.*[166] He revisited and expanded them in his final book, *Unbelievable,* in 2018.[167] In 1999 he made the first of 12 visits to the Library to deliver a course. Each visit was always a sell-out.

In June 2017, Jack had a stroke from which he has recovered well – except his handwriting is now terrible! It is almost certain that *Unbelievable* will be his very last book – he has written 26. *Unbelievable* is a fine summation of his thought, belief and passion for truth.

Spong's importance for my generation of clergy, and those that flock to hear him speak, is that he lived through and fought the same battles that we, if we were liberals, have all had to face: he was deeply involved in the Civil Rights Movement, the ordination of women, inter-faith dialogue, gay liberation. In each of these movements he was re-educated by friends and those under his pastoral care as well as by study. He studies furiously and his zeal for truth is clear. Once he has found it, he professes it with the same fervour as the Southern Preachers of his youth. It is a message he wants to convey with wit and conviction. He addresses the real questions and profound hesitations that his contemporaries have about Christianity. Put another way, it provides the basis for a new reformation for all those who are hanging on by a thread to a church or the Christian faith or those who have left the church in despair as well as those who will never darken its doors because of the intellectual non-sense and constricted life that are believed to be required by its followers. Jack Spong asks us not to check out our brains at the door but to think deeply, 'to live fully, love wastefully, and be all that God want us to be'.

Jack Spong has a great gift of being able to interpret the work of the academy for a wider audience. His books are frequently *New York Times* bestsellers and his travelling and lecturing have fed thoughtful enquirers and adherents of Christianity in many countries. He has, in the service of his quest for truth, been pilloried by many in the established churches and especially by fundamentalist Christians. Hosting him at the Library often ensures that a delegation of fundamentalist Christians will come knocking on our door. To witness the encounter is fascinating as Jack is far more au fait with the Bible than they are and can defeat their narrow logic quite easily. He was very capable of out-quoting them not only on chapter and verse but the historical context of biblical texts. They departed slightly bemused as they obviously were surprised to encounter such a passionate advocate of the Bible, whose message was so starkly different from their own.

In the early 2000s I suggested making him a Fellow of the Library. Rowan Williams (Archbishop of Wales and later to become Archbishop of Canterbury), who at the time was a trustee and regular user of the Library, objected and claimed that Jack was not of sufficient intellectual calibre to be honoured in such a way. I was furious but persisted and sent copies of one of Jack's books to some of the Trustees, who thankfully agreed with me, and the objection from Rowan Williams was gracefully withdrawn. Some years later, Jack and his family celebrated his 80th birthday at the Library with a wonderful meal and speeches. When Jack dies, he has indicated that half of his ashes will be buried at Gladstone's Library. I find this very moving; the liberal influence of Gladstone's Library has also been part of his journey.

Don Cupitt was someone else I invited to visit the Library. Don's thought has been influential in my own life and theology as has been obvious from reading these chapters. Don was an Anglican clergyman and is a philosopher of religion. I've been reading Don's work longer than Jack's. His views have been a compulsive irritant to me, always urging more radical thought. Don has a non-realist approach to God. His idea is that God is 'the sum of our values' and that our thought and speech is all we have to shape the world, for without language there is no God. This world is all that there is and there is no beyond. We have to live fully for the moment. In brief notes, now deposited in his Gladstone's Library archive, Don shows a pathway from his thought about religion in general to the Christian faith and his belief that Jesus provides an ethical approach that is worth following.

> Thinking is internalized speech; all our thoughts depend on language …

> We invented language, every word of it …

> We developed our whole picture of the world through our conversation amongst ourselves. We even developed our own consciousness … We evolved all the symbols of religion and morality …

> Our human life-world, being the only world, is also the world with no beyond, the last world we will ever know. It follows if we are ever to achieve the Highest Good (= salvation, = eternal happiness), we must realise it here and now in this world …

> Religion therefore must now take the new form of an immediate, belief-less and 'solar' commitment to this life now. Expressive, self-outing, 'solar' living = 'the Kingdom of God.'

> Ethics needs to be as purely affirmative as possible. It is an effort to revalue the world.[168]

Don has been ill-treated and misunderstood by the church, as have those who belonged to the movement that he started, the Sea of Faith Network. *Sea of Faith* was the title of a BBC series that Don presented and the title was taken from Matthew Arnold's poem 'Dover Beach':

> The Sea of Faith
> Was once, too, at the full, and round earth's shore
> Lay like the folds of a bright girdle furled.
> But now I only hear
> Its melancholy, long, withdrawing roar,
> Retreating, to the breath
> Of the night-wind, down the vast edges drear
> And naked shingles of the world.[169]

Cupitt has often been cold-shouldered by his fellow theologians in academia, not least Rowan Williams again. Many traditionalists in the church would say that if you do not believe in the reality of God and the divinity of Jesus, you should not be a clergyperson. Don knows from conversations with many leading theologians and clergy that many believe what he believes (i.e. that Jesus was not divine, God is not a being and religion is a human construct), but have chosen to be quiet to protect their role in church and academia. He regrets that more theologians haven't 'come out' and been honest about what they believe or don't believe. Most have chosen career security and preferment over public intellectual honesty. He cites a strong friendship with John Robinson, the author of *Honest to God*, who was always supportive of Don, while at the same time not necessarily agreeing with him. Interestingly, Ruth Robinson, John's wife, was an active member of the Sea of Faith Network and was more in tune with Don's theology.

Cupitt's philosophy is much more sophisticated than those few phrases of mine try to summarise. What I am always interested in is his understanding of Jesus. For in spite of his philosophical stance, he cannot rid himself of the importance of Jesus. He has written 51 books and his developing understanding about Jesus occupied a number of them. *Jesus and Philosophy* (2009) marked his last specific focus on Jesus.[170] This book is interesting as it reflects his involvement with the Jesus Seminar and the influence of its founder Robert Funk.

Like Jack Spong, his affection for Gladstone's Library and its open and liberal stance, has led him not to donate his ashes but deposit his archive with the Library.

During my time in Scotland, I got to know and admire Richard Holloway. He has subsequently visited Gladstone's Library several times and I have always relished our talks together. He is a friend of both Jack Spong and Don Cupitt. He is clearly on the radical edge of the church but unlike many others would, as a bishop, always prefer to support friends or articulate the truth as he saw it rather than choose theological or ecclesiastical expediency. He is a very charismatic figure and much loved by his friends. In belief terms, when he finished being a bishop in the Scottish Episcopal Church, he was somewhere between a critical-realist and a non-realist (roughly representing the spectrum of views between the critical-realism of Spong and the non-realism of Cupitt). My sense is that since throwing his bishop's mitre in the Thames (yes, really!) and walking away from a formal role in the church, he has become more non-realist – no longer a closet sceptic that has definitely come out, but not with absolute certainty, as the wonderful end of his theological memoir, *Leaving Alexandria,* suggests:

> In October 2000 I preached my last sermon as bishop and used it to look back. A closet sceptic, I had now become the kind of bishop I had despised thirty years earlier. I have come back to where I had started from – I could no longer talk about God.
>
> I headed for the hills – the Pentlands ... In my walks I discovered my real dilemma – I wanted religion still around, purged of cruelty, because it gave us space to wonder and listen within ...
>
> What's left to say? Only this, when I die, I hope my children will bring me back up here. I don't want a stone, or a sign left anywhere

to mark the fact that I had a life on earth before I went down to join the unnumbered dead. They can take it in turns to carry what's left of me in my old rucksack. They will open the box to let me blow away across the heather and then make their way back down and home.

And that'll be that. Well, almost certainly ...[171]

I like that hint of uncertainty at the end of the book. Once, I emailed him to say how much my views chimed with a phrase he quotes by the nineteenth-century Russian Vasilli Rozanov: 'All religions will pass, but this will remain: Simply sitting in the chair and looking in the distance.'[172] Richard replied, 'Ah, but Peter, think of the view, the view!' Perhaps his greatest gift to me was his love of poetry. Indeed, I think he would prefer all religion to be poetry rather than prose. He quotes poets in all his later books and I started reading the works of those poets he quoted and became a convert to poetry.

It was Richard Holloway who first alerted me to this short poem, 'Outwitted', by Edwin Markham that is perhaps a suitable epitaph for these three wise men:

> He drew a circle that shut me out —
> Heretic, rebel, a thing to flout.
> But Love and I had the wit to win:
> We drew a circle that took him in![173]

Spong, Cupitt and Holloway have helped to shape my theology. I can see within my own theological thought so many of the building blocks of my belief in their words. I owe them a great debt of gratitude. They have saved my faith. They have excited and fed my questing. However, the greatest influence on my theological thought, and indeed the whole of my life, has been my wife, Helen. It is for her and our daughter, Lucy, that this book has been written. For they deserve the real thanks.

Helen and her influence throughout is obvious to me but probably not to her. Life with Helen has been life changing for me. I was frankly just treading water in life and somewhat aimless on a personal level and in terms of my faith. Helen woke me up from a sort of limbo, not only personally, but also I have to admit, because she is so very sceptical about religion. I had been wrapped in the cocoon of a cosy Christian ghetto where there are shared understandings, shortcuts and probably such a familiarity with religious assumptions that we forget to question and challenge, Helen encounters religious statements with the freshness of an inquisitive outsider. And she treats most dogmatic religious statements as evidence of sloppy thinking and poor research. Jesus is to her as unlikely to have lived in the way the New Testament described as the naïve idea that Adam and Eve actually lived in the garden of Eden. She, as a five-degree holding social scientist, wants evidence, copious footnotes and verifiable citations. My freewheeling interpretation of a Jesus of history might be, in her view, less unacceptable and less harmful than a biblical fundamentalist's interpretation but is still lacking in hard evidence. And you know what, she's right. My understanding of Jesus (and everyone else's understanding) is just a working hypothesis and should not be peddled as certainty.

Helen's scepticism has influenced my understanding of faith more than anyone or anything else. What on earth can the life of a first-century Palestinian male say to her? From an historical perspective there are centuries of abuse and silencing of women by followers of Jesus to answer for. And there remains in Islam and within many branches of Judaism, Hinduism and Christianity a continued bias against women that is bolstered by the uncritical reading of sacred texts, the maleness of the godhead and the entitlement of male clerical hierarchies.

Helen's worldview is strongly feminist. Feminism is the theoretical framework through which she sees the world. Can a male Saviour 'save' a woman? She finds Christian practice (or that of other major religions) excessively patriarchal. From her perspective Christian faith and practice is often, frankly, on the side of injustice and inequality. Helen has altered my religious outlook by interrogating me about questions that have no definite answer and remain questions, uncertainties and doubts that we just have to live with. Any wishy-washy claim that faith enables us to live with uncertainties is to her just lazy thinking.

Helen has raised many more question marks in my faith which I would have lazily left unexamined when I was in a Christian environment as priest and pastor. Nowadays, when I try to explain a theological doctrine or listen to someone else explaining it, I have become more aware of this and ever more careful as I try to explain church polity or the Christian faith.

And if Christians are meant to be caring, loving and selfless, then Helen puts most Christians I know, myself included, to shame. I only have to think of the extraordinary exemplary care she showed to my mother in the last years of her life, or to an elderly couple, Heather and David in the village where we live. How quick are we Christians to claim the moral and caring high ground? Helen's simple humanitarian care was extraordinary. What need has someone like Helen for the hang-ups of a Christian faith? Would it make her a better person? A happier person? We know that unbelief is not going to condemn her to everlasting torment – for, as she and I both know, hell does not exist.

There are, of course, moments when the feminist mindset and a progressive Christian humanist perspective overlap. There was a moment of absolute religious consensus between Helen and I when our daughter, Lucy, went away to Bath Spa University and shared a flat in her first year with a group of young women. The only serious worry we had (beside the trauma of leaving her in a damp and grotty flat) was when she told us that she was going to a 'house church' with an evangelical and fundamentalist flat-mate. We were worried that she would be sucked into that particular Christian ghetto. Oh, we of little faith! We needn't have worried – thank God – she was far too sensible to fall for all that spiritual manipulation.

Helen and Lucy have brought such joy into my life and relaxed me enough to enjoy that happiness. After believing that I would never have children, I now have a daughter, Lucy, of whom I am immensely proud. Lucy is a teacher, a woman with her own yoga business, a gifted musician and artist, a liberal thinker, a happily married young woman whose gift of friendship, generosity and hospitality together with her infectious enthusiasm is cherished by many. She inherits from her mother an easy way with people that creates strong relationships. A few minutes in her company revives the soul.

Lucy and her husband Phil have a son. I found her pregnancy and the birth of Rupert exciting and amazing. One of the most thrilling and awe-inspiring experiences of my life. Because I had missed out on childbirth as a parent it was a new and precious experience. One of the very biggest thrills and proudest moments of my life was quietly holding Rupert for the first time.

For me, Lucy is an important influence on this book as I have her constantly in mind as I seek to present a life-affirming faith not only for her generation but for Rupert's too. I want my family to see that Christian faith can be rational, progressive, inclusive. It can offer a creed that deals with disappointment, defeat and still urge us on in hope. Christianity does not have to be occult, esoteric or apolitical; Christianity can be something that is inspiring, hopeful and progressive. It can be worth following. What it doesn't do is provide a ticket to a heavenly afterlife but it does provide the possibility, if we dare to follow, of life in all in its fullness and a tantalising glimpse of a wide and inclusive world.

NOTES TO THE TEXT

Most biblical citations are from the New Revised Standard Version (National Council of the Churches of Christ in the USA, 1989). In one or two cases I have preferred the Scholars' Version contained in Robert W Funk, Roy W Hoover, and the Jesus Seminar, *The Five Gospels* (San Francisco: Harper Collins, 1997).

1 Anne Applebaum, *Twilight of Democracy* (London, Penguin, 2020).
2 https://archbishopcranmer.com/just-6-of-anglican-clergy-voted-conservative-in-2019/
3 Greg Smith and Linda Woodhead, 'Religion, Brexit, populism and the Church of England' in *Religion, State and Society*, 46(3), 2018, pp. 206–223.

Notes to Chapter 1 – Schooled
4 A A Milne, 'Vespers' (1923). Retrieved from:
   https://www.oatridge.co.uk/poems/a/aa-milne-vespers.php
5 John A T Robinson, *Honest to God* (London: SCM Press, 1963).
6 J M Barrie, *Peter and Wendy* (London: Hodder & Stoughton, 1911), p. 1.
7 *Our Bounden Duty* (London: SPCK, 1943).
8 *The Independent*, 9 December 1993. http://www.independent.co.uk/news/business/pembroke-harvey-jones-goes-gladly-back-to-school-1466383.html
9 John Harvey-Jones, *Getting It Together* (London: Heinemann, 1991), p. 40.
10 *Reach for the Sky* (Lewis Gilbert, 1956).
11 Rudyard Kipling, *Rewards and Fairies* (London: Macmillan 1910), p. 155.
12 Colin Duriez, *C.S. Lewis: A Biography of Friendship* (Oxford: Lion, 2013), p. 38.
13 Duriez, p. 37.
14 *The War Game* (Peter Watkins, 1966).
15 Gerome Ragni and James Rado, 'Sodomy' from *Hair* (RCA Victor Records, 1967).
16 G A Studdert Kennedy, *The Unutterable Beauty* (London: Hodder & Stoughton, 1927), p. 24.
17 Monica Furlong, *Prayer and Poems* (London: SPCK, 2004), p. 44.
18 *If....* (Lindsay Anderson, 1968).
19 Ralph Blumenau, *Philosophy and Living* (Exeter: Imprint Academic, 2002).
20 Viktor E Frankl, *Man's Search for Meaning: The Classic Tribute to Hope from the Holocaust* (London: Rider, 2004).

21   John Hemming, *Conquest of the Incas* (London: Pan Macmillan, 1970).
22   Peter Shaffer, *The Royal Hunt of the Sun* (London: National Theatre, 1964), Act II, Scene XII.

Notes to Chapter 2 – Called
23   *The Ten Commandments* (Cecil B DeMille, 1956).
24   David Watson, *My God is Real* (Eastbourne: Kingsway, 1970), p. 37.
25   Don Cupitt, *Jesus & Philosophy* (London: SCM Press, 2009), pp. 24–25.
26   Eberhard Bethge, *Dietrich Bonhoeffer* (London: Collins, 1970), p. 524.
27   Dietrich Bonhoeffer, *Letters and Papers from Prison* (London: SCM Press, 1971), p. 17.
28   E F Schumacher, *Small is Beautiful* (London: Blond and Briggs, 1973).
29   Harvey Cox, 'The Prophetic Purpose of Theology' in Dean Peerman (Ed), *Frontline Theology* (London: SCM Press, 1967), p. 149.
30   Peter Shaffer, *The Collected Plays of Peter Shaffer* (London: Random House, 1984).
31   David Storey, *Plays: 1 – The Contractor, Home, Stages, Caring* (London, Methuen, 1992); *Plays: 2 – The Restoration of Arnold Middleton, In Celebration, The March on Russia* (London, Methuen, 2016); *Home, The Changing Room & Mother's Day* (Harmondsworth, Penguin, 1978).
32   Edward Bond, 'Drama and the Dialectics of Violence' in *Theatre Quarterly*, 2, 1972, pp. 81–100.
33   Edward Bond, *Plays: 1 – Saved, Early Morning, The Pope's Wedding* (Methuen, 1977).
34   Elif Shafak, *How to Stay Sane In An Age of Division* (London: Wellcome Press, 2020), p. 87.
35   Franz Kafka, *Letters To Friends, Family and Editors* (New York: Shoeken Books, 1977), p. 17.
36   This was originally written some time in the spring of 1977 at the University of St Andrews when I should have been revising. The version I have reproduced here was written in March 1986 for the Student Christian Movements Congress held at Queen Mary College in the University of London. I have borrowed an idea from Peter Brook who writes at the very end of his book *The Empty Space* (London: Penguin, 1968) about the theatre as allowing us to see the 'if' we hope for actually happening on stage (p. 57).
37   John Hick (Ed), *The Myth of God Incarnate* (London: SCM Press, 1977).

38 I was ordained deacon at Hagley (being a deacon is almost an apprenticeship before becoming a priest) and then ordained priest in Worcester Cathedral the following year.

39 Don Cupitt, *Taking Leave of God* (London: SCM Press, 1980), p. 82.

Notes to Chapter 3 – London E1

40 Commission for Urban Priority Areas, *Faith in the City: A Call for Action by Church and Nation* (London: Church House Publishing, 1985).

41 Monica Furlong, 'The St Hilda Community', *Christian*, May/June 1988, p. 11.

42 Naomi Alderman, *The Liars' Gospel* (London: Penguin, 2013). Informal discussion with the author, January 2013.

43 Mark 5:25ff.

44 Luke 7:36ff.

45 Matthew 19:3–10; Mark 10:22ff.

46 Luke 10:38–42.

47 Luke 8:1–3.

48 Mary Daly, *The Church and The Second Sex* (San Francisco: Harper & Row, 1968).

49 Karen L King, *The Gospel of Mary Magdala* (Salem: Polebridge, 2003) and Marvin Meyer, *The Gospels of Mary* (San Francisco: Harper Collins, 2004).

50 Brian Wren, *What Language Shall I Borrow?* (London: SCM Press, 1989), pp. 116–117.

51 Janet Morley, 'Liturgy and Danger' in Monica Furlong (Ed), *Mirror to the Church* (London: SPCK, 1988), p. 33.

52 Monica Furlong, *The C of E: The State It's In* (London: Hodder, 1999), p. 350.

53 Mary Daly, *The Church and The Second Sex* (San Francisco: Harper & Row, 1968); *Beyond God the Father* (New York: Beacon Press, 1973).

54 Daly, *Beyond God the Father*, p. 9.

55 Rosemary Radford Ruether, *Women–Church: Theology and Practice of Feminist Liturgical Communities* (San Francisco: Harper Collins, 1985), p. 137.

56 Ruether, *Women–Church*, p. 137.

57 Church of England, *Making Women Visible* (London: Church Information Office, 1988), p. 9.

58 Deborah Cameron, *Feminism and Linguistic Theory* (London: St Martin's Press, 1985), p. 72.

59 Matthew 23:9.

60 William Oddie, *What Will Happen To God?* (London: SPCK, 1984).

61 Catherine Lacunga, *Freeing Theology* (San Francisco: Harper Collins, 1993), p. 9.
62 Gaye Ortiz, *Getting a Look In* – unpublished lecture at St Deiniol's Library, April 1998.
63 Daphne Hampson, 'On Power and Gender' in Elizabeth Stuart & Adrian Thatcher (Eds), *Christian Perspectives on Sexuality and Gender* (London: Eerdmans, 1996), pp. 128–129.
64 Mary Beard, *Women and Power* (London: Profile Books, 2017), p. 86.

Notes to Chapter 4 – Scotland
65 Carl Jung, *Modern Man in Search of His Soul* (New York: Routledge, 2001), p. 235.
66 Mark 9:33f. and 18:1f. and synoptic parallels.
67 John Dominic Crossan, *Jesus: A Revolutionary Biography* (New York: Harper Collins, 1994), p. 63.
68 Crossan, pp. 66–71.
69 Mark 2:13f and synoptic parallels.
70 Kathy Galloway (Ed), *Dreaming of Eden* (Glasgow: Wild Goose Publications, 1997), pp. 105–106.
71 Matthew 8:5–13.
72 Alan Cadwallader, *Pieces of Ease and Grace* (Adelaide: AFT Theology, 2013), pp. 85–100.
73 Cadwallader, p. 90.
74 Kyle Harper, *From Shame to Sin* (Harvard: Harvard University Press, 2013), pp. 22–37.
75 John A T Robinson, *Exploration Into God* (London: SCM Press, 1967), pp. 36.
76 David Hare, *Racing Demon* (London: Methuen, 1990), p. 1.
77 Don Cupitt, A Summary Philosophy of Religion. 2007. Notes deposited in the Cupitt archive at Gladstone's Library.
78 Richard Rorty, *Contingency, Irony and Solidarity*. (Cambridge: Cambridge University Press, 1989), pp. 4–5.
79 Paul Tillich, *The Shaking of The Foundations* (London: Penguin, 1949), p. 63.
80 Don Cupitt, *The Sea of Faith* (London: BBC, 1984), p. 269.
81 Don Cupitt, *The Revelation of Being* (London: SCM Press, 1998).
82 Tom Stoppard, *Jumpers* (London: Faber, 1972), p. 65.
83 Scott Holland, 'Theopoetics is the Rage', *The Conrad Grebel Review*, 31(2), Spring, 2013, pp. 121–129.
84 Philippians 12:2 KJV.

85   Don Cupitt in discussion with John Robinson at Great St Mary's, Cambridge, 25 April 1982.

Notes to Chapter 5 – Living in a Library
86   T W Pritchard, *A History of St Deiniol's Library* (Hawarden, Monad Press, 1999), p. 35.
87   Pritchard, p. 36.
88   Hermione Lee, *Penelope Fitzgerald: A Life* (London: Chatto & Windus, 2013), pp. 218–219.
89   2012: Ian Parks, Nadene Ghouri, Naomi Alderman, Stella Duffy. 2013: Angela Topping, Katrina Naomi, Peter Jukes, Richard Beard, Sarah Perry. 2014: Lesley McDowell, Melissa Harrison, Patricia Bracewell, Peter Moore, Rebecca Abrams, Tania Hershman. 2015: Jessie Burton, Pascale Petit, Rachel Holmes, Robyn Cadwallader, Salley Vickers, Sarah Butler, Wendy Cope, Lachlan Mackinnon. 2016: Amy Liptrot, Natasha Pulley, Rebecca Farmer, Susan Barker. 2017: Penny Boxall, Rowan Hisayo Buchanan, Ruth Scurr, William Atkins. 2018: Cal Flyn, Keggie Carew, Polly Atkin, Rachel Malik. 2019: Sophie Mackintosh, Susannah Forrest, Oliver Emanuel, Emily Morris, Suzannah Evans, Sarah Day.
90   Aida Edemariam quoting Zadie Smith, *Guardian Review*, 3 September 2005. https://www.theguardian.com/books/2005/sep/03/fiction.zadiesmith
91   Quoted by Philip French in *The Observer,* 6 October 2002.
92   Clive Marsh and Gaye Ortiz (Eds), *Explorations in Theology and Film* (Oxford: Blackwell, 1997).
93   Eric Christianson, Peter Francis and William Telford (Eds), *Cinéma Divinité* (London: SCM Press, 2005).
94   *Celui qui doit mourir* (Jules Dassin, 1957); *Jésus of Montréal* (Denys Arcand, 1989); and *Son of Man* (Mark Dornford-May, 2006).
95   *Vera Drake* (Mike Leigh, 2008).
96   Peter Francis, Sermon at St Deiniol's Church, Hawarden, September 2008. See also my 'Face to Faith' article in *The Guardian*, 20 September 2008, on the same theme: https://www.theguardian.com/commentisfree/2008/sep/20/islam.religion
97   Kofi Annan, *We The Peoples* (London: Paradigm Publishers, 2014), p. 226.
98   Hans Küng, *Christianity* (London: SCM Press, 1995), p. 783.

99   Philip Kirby, *Leading People 2016: The Educational Backgrounds of the UK Professional Elite* (London: Sutton Trust, 2016). https://www.suttontrust.com/wp-content/uploads/2020/01/Leading-People_Feb16.pdf, pp. 2–3.

100 Danny Dorling, *Peak Inequality* (Bristol: Policy Press, 2018), p. 142.

101 Naomi Alderman. A short piece that Naomi wrote when she was writer in residence at Gladstone's Library, 2012.

102 Kofi Annan, *We The Peoples* (London: Paradigm Publishers 2011), p. 239.

Notes to Chapter 6 – Gladstone: A Toppled Hero?

103 Michael Foot (Ed), *Gladstone Diaries – Volume II* (Oxford: Oxford University Press, 1968), pp. 623–624.

104 Foot, p. 358.

105 S G Checkland, *The Gladstones: A Family Biography 1764–1851* (Cambridge: Cambridge University Press, 1971).

106 British Library, *Gladstone's address to the Newark electors, 8 Oct. 1832* (British Library, Gladstone papers, Add. MSS 44722). Fos 63–64.

107 Checkland, *The Gladstones*, p. 416.

108 John Morley, *Life of Gladstone Vol. III* (London: Macmillan, 1903), p. 475.

109 Morley, *Life of Gladstone Vol. II*, p. 137.

110 Morley, *Life of Gladstone Vol. II*, p. 104.

111 Gladstone speaking in Parliament, 19 March 1850 (Westminster: *Hansard*, 1850).

112 W E Gladstone, 'Memorials of a Southern Planter' in *The Nineteenth Century*, 154 (1889), pp. 984–985.

113 Gladstone speaking at Hawarden School, 16 January 1877.

114 John Micklethwaite and Adrian Wooldridge, *The Wake Up Call* (London: Short Books, 2020), p. 33.

115 John Micklethwaite was editor-in-chief of *The Economist* and is now editor-in-chief of *Bloomberg*. Adrian Wooldridge is the political editor of *The Economist*.

116 W E Gladstone: Foresters Hall, Dalkeith, Midlothian, 26 November 1879.

117 *Hansard*, 26 April 1870.

118 Welsh Government, *The Slave Trade and the British Empire: An Audit of Commemoration in Wales*. https://gov.wales/sites/default/files/publications/2020-11/the-slave-trade-and-the-british-empire-an-audit-of-commemoration-in-wales.pdf

119 Galatians 3:28.

120 Roland Quinault, 'Gladstone and Slavery' in *The Historical Journal*, 52(2) (June 2009), pp. 363–383.

121 Parliamentary Debates, Third series, 216 (1873), pp. 943–947.

122 Adam Shatz in conversation with Keeanga-Yamahtta Taylor, *London Review of Books* Podcast, 30 June 2020. https://www.lrb.co.uk/podcasts-and-videos/podcasts/lrb-conversations/how-do-you-change-things

123 Priya Satia, 'The whitesplaining of history is over' in *The Chronicle*, 28 March 2018.

124 John Stuart Mill, reported speech to the Westminster Reform meeting, *The Daily Telegraph*, 13 April 1866.

Notes to Chapter 7 – Yeshua

125 Rosemary Radford Ruether, *To Change the World* (London: SCM Press, 1981), p. 3.

126 Robert W Funk, Roy W Hoover and the Jesus Seminar, *The Five Gospels* (San Francisco: Harper Collins, 1997), pp. 1–3.

127 Hans Küng, *On Being a Christian*. (London: Collins, 1976).

128 Robert W Funk and the Jesus Seminar, *The Five Gospels: What Did Jesus Really Say?* (San Francisco: Harper Collins, 1997).

129 Robert Funk and the Jesus Seminar, *The Acts of Jesus: What Did Jesus Really Do?* (San Francisco: Harper Collins, 1998).

130 Jane Shaberg, *The Illegitimacy of Jesus* (Sheffield: Sheffield Academic Press, 1995).

131 Daniel C Maguire, *Jesus without God* (New York: SUNY Press, 2014), p. 67.

132 Robert Funk and the Jesus Seminar, *What Did Jesus Really Do?* (San Francisco: Harper Collins, 1998), pp. 530–531.

133 Thomas 113:1–4 but also Luke 17:20–21.

134 Don Cupitt archive, (Jesus and Philosophy handout 2009). Gladstone's Library.

135 Edward Schillebeeckx, *Christ* (London: SCM Press, 1977), pp. 848–849.

136 Philip Potter, *Life in All Its Fullness*. (Geneva: WCC Publications, 1981), pp. 1–15.

137 Thomas 113:1–4 but also Luke 17:20–21.

138 Dorothee Sölle, *Revolutionary Patience* (London: Lutterworth Press, 1979), p. 36.

139 Arthur J Dewey (Ed), *The Authentic Letters of Paul* (Salem: Polebridge, 2010), pp. 1–11.

140 Larry Siedentop, *Inventing the Individual* (London: Allen Lane, 2014), pp. 57–58.

141 Galatians 3:28.

142 Arthur J Dewey (Ed), *The Authentic Letters of Paul* (Salem: Polebridge, 2010), pp. 57–58.

143 Galatians 3:28; Colossians 3:11.

144 Siedentop, pp. 51–66.

145 John D Davies, *The Faith Abroad* (Oxford: Blackwell, 1983), p. 12.

146 Kathy Galloway, *Struggles to Love* (London: SPCK, 1994), p. 2.

147 John Lennon, *Imagine* (Apple Music, 1971).

Notes to Chapter 8 – Present-ing Jesus

148 Mary Oliver, *Devotions* (New York: Penguin Books, 2017), p. 131.

149 Andrew Copson and Alice Roberts, *the little book of humanism* (London: Piatkus, 2020), p. 214.

150 Copson and Roberts, p. 215.

151 Mark 2:27.

152 Philippians 4:8.

153 The Church of the Province of New Zealand, *The Liturgy of the Eucharist* (Christchurch: Genesis Publications, 1984), p. 50.

154 Janet Morley (Ed), *Bread of Tomorrow* (London: SPCK, 1992), p. 133.

155 Maya Angelou, *Amazing Peace* (New York: Penguin, 2005), p. 208.

156 Micah 6:8.

157 Maya Angelou, *The Complete Collected Poems* (London: Virago, 1994), p. 269.

158 Joe Moran, *Guardian Review*, 11 July 2020. https://www.theguardian.com/books/2020/jul/11/out-of-office-has-the-homeworking-revolution-finally-arrived

Notes to Chapter 9 – Inevitable Death

159 T S Eliot, *Selected Poems* (London: Faber, 1954), p. 80.

160 Seamus Heaney, *Aeneid Book VI* (London: Faber, 2016), p. 38.

161 Leonard Cohen, *Stranger Music* (London: Jonathan Cape, 1993), p. 363.

162 Matt Haig, *How to Stop Time* (Edinburgh: Canongate, 2017), p. 219.

163 Dietrich Bonhoeffer, *Letters and Papers from Prison* (Minneapolis: Fortress, 2009), p. 238.

164 W N P Barbellion (Bruce Frederick Cummings), *Journal of a Disappointed Man* (London: Chatto & Windus, 1920), p. 7.

Notes to Coda – Three Men, Two Women and a Little Chap

165 Galatians 3:8; John 8:32; John Shelby Spong, 'A Call for A New Reformation' in *The Voice* (Diocese of Newark Newsletter, 1998).

166 John Shelby Spong, *Why Christianity Must Change or Die: A Bishop Speaks to Believers in Exile* (San Francisco: HarperOne, 2001).

167 John Shelby Spong, *Unbelievable: Why Neither Ancient Creeds Nor the Reformation Can Produce a Living Faith Today* (San Francisco: HarperOne, 2018).

168 Don Cupitt, *A Summary Philosophy of Religion* (January 2007, Archive at Gladstone's Library).

169 Matthew Arnold, *New Poems* (Oxford: Oxford University Press, 1867), p. 112.

170 Don Cupitt, *Jesus and Philsophy* (London: SCM Press, 2009).

171 Richard Holloway, *Leaving Alexandria* (Edinburgh: Canongate, 2012), pp. 351–352.

172 Richard Holloway, *Looking in the Distance* (Edinburgh: Canongate, 2004), p. 3.

173 Edwin Markham, *The Shoes of Happiness* (New York: Doubleday, 1921), p. 1.